A HISTORY OF 1
SPEEDWAY
ASHES

A HISTORY OF THE
SPEEDWAY
ASHES

PETER FOSTER

TEMPUS

First published 2005

Tempus Publishing Limited
The Mill, Brimscombe Port,
Stroud, Gloucestershire, GL5 2QG
www.tempus-publishing.com

British Library Cataloguing in Publication Data.
A catalogue record for this book is available from the British Library.

ISBN 0 7524 3468 3

Typesetting and origination by Tempus Publishing Limited
Printed in Great Britain

CONTENTS

ACKNOWLEDGEMENTS

As always, when writing a book, there are many people to thank who have been instrumental in its completion. The history of the Ashes covers a period of over seventy years, and began well before I was a twinkle in my mother's eye. Therefore, research, especially into the early days, has been an adventure to me. I pay homage to those early speedway reporters who stood through rain, wind, hail and fog to bring us the reports that have become such an important part of speedway's history; and also to the photographers who have recorded many wonderful images for posterity. Plates 1, 3, 5-7, 13-24 and 28-9 are from the Wright Wood archive, courtesy of John Somerville; 25-7 were supplied by Geoff Bennett; 30-1, 35, 37 and 40 are from *Speedway Star*; 36 and 45-7 are courtesy of John Hall and 41-4 and 48-53 are Mike Patrick images. Where I have been unable to trace copyright I thank the anonymous donors and encourage them, where possible, to contact the publishers who will be happy to credit them in any future edition of this work.

Speedway supporters are amongst the most generous in any sport, always prepared to put themselves out and help any serious project along. I could not have written this book without the help of Alan Hunt, who put his considerable speedway collection at my disposal, and Barry Stephenson (the walking speedway encyclopaedia) who generously supplied the programme covers. Nigel 'statistics' Nicklin is always a useful friend to have in your corner, and Phil 'Cradley Website' Johnson never lets me down in my hour of need. It is almost unimaginable to write a speedway book without referring to the *Speedway Star*. It has become the Speedway Bible, and its excellent coverage of our sport gets better every year.

Apologies to anyone who I have omitted and, as the book covers so many years, there must be many. I can only thank the unknowns for helping to develop speedway into the great spectacle that it is today.

FOREWORD

The history of the Ashes has been complicated to chronicle. The Ashes was originally devised as a Test-match series between England and Australia, and for many years, it remained exclusively so. However, some of the England teams that toured Australia in the early days, notably some of Jack Parker's 'Pirates' were not officially recognised by the British speedway authorities, and are therefore 'unofficial'. Even so, these have been included, because they are an important part of the development and history of the Test Series.

Next comes the thorny subject of the Australasians who, of course, embraced New Zealand. I could have written this book about the history of England vs Australia, but many sparse years would have been omitted from both countries' development, and, as the series was still called 'The Ashes', I have included them, although they do not feature in the 'Test match Scorers' section.

I have not featured any 'Second Division' matches, between England and Australia and Australasia, although many have taken place. The book is a record of the best that both teams had to offer at the time. Apologies to any rankles that this may cause the purists, but, for the sake of continuity, I consider all matches included in this book to be of historical significance.

If one considers that, in the fifties, England were virtually sacked from touring Australia, one has to ask why? And therefore, it seemed important to include the early unofficial tours which were taken by some of the worst teams ever to be called 'England'.

English riders have played a less important role in Australian speedway history for some years now, but Jack Parker, Ken McKinlay and

Nigel Boocock remain legends 'down under'. The legacy continues in Britain. It began with Vic Huxley, Max Grosskreutz and Lionel Van Praag, and it continued with Vic Duggan and Graham Warren. Jack Young saw the Aussies through a very bleak period, as did Jim Airey and Phil Crump, but in modern times the Aussies have bounced back, treating us to the exploits of Jason Crump, Leigh Adams and Ryan Sullivan. They are a hardy race of riders who have graced our shores for over seventy years now, and, as the country who introduced us to speedway, we owe them a great debt.

Speedway is presently dominated by the Grand Prix. The World Team Cup has also become a 'major event' being staged over a week. Speedway enthusiasts have pleaded for more television coverage of their beloved sport, and now we have it – but at what price? In years gone by, we could only dream about the fabulous coverage that is now given to our sport every single week of the speedway season, but now the two major events threaten British speedway with destruction. As we are bought to heel with the demands of the Grand Prix series, and World Team Cup, British League racing (which has spawned the greatest riders in the sport) appears to have lost control and seems to be under threat.

Make no mistake about it: Huxley, Wilkinson, Young, Moore, Briggs, Fundin, Mauger, Olsen, Penhall, Gundersen, Nielsen, Hancock and Rickardsson (apologies to the fifty or so riders omitted) were all superb exponents of the sport, but would not have been so without their time spent in Britain.

With the advent of these two major competitions, and riders spending so much time on the continent, Test matches may soon become a thing of the past, but they will still remain an important part of the development of speedway in Britain. Modern-day promoters can only dream about the size of the crowds that flocked to see the early Test matches between England and Australia. Spectators were prepared to queue for hours in order to make sure that they got into the stadia before the 'House Full' signs went up. Once they were inside, they were usually treated to a top-class speedway match between deadly rivals, run amid a carnival atmosphere.

There have been many great Australian riders over the years (and English ones too of course) and I'm sure I speak on behalf of all British speedway supporters when I thank them all for visiting our shores and entertaining us for the last seventy-odd years.

INTRODUCTION

Australia introduced speedway to England in 1928, when the Aussies had already enjoyed a number of years in the sport themselves. The speedway season in Australia covers our winter, so the top Aussies were able to ride in their own country during the winter months, and ride in Britain during the spring and summer. As such, they were more experienced than our lads, so much so that the very first 'Star Championship' (the predecessor to the World Championship) held in 1929 was split into two sections – the Overseas Final, and the British Final.

Although the official Test matches did not begin until the following year, England met Australia at Coventry in September 1929 in an 'International'. England were represented by Jack Parker, Arthur Jervis, Wilmott Evans and Sid Jackson, whilst the Aussies fielded Overseas Champion Frank Arthur, Max Grosskreutz, 'Cyclone' Billy Lamont and Col Stewart. Sixteen two-man match races were ridden, with the winner being awarded 1 point and, at the end of it, England surprisingly won by 3 points. A reported crowd of 25,000 were admitted before the gates were locked, and the 1,000 or so unlucky fans who were locked out broke down the barriers by the pits to gain entrance into the stadium. It was a sign of the hysteria that was to follow.

Speedway in Britain had obviously become popular very quickly, and by 1930, there were no fewer than twenty-six clubs competing in the Southern and Northern leagues. With the English riders progressing steadily, a Test match series was devised between an England team and their speedway forefathers, the Australians, that same year. It began in June, at the same time that the England cricket team were entertaining Australia at Lords, and appropriately, the speedway Test Series was christened 'The Ashes'. They may have been mythical Ashes, but they were speedway's 'Ashes'.

The first official Test match between the two countries was staged at Wimbledon, and it immediately caught the public's imagination. The start of the match was held up for 45 minutes as thousands of spectators queued to get through the turnstiles, and the traffic outside the Plough Lane Stadium became gridlocked.

The Aussies had only a handful of top class riders in Britain in 1930, but they featured arguably the best rider in the world in the magnificent Vic Huxley, and they also had the mighty warrior, Max Grosskreutz, and one of the most exciting pioneers of the sport in 'Cyclone' Billy Lamont. England were led by the Wimbledon captain Jim Kempster, and featured twenty-three-year-old Jack Parker in the team, a rider who was to become a thorn in the Australians' side for many years to come.

England won the inaugural series, and indeed triumphed the following year also, as the matches drew thousands upon thousands of supporters to what had become the largest speedway event in the calendar. England were successful for the next couple of years, thanks to the efforts of Eric Langdon, Ginger Lees, Frank Varey, and of course Parker, but they had a multitude of riders to take their pick from, whereas the Aussies only had a handful.

Perhaps this shortage of Colonials bred the legendary Australian fighting spirit. They were true battlers, who never knew when they were beaten. Besides that, they were nurturing new talent in the form of Bluey Wilkinson and Lionel Van Praag. In 1934 Australia won their first ever Test Series, and over 50,000 fans turned out for the opener at Wembley, ironically, a track that the Aussies did consistently well on over the years.

That winter saw the first ever England touring team ride a Test Series 'down under'. England failed to regain the Ashes but they gave a good account of themselves in front of massive crowds. This was to become very much the *status quo* over the next years, with the home team winning and the visitors performing creditably.

There was still a shortage of top class Australians in Britain throughout the thirties. So much so that the team usually 'picked itself'. There was a nucleus of six good riders, who made up the main body of the team, and there was usually a 'bunfight' for the two reserve spots. Although they were great battlers, it did make Australia a 'fragile' team and, in 1937, when, after just one match, Bluey Wilkinson sustained a long-term injury, the rest of the series was cancelled.

It was a hiccup however, and business returned to normal in Australia in the winter, and indeed the following summer in England. The rivalry between the two teams, following a decade of battles, had become intense, but it all came to an abrupt end in September 1939 when England declared war on Germany. The deadly on-track rivals became united off it, as they joined forces, marching off to fight the Hun.

When Germany surrendered in the spring of 1945, speedway returned to Britain and, following an initial 'sorting out' period, hostilities resumed between England and Australia in 1947. Most of the old faces on both teams returned (there had not yet been time to train new ones) but Australia had a new star in Vic Duggan, whilst Jack Parker had re-established himself as England's favourite. Speedway was once again booming, and a crowd of 47,000 welcomed the Aussies back to Test match action at Bradford. As an event, only the World Championship eclipsed the Test Series.

Parker and the England team resumed their winters in Australia but, by the turn of the decade, the standard of the touring teams had began to decline. The reason was that most of the riders now held full-time jobs and were unable to commit to a three-month trip.

In the early fifties, the post-war riders began to make their presence felt in both teams. Tommy Price, Alan Hunt and Freddie Williams were England regulars, and Australia boasted Aub Lawson, Ken Le Breton, Graham Warren and the mighty Jack Young. However, the England winter tour of 1950/51 was a complete disaster. Parker scrambled a last-minute team together, which due to time constraints was the poorest 'England' team ever assembled. It was so poor in fact that the Board of Control refused even to recognise it as an 'England' team. They were met with torrential rain and power cuts, and never got near to winning any of the seven matches in which they rode. But the fated tour held even worse than that. In the second Test at the Sydney Sports Ground, 'White Ghost' Ken Le Breton crashed, and became the first rider ever to lose his life in a Test match.

As quickly as it had boomed after the war, British speedway went into decline, but the Test matches continued to draw huge crowds. Australia had by now outshone England as the number one speedway nation in the world and won the 1951 and 1952 Test Series in England. Warren was awfully unlucky not to win the 1950 World Championship, and Jack Young had been World Champion in 1951 and 1952. By that time they had a new star in nineteen-year-old 'wonderboy' Ronnie Moore. In fact, these were the halcyon days of Australian speedway.

The post-war Australians were a new breed. In the late forties and early fifties they were considered to be the 'cowboys' of speedway, with many reputed to have carried firearms. There was also what was dubbed the 'Australian Mafia'. If any British rider were to commit a misdemeanour against a Colonial then all other Australian riders would hear of it. The Australian Mafia ensured that retribution was swift and severe. The Aussies were colourful, ebullient and crazy, and they all rode like demons in England because if they didn't earn enough money, then they were stranded without the means to return home for the winter.

Jack Parker continued to take his England 'Pirates' down under in the winter, but the matches in Australia had become a travesty, as the Aussies were forced to 'dilute' their teams in order to make the matches competitive. The Australian promoters eventually got fed up with the sub-standard teams that were masquerading as England and pulled the plug in the winter of 1952/53.

It was around this time that things began to go wrong for Australia. Grahame Warren sustained serious head injuries while riding in New Zealand and, although he recovered, he was a shadow of his former brilliant self. But a second blow was one of a far more bizarre nature.

In 1953, England rode a three match Test Series against New Zealand. Although Ronnie Moore had been born in Australia, he had lived almost all of his life in New Zealand, and so he chose to represent them in the rubber. In so doing, he lost his eligibility to ride for Australia, and that, coupled with the demise of Warren and the retirement of Duggan, finished them as a team. It was the old problem: great riders, but not enough of them.

Although attendances continued to fall in 1954, the public still wanted to see Test matches. So the Ashes were kept alive by the formation of the Australasian team – a hybrid of Australia and New Zealand – which was pitted against England for the next seven years.

The early sixties saw British speedway begin a long haul back to popularity. By that time Sweden, led by the mighty Ove Fundin, was emerging as a top-flight speedway nation. Maybe it was because they were a thoroughbred team as opposed to the mongrel Australasians, but they captured the public's imagination and replaced the Aussies as England's Test opponents for the next few years.

The highly successful British League was formed in 1965, and thus began another boom in British speedway. Jack Young and Ronnie Moore had retired, and Australia lay dormant for some years. However, a new breed of Aussies was infiltrating the League, and even though none of them were yet world class, England were invited back to Australia to take them on in the winter of 1967/68. It was the first visit for a decade, and both teams were of course unrecognisable from their last encounter.

Thankfully, England sent a realistic 'England' team, winning the series. The tour was a huge success, so much so that they were invited back for the next ten years. In 1969 and 1970, England rode Test Series against the Aussies in England, but apart from Jim Airey and Charlie Monk, the Australians had little to offer in England.

The Aussies threat slumbered for many years as firstly America and then the mighty Danes engaged England. But in the nineties, Australia again rose like the Phoenix with the emergence of riders like Jason Crump, Leigh Adams and Ryan Sullivan, and the Test matches again resumed. Of course, they didn't draw 50,000 spectators, and probably never will again. Those days are locked in the vaults of speedway history.

CHAPTER 1

THE THIRTIES

ENGLAND v AUSTRALIA TEST SERIES 1930

1st Test	Wimbledon	June 30th	'30	Eng 17	Aust 35	L
2nd Test	Belle Vue	July 23rd	'30	Eng 56	Aust 39	W
3rd Test	Stamford Bridge	Aug 20th	'30	Eng 49	Aust 46	W
4th Test	Belle Vue	Sept 3rd	'30	Eng 51	Aust 45	W
5th Test	Wembley	Sept 26th	'30	Eng 49	Aust 45	W

England win series 4–1

Having enjoyed some years in the sport before introducing England to speedway, the Aussies were therefore more experienced, and it was not until 1930 that it was thought that the time was ripe to stage a Test-Match Series in England against Australia.

The first ever Test match was staged at **Wimbledon** in June 1930, and drew a capacity crowd to Plough Lane. It was staged over 9 heats, and was competed by six-man sides. England's first captain was Wimbledon's own 'Smiling' Jim Kempster who was joined by Frank Varey, Jack Parker, Roger Frogley, Jack Ormston, Wal Phillips and reserve Gus Kuhn.

Australia were skippered by arguably the best rider in the world at that time – twenty-four-year-old Vic Huxley - and his team included Max Grosskreutz, Dick Case, Billy Lamont, Frank Arthur and Ron Johnson. The presentation of the inaugural event has rarely been

Price 6d.

FIRST SPEEDWAY
TEST MATCH
ENGLAND v AUSTRALIA
Wimbledon, June 30th, 1930

THE AUSTRALIAN TEAM HAS BEEN APPROVED BY THE
AUSTRALIAN AUTHORITIES, WHO RECOGNISE THIS EVENT
AS THE FIRST OFFICIAL SPEEDWAY TEST MATCH.

TEAMS

ENGLAND COLOURS—WHITE	AUSTRALIA COLOURS—RED
No.	No.
1.—JIM KEMPSTER (Capt.) WIMBLEDON.	1.—VIC HUXLEY (Capt). HARRINGAY.
4.—ROGER FROGLEY CRYSTAL PALACE.	4.—DICKY CASE WIMBLEDON.
2.—FRANK VAREY MANCHESTER.	2.—FRANK ARTHUR STAMFORD BRIDGE.
5.—WAL PHILLIPS STAMFORD BRIDGE.	5.—RON JOHNSON CRYSTAL PALACE.
3.—JACK PARKER COVENTRY.	3.—MAX GROSSKREUTZ MANCHESTER.
6.—JACK ORMSTON WEMBLEY.	6.—BILLY LAMONT WIMBLEDON.
7.—GUS KUHN STAMFORD BRIDGE (Res.)	7.—ARNIE HANSEN SOUTHAMPTON (Res).

bettered, the Englishmen resplendent in their white jerseys with a red lion emblazoned on the back, and the Aussies in their red jerseys sporting a white kangaroo. However, the 9-heat format favoured the visitors, with Huxley undefeated in his 3 races, beating Kempster's track record. Despite England's 37-17 point defeat, the fixture was a huge success, and it was obvious to all that Test matches were here to stay.

ENGLAND 17: R.Frogley 6, B.Kempster 5, W.Phillips 4, J.Parker 1, J.Ormston 1, F.Varey 0.

AUSTRALIA 35: V.Huxley 9, M.Grosskreutz 6, F.Arthur 6, B.Lamont 6, R.Johnson, 5, D.Case 3.

England decided that eight-man teams riding over 16 heats was the 'way to go' (Australia having basically only six top-class riders in Britain), and this was instituted in the second Test at **Belle Vue.** The Manchester gates were closed with hundreds of fans still trying to get in. England went for a 'horses for courses' policy, with the team mainly comprising Northern riders. In fact, Kempster, and new skipper Varey, were the only riders retained, as Squib Burton, Joe Abbott, Frank Charles, Wally Hull, Colin Watson, and the Langton brothers, Eric and Oliver, were bought in to stem the tide.

As a tactic it worked and despite Australia's Max Grosskreutz's brilliant maximum, England won the day with a convincing victory,

ENGLAND 56: J. Kempster 10, S. Burton 9, F. Varey 9, E. Langton 8, J. Abbott 7, F. Charles 5, W. Hull 5, O. Langton 2, C. Watson 1.

AUSTRALIA 36: M. Grosskreutz 12, V. Huxley 7, F. Arthur 6, B. Lamont 5, D. Case 4, D. Wise 3, B. McCallum 2, J. Chapman 0.

The third Test at **Stamford Bridge** was the scene of high drama, as an over-ambitious move by England's Frank Varey in heat two, saw him crash into the fence, only to be catapulted head first onto the track, where he lay motionless. As he was stretchered off, the many thousands of spectators fell into stony silence and, as they awaited the doctor's verdict, they were suddenly plunged into darkness when a main fuse blew.

STAMFORD BRIDGE SPEEDWAY

Third Test Match

ENGLAND

AUSTRALIA

on

Wednesday, 20th August, 1930

at 8.0 p.m.

SOUVENIR PROGRAMME

PRICE - SIXPENCE

The more superstitious among them shuddered, but although the lights had gone out in the stadium, they had not gone out for Varey, and it was announced that he had regained consciousness. The 'blackout' lasted for some 30 minutes. With the lights back on, in a moment of high drama, Varey staggered out onto the track to acknowledge the rapturous crowd and to resume his place in the side.

Varey was tough. He returned to win heat six adding another win to his credit in a subsequent heat. The match itself proved to be a close-fought battle with both sides refusing to give an inch and, with only two races remaining, the scores were tied at 42 points apiece. In the penultimate race, Aussie skipper Huxley led from England's Wal Phillips and Frank Charles with Bluey Wilkinson at the rear. Huxley fell and the home riders moved into first and second places. However Charles' back tyre burst and Wilkinson also took a tumble. By this time Huxley had re-mounted and followed Phillips home. Despite this misfortune England still took a 1-point lead into the final heat.

As the riders broke from the first bend England's Syd Jackson led the field, with teammate Harold Stevenson third, the two riders being separated by Max Grosskreutz, with Billy Lamont trailing on a sick bike. That was the way it stayed, leaving England 3-point winners in a thrilling match.

ENGLAND 49: W. Phillips 12, H. Stevenson 7, F. Varey 7, A. Warwick 6, S. Burton 5, S. Jackson 3, F. Charles 3, A. Jervis 3, R. Frogley 2, J. Kempster 1.

AUSTRALIA 46: V. Huxley 11, F. Arthur 8, M. Grosskreutz 7, R. Johnson 7, D. Case 5, J. Chapman 4, C. Spinks 3, B. Lamont 1, B. Wilkinson 0, D. Wise 0.

It was back to **Belle Vue** for the fourth Test match and over 40,000 wildly enthusiastic fans turned out to see what was proving to be an unqualified success. England appeared to suffer an early blow when captain Frank Varey missed the boat from the Isle of Man, where he had been practising for the Manx Grand Prix. Never one to let England down, Frank made it to Hyde Road just in time, but he had damaged his ankle in the practice, and was not 100 per cent fit. Although the scores were fairly close, it was only the efforts of Vic Huxley and Jack

Chapman that kept the Aussies in the hunt, and at the final reckoning, the strength in depth of England saw them win the match by 6 points and claim the Ashes in its inaugural year.

ENGLAND 51: J. Parker 9, E. Langton 9, F. Varey 8, B. Harrison 8, W. Hull 6, S. Burton 5, F. Charles 5, J. Kempster 1.

AUSTRALIA 45: V. Huxley 12, J. Chapman 8, D. Case 7, F. Arthur 6, R. Johnson 6, M. Grosskreutz 5, B. Lamont 1, D. Wise 0.

It rained heavily for hours before the final match of the series at **Wembley**, and the rain continued throughout the match. In spite of this racing was close, but England were dogged by bad luck. Both Burton and Charles were leading in separate races when their bikes failed, and Australia seized their chance, creeping ahead just after the interval. Heat eleven alone was worth the price of admission, as Squib Burton and Billy Lamont rode 'tied together' for four laps, before Burton claimed the victory by a tyre's width. The race inspired the Lions, and they staged a comeback to overhaul the Roos and win the match by 4 points.

ENGLAND 49: J. Ormston 8, C. Watson 8, J. Parker 7, S. Burton 7, G. Kuhn 6, R. Frogley 5, F. Charles 4, F. Varey 4.

AUSTRALIA 45: V. Huxley 12, B. Lamont 10, J. Chapman 7, M. Grosskreutz 4, R. Johnson 4, D. Case 3, C. Spinks 2, B. Wilkinson 2, A. Hansen 1.

ENGLAND v AUSTRALIA TEST SERIES 1931

1st Test	Crystal Palace	June 27th	'31	Eng 55	Aust 37	W
2nd Test	Leicester	July 20th	'31	Eng 46	Aust 47	L
3rd Test	Wembley	Aug 24th	'31	Eng 53	Aust 43	W
4th Test	Belle Vue	Sept 5th	'31	Eng 53	Aust 41	W
5th Test	Stamford Bridge	Sept 23rd	'31	Eng 48	Aust 46	W

England win series 4–1

The inaugural 1930 Test Series had so captured the speedway public's imagination that a repeat performance the following year was deemed a necessity.

Colin Watson was selected as England's skipper and, at thirty-two years old, he was the oldest rider in the series. Eric Langton, Squib Burton and Wal Phillips were all recalled. Jack Ormston, Dusty Haigh, Joe Francis and twenty-three-year-old Jack Parker completed the main body of the Lions team.

The fabulous Vic Huxley once again led the Aussies, who also boasted the formidable Dickie Case, Bluey Scott and Max Grosskreutz. Ron Johnson, Dick Smythe and Frank Arthur also turned out for Australia in the first Test match of the series.

A bumper crowd arrived at **Crystal Palace** on the first dry Saturday in London since the speedway season had begun. The anticipated 'Megamatch' never materialised though and, before the interval, England were home and dry. Twenty-three-year-old Eric Langton won all of his four races and, as a pairing, he and Jack Parker were only split once, in the last heat of the match. The Aussies had their fair share of mechanical difficulties. In fact Grosskreutz and Woods, who should have had three machines at their disposal, only had one – and not the fastest at that.

ENGLAND: 55: E. Langdon 12, C. Burton 10, W. Phillips 10, J. Parker, 7, J. Ormston 5, H. Haigh 4, C. Watson 4, J. Francis 3.

AUSTRALIA 37: F. Arthur 9, M. Grosskreutz 7, V. Huxley 6, D. Case 6, B. Wilkinson 4, R. Johnson 3, L. Woods 2, D. Smythe 0.

The second Test took place on an appalling track at **Leicester** and, where the English riders exercised discretion at the expense of valour on the bumpy track, the Aussies threw caution to the wind. It led to many Australian fallers but, ironically, it was England who suffered the injuries. In the first heat, Squib Burton's motor seized, throwing him to the ground and Ron Johnson, who was in pursuit, ran into him. Johnson took no further part in the meeting for Australia and Burton was found to have a broken thigh, which ended his season. In a later race Wal Phillips fell and was run over by Arne Hansen. Phillips was also an early retiree from the match.

Twenty-two-year-old Lionel Van Praag had been called up for the visitors, and topped the Australian scorechart in a nail-biting match. Australia led from the outset, but when both Arthur and Hansen fell in heat nine, the resulting 5-0 from Sid Jackson and Joe Abbot gave England a 3-point lead. Thanks to Arthur Jervis, England, despite some gritty riding from the Aussies, held on, and going into the final heat, they held a 1-point lead.

As the tapes went up, Eric Langton's motor failed, leaving Jack Parker to try and catch the flying Frank Arthur. As hard as he tried, Parker could not match the Stamford Bridge skipper, and with Arne Hansen trailing in third, Australia won a thrilling match by a single point.

ENGLAND 46: A. Jervis 9, J. Abbott 8, E. Langdon 7, J. Parker 7, D. Haigh 6, H. Herbert 3, S. Jackson 3, F. Wilkinson 3, S. Burton 0, W. Phillips 0.

AUSTRALIA 47: L. Van Praag 9, D. Case 8, F. Arthur 7, V. Huxley 6, B. Blake 5, A. Hansen 5, M. Grosskreutz 4, B. Wilkinson 3, R. Johnson 0.

England, of course, had to replace Burton and Phillips for the third match at the Empire Stadium, **Wembley**. Tommy Croombs was making a comeback from injury and was an automatic choice. Wembley's own Harry Whitfield joined him, with twenty-three-year-old Tom Farndon being brought in at reserve.

An enormous crowd turned out to witness the spectacle and England did not disappoint. When Aussie skipper Huxley came to grief following an over-ambitious move on Colin Watson in heat one, England took an early lead, which they never relinquished throughout the match.

It was very much Jack Parker's night, as he rode to the fastest time around Wembley all year (79 seconds), and was unbeaten by an opponent in the match for England. Reg Bounds made an impressive debut for the home side, while Frank Arthur continued to improve as Australia's outstanding rider of the series so far.

England were 6 points up going into the interval, but they had lost Whitfield with an ankle injury in heat five. When Frank Arthur and Col Stewart began the second half with a 5-1 over Whitfield's replacement, Tom Farndon, the Aussies reduced the deficit to only 2 points. They

looked about to draw level in the following race, as Ron Johnson led from the struggling Eric Langton, but Johnson's back tyre came away from the rim, and England further increased their lead, to cruise home to a 10-point win.

ENGLAND 53: J. Parker 11, R. Bounds 10, G. Lees 8, E. Langton 7, D. Haigh 5, T. Croombs 4, C. Watson 3, H. Whitfield 2, T. Farndon 2, A. Warwick 1.

AUSTRALIA 43: F. Arthur 11, C. Spinks 7, R. Johnson 6, M. Grosskreutz 6, B. Wilkinson 5, L. Van Praag 4, C. Stewart 3, V. Huxley 1, A. Hansen 0.

For the fourth Test at **Belle Vue**, Australia played what was considered by some to be a trump card – they recalled the legendary 'Cyclone' Billy Lamont to the side. In the early days of speedway, along with 'Sprouts' Elder, full-throttle Billy was the biggest draw in the sport, but he was making a late return, and his match-fitness was in question. Eric Langdon took over as skipper for England, who recalled Frank Varey.

Track conditions at Hyde Road were treacherous, due to the amount of rain that had fallen. This suited the English riders more than the Australians. England rode as a team, whereas the Aussies rode as individuals, but track conditions considered, it was an intelligent performance by the home team, who kept their heads and were prepared to wait and take their opportunities as they were presented.

One such individual was Jack Parker, who had been in bed most of the week with influenza. He failed to make the gate in any of his four rides, and yet ended up with a 12-point maximum, in fact he and partner Dusty Haigh scored 18 points out of a possible 20. Ginger Lees was also a revelation for England, and dropped his only point to Bluey Wilkinson. For the Aussies, Vic Huxley returned to form and Wilkinson and Grosskreutz supported well, but the rain-soaked track was not to the liking of Van Praag and Lamont.

Australia flourished in the early stages and, after heat five, they led by 2 points. But in the next race, the dynamic duo of Parker and Haigh put England back in front and they steadily built on their lead to win the match comfortably.

ENGLAND 53: J. Parker 12, G. Lees 11, T. Croombs 7, C. Watson 6, D. Haigh 6, F. Varey 5, E. Langton 4, J. Abbott 2.

AUSTRALIA 41: V. Huxley 10, M. Grosskreutz 9, B. Wilkinson 8, F. Arthur 6, C. Spinks 4, L. Van Praag 2, B. Lamont 1, L. Woods 1, R. Johnson 0.

Parker was named as the England captain for the final Test at **Stamford Bridge**, and Reg Bounds, who had been so impressive at Wembley, was given another chance to shine. 'The Bridge' was one of the Australian's favourite tracks, and Frank Arthur was the current track record holder, so, even with the Ashes 'in the can', England appeared to have their hands full.

In the event, the match was all about Jack Parker, as indeed the series itself had been. In his opening heat, he smashed the British Mile Record, and in his next race, he lowered it by another 0.2 seconds. He completed a peerless performance by winning his remaining two races.

Local rider Gus Kuhn, who had replaced Croombs, gave a good account of himself, and got one of the biggest cheers of the night when he got the better of both Van Praag and Wilkinson in heat ten. It gave England a 10-point lead, but the Aussies, inspired by the team riding of skipper Huxley and partner Lamont, staged a comeback, and they trailed by a mere 2 points going into the last heat. After three false starts, the riders finally got away, led by Frank Arthur. Eric Langton was in second place, followed by partner Reg Bounds, but towards the end of the race, Langton's bike slowed alarmingly, and it was left to some heroics by Bounds to keep a lively Dick Smythe at the back to secure a 2-point win for England.

ENGLAND 48: J. Parker 12, C. Watson 8, G. Kuhn 7, E. Langton 7, D. Haigh 5, A. Warwick 4, R. Bounds 3, G. Lees 2.

AUSTRALIA 46: V. Huxley 10, F. Arthur 8, M. Grosskreutz 7, B. Lamont 5, R. Johnson 4, L. Van Praag 4, B. Wilkinson 4, D. Smythe 3, D. Wise 1.

The 1931 series had been a huge success, watched with great enthusiasm by thousands of speedway supporters, and it had made Jack Parker one of the most popular riders in the country.

ENGLAND v AUSTRALIA TEST SERIES 1932

1st Test Stamford Bridge	June 4th	'32	Eng 50	Aust 41	W
2nd Test Wembley	June 23rd	'32	Eng 35	Aust 59	L
3rd Test Belle Vue	July 26th	'32	Eng 53	Aust 43	W
4th Test Crystal Palace	Aug 6th	'32	Eng 45	Aust 49	L
5th Test Wembley	Sept 15th	'32	Eng 51	Aust 42	W

England win series 3-2

The 1932 season saw support for speedway in Britain flagging with attendances down all around the country, but the England v Australia Test Series once again received phenomenal support and played a major part in keeping the sport going in the UK.

The Aussies had their 'ready-made' team, and England, for the first Test at **Stamford Bridge**, included regulars Eric Langdon, Wal Phillips, Tommy Croombs and Colin Watson. Frank Varey and Arthur Warwick were given another run, as was young Tom Farndon and George Greenwood and Nobby Key made their International debuts.

Farndon had a terrifically impressive match for the home team, and it was his 5-1 with Greenwood in heat four, which put England back on track after Australia had taken an early 3-point lead. The Colonials regained the lead only to be thwarted again by the combination of Greenwood and Farndon in heat seven and from then on the Lions remained steadfast. Both skippers had off-nights with England's skipper Colin Watson failing to score, and his counterpart Huxley netting only 5 points.

ENGLAND 50: T. Farndon 11, W. Phillips 10, A. Warwick 8, F. Varey 8, N. Key 6, G. Greenwood 5, E. Langton 2, C. Watson 0, T. Croombs 0.

AUSTRALIA 41: M. Grosskreutz 7, D. Case 6, F. Arthur 6, V. Huxley 5, B. Wilkinson 5, R. Johnson 4, B. Lamont 4, L. Van Praag 2, J. Chapman 2, D. Smythe 0.

For the second Test at **Wembley** Watson was dropped and Jack Parker came in to replace him as England's captain. Ginger Lees and Jack Ormston were also reinstated. The match itself was a torrid affair, with several riders being disqualified, causing an uproar in the crowd, which resulted in the steward being given a police escort out of the stadium. The Aussies had come for a fight, and the 'rough and tumble' manner in which the match was ridden suited them down to the ground. Dick Case and Billy Lamont made history by becoming the first unbeaten partnership in a Test match and thus dictated the result.

England, as a team, just didn't hit it off. Farndon, their last top-scorer, failed to gain a single point, Parker was mounted on an under-powered bike and Langdon was involved in a crash that tore his boot clean from his foot. But that is to take nothing from the Australians, whose spirited performance saw them easily win the match 59-35.

ENGLAND 35: G. Greenwood 8, J. Ormston 7, E. Langdon 6, J. Parker 5, G. Lees 5, W. Phillips 4, T. Farndon 0, N. Key 0, A. Warwick 0, J. Francis 0.

AUSTRALIA 59: D. Case 12, V. Huxley 9, B. Wilkinson 9, B. Lamont 8, F. Arthur 8, D. Smythe 5, M. Grosskreutz 4, R. Johnson 3, C. Spinks 1.

Frank Varey returned for the third Test at **Belle Vue**, and stabilised the team. Thousands were turned away, as the Hyde Road gates were closed behind a full house as the series began to gain impetus.

Australia were at an immediate disadvantage when they were informed that Ron Johnson had broken down en route, and was not going to make it. The visitors still showed their fighting qualities, but Farndon, Lees and Varey were all on top form, and England stormed to a 10-point win.

ENGLAND 53: G. Lees 11, T. Farndon 11, F. Varey 11, J. Parker 9, E. Langdon 6, D. Haig 2, A. Warwick 2, J. Ormston 1, W. Phillips 0, G. Greenwood 0.

AUSTRALIA 43: D. Case 10, V. Huxley 6, B. Wilkinson 6, B. Lamont 6, F. Arthur 5, M. Grosskreutz 5, L. Van Praag 3, C. Spinks 2, D. Smythe 0.

England arrived at **Crystal Palace** determined to win the Ashes – but no more determined than Australia. The Test matches were currently the best thing in speedway, and the fourth Test was another heart-stopper. England were dealt a double blow as Farndon injured a leg in heat four, and in the following heat, Parker withdrew from the meeting after colliding with Ron Johnson. In spite of this, England still led by 6 points at the interval, and looked likely winners of the match.

In heat fourteen, Case and Lamont scored maximum points to pull the Aussies within 2 points of the home side and, in a classic heat fifteen, Huxley rode around Lees, to score a 4-2 with Grosskreutz to level the scores. In the deciding last race, Frank Varey led from Ron Johnson and Bluey Wilkinson, but a burst tyre saw him overtaken by the two Aussies who scored a 5-1 to win the match 49-45, and level the series.

ENGLAND 45: E. Langdon 10, J. Francis 8, F. Varey 7, N. Key 6, G. Lees 4, S. Jackson 4, J. Parker 2, T. Farndon 2, W. Phillips 1, A. Warwick 1.

AUSTRALIA 49: D. Case 10, V. Huxley 9, B. Lamont 8, B. Wilkinson 6, F. Arthur 5, R. Johnson 5, D. Smythe 4, M. Grosskreutz 2.

Three hours before racing commenced at **Wembley**, queues were forming outside the Empire Stadium to witness the climax of the best Test Series so far. The 53,000 supporters formed the largest crowd ever to watch a speedway match, and they weren't to be disappointed. Australia's skipper Huxley tried hard, being unbeaten by an opponent and equalling Ginger Lees' Wembley track record, but Grosskreutz's worst ever Test performance was a telling factor as England won another thrilling encounter by 9 points and, in the process, retained the Ashes.

ENGLAND 51: E. Langdon 10, G. Lees 10, W. Phillips 8, T. Farndon 7, J. Parker 6, H. Stevenson 5, N. Key 4, G. Byers 1.

AUSTRALIA 42: V. Huxley 12, R. Johnson 7, L. Van Praag 7, D. Case 5, D. Smythe 5, B. Wilkinson 3, F. Arthur 2, J. Chapman 1, M. Grosskreutz 0.

ENGLAND v AUSTRALIA TEST SERIES 1933

1st Test	Wembley	June 29th '33	Eng 76	Aust 47	W
2nd Test	Belle Vue	July 15th '33	Eng 61	Aust 65	L
3rd Test	Crystal Palace	July 29th '33	Eng 63½	Aust 62½	W
4th Test	Wimbledon	Aug 21st '33	Eng 62	Aust 64	L
5th Test	West Ham	Sept 4th '33	Eng 74	Aust 52	W

England win series 3-2

Before the 1933 Test Series got underway, there was a worry that there were not enough Australians riding in Britain to put together a competitive team at international level. The six-man team virtually picked itself, as Huxley, Wilkinson, Van Praag, Case, Johnson and Grosskreutz were all named and Ernie Evans and Jack Sharp were selected as reserves.

The Speedway Control Board selected the England team and appointed Harold Stevenson as captain. He was joined by Eric Langdon, Wal Phillips, Tom Farndon, Claude Rye, Ginger Lees and reserves Syd Jackson and Jack Parker, to ride against the Aussies in an eighteen-heat formula match, which was scored on a 4-2-1 basis.

Many thought that the Australians took the Test Series more seriously than the English did, and therefore rode the matches with more determination, but this was certainly not the case in the first Test at **Wembley**, where England put on a committed workmanlike performance. Eric Langdon was outstanding, winning his first four races in fine style, but when he overslid and went onto the grass in his next outing and finished second, the referee excluded him. Any public sympathy that Eric had gained was lost when he refused to come out for his final ride.

Ginger Lees set a new record by being the highest scorer ever in a Test match scoring 21 points out of a possible 24, but England's reserve Syd Jackson got the biggest cheer of the night scoring 15 points and winning three races. Indeed, the reserves played a significant part in the night due to the number of injuries sustained by the participants. In the second heat Claude Rye and Max Grosskreutz were both put out of the match and they were later followed by Tom Farndon in heat eight, and Wal Phillips in heat twelve, but such was the strength of England at reserve, that they were hardly missed.

ENGLAND 76: G. Lees 20, E. Langdon 16, S. Jackson 15, H. Stevenson 13, J. Parker 7, W. Phillips 4, T. Farndon 1, C. Rye 0.

AUSTRALIA 47: V. Huxley 12, D. Case 8, R. Johnson 8, B. Wilkinson 8, L. Van Praag 5, E. Evans 3, J. Sharp 3, M. Grosskreutz 0.

The second Test at **Belle Vue** left the England critics saying, 'I told you so'. The main criticism levelled at the English riders was their lack of consistency and sure enough, at Hyde Road, a traditionally happy hunting ground for the Aussies, that proved to be the case.

For England, Frank Varey, Bill Kitchen and Bob Harrison replaced Langton, Phillips and Farndon, while Australia made just one change, bringing in John Chapman for Jack Sharp. Ginger Lees was again in record-breaking form, this time scoring 22 points for England and breaking the track record. But apart from him and Syd Jackson, the home nation was, in the main, disappointing. Once Australia had nosed ahead in heat four, they never again fell behind and the difference was twenty-two-year-old Bluey Wilkinson, who at last performed at international level as he had been doing at club level for West Ham. He and Huxley never lost their focus all the way through the match, and although the Aussies were virtually a five-man team, their determined riding earned them a 4-point win.

Bill Kitchen deserves a mention for being unbeaten by an opponent in his two outings from reserve.

ENGLAND 61: G. Lees 22, S. Jackson 12, F. Varey 8, H. Stevenson 7, B. Kitchen 6, J. Parker 4, B. Harrison 2, T. Farndon 0.

AUSTRALIA 65: V. Huxley 16, B. Wilkinson 16, D. Case 12, E. Evans 9, M. Grosskreutz 9, J. Chapman 1, R. Johnson 1, L. Van Praag 1.

England arrived at **Crystal Palace** for the third match in the series without the injured Wal Phillips and Claude Rye and Eric Langdon riding for his club Belle Vue. So Joe Francis and Tom Farndon were brought in as replacements. The match however marked the return to form of Jack Parker which made the difference – but only just! Ginger Lees was rewarded for his record-breaking achievements by being appointed captain of the England side.

Farndon got the show on the road by beating Huxley in the first heat, but the early races saw the fortunes sway one way and then the other. A dead heat between Huxley and Joe Francis in heat five made a mess of everyone's programmes and, by the interval, the scores were locked at 31½ points apiece. England were looking the stronger of the two teams at that point, but the Australian pair of Dickie Case and Max Grosskreutz had yet to be beaten. Parker saw to that in heat twelve, as he established himself as the best rider on the night, scoring 17 points overall.

By the end of heat seventeen, England had won the match. But in the final race, the Aussies were flattered. Harold Stevenson had overtaken the formidable pairing of Case and Grosskreutz, when his con-rod made an appearance out of his crankcase leaving the 'Tiger' toothless. The resulting 6-1 to the Australians left England as the winners by a single point.

ENGLAND 63½: J. Parker 17, G. Lees 13, H. Stevenson 12, T. Farndon 11, J. Francis 6½, S. Jackson 4, B. Kitchen 0. T. Gamble 0.

AUSTRALIA 62½: D. Case 15, B. Wilkinson 14, M. Grosskreutz 13, R. Johnson 9, V. Huxley 8½, L. Van Praag 2, E. Evans 1, J. Chapman 0.

At **Wimbledon**, the close result belied the action, or rather the lack of it. After eighteen processional heats, in a match that was described as the most uninteresting Test so far. England's Syd Jackson was due to meet Australia's Ron Johnson for the final leg of the British Individual Championship a few days later and both rode sparingly. Ginger Lees and Tom Farndon proved to be a prolific pairing for England and, by the interval stage, the home team were 9 points ahead. But after the break the Australians came out fired up with adrenaline, while the English performance thereafter was laced with lethargy.

In heat fourteen, Australia replaced the reticent Johnson with Jack Chapman, and the Aussie reserve led Bluey Wilkinson home for a 5-1 for the visitors. In the very next race Grosskreutz and Case repeated the performance, as stricken Jack Kitchen was stretchered away from the track. Chapman was given another outing in heat sixteen at the expense of Evans and raced to another victory and, although England's

4TH OFFICIAL TEST MATCH
Monday, August 21st, 1933

WIMBLEDON
SPEEDWAY

OFFICIAL
SOUVENIR
PROGRAMME
4D.

Bob Harrison finished in front of Huxley, Australia took a 1-point lead. After all the hard work that they had put in, the Aussies were never going to let it go. At the end of the match they were 2-point winners and, although the meeting had been an uninspired affair, with the progressive score at 2 matches each, it did make for an intriguing finale at West Ham.

ENGLAND 62: G. Lees 17, H. Stevenson 13, T. Farndon 11, J. Parker 9, B. Kitchen 6, B. Harrison 4, Syd Jackson 1, J. Francis 1.

AUSTRALIA 64: M. Grosskreutz 18, B. Wilkinson 14, V. Huxley 12, D. Case 10, J. Chapman 8, E. Evans 2, R. Johnson 0, J. Sharp 0.

England's hopes received a blow in the run up to the final Test, as Kitchen remained injured, and was joined by Lees and Wal Phillips to add to the unavailability of Parker and Langdon. So Australia began as red-hot favourites to take the series. Stevenson again took on the captain's role and Farndon, and Bob Harrison were retained. The dearth of available riders meant a recall for Colin Watson, Frank Varey, Tommy Croombs and Squib Burton with Gordon Byers being given a crack at reserve.

England's makeshift side turned out to be a team with a point to prove. The substitutes did not revel in being considered second-best, and put on a determined show that left the Aussies reeling. In the first international staged at **West Ham**, Harold 'Tiger' Stevenson set the scene in the opening race when he clipped almost a full second off his home track record. Heat wins followed by Farndon, Varey and Watson. In fact, an English rider was first past the post in every race before the interval and England went into the break 42-21 points ahead of Australia.

In the interval the English euphoria diminished slightly and they returned to the track more subdued, whereas the Aussies returned determined to salvage some national pride. Led by the increasingly impressive Bluey Wilkinson and the never-say-die attitude of Vic Huxley, Australia applied themselves. But the damage had been done, and the mountain was too big to climb. At the end of eighteen heats, England were the unlikely winners by 74-52, and the Ashes were retained. It was no fluke however and the victory had been thoroughly deserved. The first nine heats at Custom House had arguably been England's finest hour and a feature of the meeting had been the riding of the English pairing of Harold Stevenson and Squib Burton.

ENGLAND 74: F. Varey 18, H. Stevenson 15, C. Burton 12, T. Farndon 10, C. Watson 9, T. Croombs 7, G. Byers 2, B. Harrison 1.

AUSTRALIA 52: B. Wilkinson 16, V. Huxley 13, D. Case 12, M. Grosskreutz 4, R. Johnson 3, J. Chapman 2, E. Evans 1, L. Van Praag 1.

The fourth Test Series once again drew huge crowds, but as a spectacle it was, compared to previous years, considered poor fare. However the series appeared to be in jeopardy. Australia had only just managed to put together a competitive team, and were lucky to steer clear of injuries. If Huxley, Wilkinson or Case had withdrawn, the result would have likely been a farce. Van Praag had been expected to join the Australian elite in 1933 but it hadn't happened at international level and, unless further top-class Australian riders were imported for the 1934 season, the continuation of the fixture looked doubtful.

ENGLAND v AUSTRALIA TEST SERIES 1934

1st Test	Wembley	June 7th	'34	Eng 38	Aust 69	L
2nd Test	New Cross	June 20th	'34	Eng 58	Aust 48	W
3rd Test	Wimbledon	July 9th	'34	Eng 51	Aust 54	L
4th Test	Belle Vue	July 21st	'34	Eng 60½	Aust 45½	W
5th Test	West Ham	Aug 21st	'34	Eng 50	Aust 57	L

Australia win series 3-2

There was not the anticipated influx of new Australian riders in 1934, but they still began as favourites for the first Test match at Wembley. The reason was that the Aussies had all hit top form in the beginning part of the season, with Vic Huxley winning the British individual title and, in the process, establishing himself as the best rider currently racing. Dick Case and Bluey Wilkinson had continued to flourish and Van Praag had, at last, begun to fulfil his fantastic potential.

The Control Board's selection for the English team was somewhat dubious. Colin Watson was reinstated as captain, and new London Champion Tom Farndon, Ginger Lees and 'Tiger' Stevenson were all recalled to the side. The board then went for in-form league riders, and Nobby Keys, Gordon Byers, Frank Charles, and Les Wotton filled the remaining places. Most were dismayed that Eric Langdon and the Parker brothers, Jack and Norman, had been overlooked and, in the event, they were costly omissions for England.

In front of a 50,000-strong crowd at **Wembley**, the Roos got off to a shaky start when Huxley collided with Wotton and appeared to be badly injured. Although he did not take his place in the rerun, the Australian skipper, although taking a knock on the knee, declared himself fit for the rest of the match. However the incident seemed to unsettle the Aussies and, after five heats, they trailed by 5 points. Heat six saw the beginning of the Case-Grosskreutz domination that would see them go on to score 28 points out of a possible 30.

Wilkinson and Johnson meted out the same punishment in heat eight, as the Australians began to take control. With the bit between their teeth the visitors put on the best display ever by an Australian side in a Test match. The English simply had no answer for antipodean exuberance and, apart from Ginger Lees, they were no match for the Aussies in this form. It spoke volumes for the match that, in the first half, the Wembley track record was broken no fewer than five times: once each by Farndon and Grosskreutz and three times by Lees.

ENGLAND 38: G. Lees 15, T. Farndon 8, C. Watson 6, F. Charles 5, N. Key 2, G. Byers 2, L. Wotton 0, H. Stevenson 0.

AUSTRALIA 69: M. Grosskreutz 15, D. Case 13, V. Huxley 12½, B. Wilkinson 12, R. Johnson 10, L. Van Praag 6½.

The England selectors had a quick re-think before the second match of the series at **New Cross**. Jack Parker chose not to ride at the Old Kent Road, but Eric Langdon was quickly drafted back into the side as were Joe Abbott and Tommy Croombs, with Joe Francis and Claude Rye being named as reserves. The Aussies, naturally, retained the nucleus of their side however, Lionel Van Praag moved down to reserve and Jack Sharp was given another outing in the starting team.

The Wembley result had rekindled the public's interest in the series, and a full house turned out in the hope of seeing England level the scores. They were not to be disappointed as the two rival teams served up a helping of thrilling speedway in what was a superb match.

New skipper Langdon made an impressive return, equalling Huxley's track record on his way to a 5-1 with Croombs in the opening heat. In heat two New Cross idol Tom Farndon overtook the Aussie pair of Wilkinson and Johnson to become the new track record holder. His celebrations were short lived because Huxley regained the record in heat four. Led by Langton and Lees, England kept up the pressure and, after nine heats, they led the match by 11 points. The torrid battle continued after the interval, but Australia suffered a blow when Huxley hit the fence in heat thirteen and jammed his leg in the rear wheel of his bike. It was the end of the match for the 'Wizard of Oz'. Meanwhile another England returnee, Joe Abbott, hit top form mid-match and was unbeaten throughout the second half of the meeting. This made the difference as England held off some determined opposition to win the match 58-48.

ENGLAND 58: E. Langdon 14, G. Lees 13, J. Abbott 13, T. Farndon 9, N. Key 6, T. Croombs 3, J. Francis 0, C. Rye 0.

AUSTRALIA 48: D. Case 13, R. Johnson 10, B. Wilkinson 9, V. Huxley 6, M. Grosskreutz 3, J. Sharp 3, F. Arthur 2, L. Van Praag 2.

The England-Australia roadshow now moved onto **Wimbledon**, and there was to be no let-up in the splendid entertainment provided by the two deadly rivals.

England knew a win at Plough Lane was important, as the final two Tests were on the large circuits of Belle Vue and West Ham which favoured the Aussies, especially on their current form. The home team was selected cautiously, with Langdon, Lees, Abbott and Farndon all being retained. Wimbledon specialist Claude Rye was given a place in the top six, as was Jack Kitchen. Geoff Pymar and Wal Phillips were named as reserves. Australia inevitably kept the same team with Frank Pearce named as second reserve.

Australia had all the bad luck though with spluttering bikes and exclusions. But their biggest setback came in heat four when skipper Huxley, still riding in pain from his injury at New Cross, fell and was run into by Joe Abbott. Vic was stretchered from the track and with him seemingly went Australia's hopes. However Jack Sharp responded brilliantly in these times of adversity to put on his best ever performance for Australia. Time and again the Aussies overcame major obstacles to win the respect of the most ardent England supporters. They established an early lead, which they maintained doggedly until heat eleven, when Johnson was excluded for exceeding the time limit and Wilkinson had machine trouble at the start. But England's lead was shortlived, as the visitors had again over-hauled them by heat thirteen and hung on grimly to win the match by 3 points.

If Australia had been impressive then conversely England had been disappointing. Although Eric Langdon was the best rider of both teams on view, Claude Rye failed to score a point on his home track and Farndon and Kitchen only scored 4 points each.

ENGLAND 51: E. Langdon 16, G. Lees 13, J. Abbott 11, B. Kitchen 4, T. Farndon 4, G. Pymar 3, C. Rye 0, W. Phillips dnr.

AUSTRALIA 54: M. Grosskreutz 15, J. Sharp 13, R. Johnson 9, D. Case 7, B. Wilkinson 4, F. Pearce 3, V. Huxley 2, L. Van Praag 1.

England desperately needed a result at **Belle Vue** to be in with a chance of retaining the Ashes and so their strongest team of the season so far took to the track at Hyde Road. Once again the side was built around Langton, Lees, Abbott and Charles. The selectors persevered with Farndon and Tiger Stevenson was recalled to the side with Croombs and Gordon Byers named as the reserves. Although there was a question over Vic Huxley's fitness Australia stayed unchanged, with Wally Little named as their number eight. However, they broke up the most profitable pairing of the series, with Dick Case joining Huxley, and Max Grosskreutz teaming up with Jack Sharp. This further fuelled fears regarding Huxley's fitness.

Those fears were realised as early as the first heat when Huxley, who was chasing Eric Langton at the time, slid to earth unaided. He continued for the rest of the meeting but was obviously not up to the job and the result was a disaster for the Aussies. Twenty-six-year-old Ron

Johnson continued to improve and top-scored for Australia with 15 points but, apart from Grosskreutz, support was thin on the ground, although the racing was keen. The Belle Vue track record disintegrated, as the existing time of 78 seconds was equalled five times (Charles, Lees, Croombs and Grosskreutz) and broken five times by Langdon, Charles, Lees, Johnson and Grosskreutz. With Huxley struggling, England took full advantage of the situation with four riders scoring double points and Langdon winning five of his six races. The home team built an early lead, which they never looked like losing and steadily increased it to win the match by 15 points and level the series.

ENGLAND 60½: E. Langton 15, G. Lees 14, F. Charles 13, J. Abbott 10, T. Farndon 4, T. Croombs 3, H. Stevenson 1½, G. Byers dnr.

AUSTRALIA 45½: R. Johnson 15, M. Grosskreutz 11, B. Wilkinson 5, L. Van Praag 4½, J. Sharp 4, D. Case 4, W. Little 1, V. Huxley 1.

There was a month's gap to the next rubber during which Vic Huxley had a chance to get himself fit – but to no avail. He was, however, present in the pits at **West Ham**, resplendent in his dapper lounge suit, at hand to give his teammates all the help, advice, and inspiration that they needed to pull off an unlikely result.

There were no surprises from the England selectors with Langton, Lees, Abbott, Charles, Croombs and Farndon making up the main body of the team and Tiger Stevenson and Norman Parker taking the reserve berths.

England skipper Langton set the scene in heat one when he broke Tom Farndon's record by over a second, beating Ron Johnson to the chequered flag. The next three races showed that the Aussies had most certainly come to win as Wilkinson, Grosskreutz and Sharp all headed the English riders home to establish a 4-point lead. In a torrid first half, the old track record was beaten or equalled a further four times, as Wilkinson and Grosskreutz put on a breathtaking display to maintain a 4-point lead for Australia into the interval.

In the second half England immediately struck back through Langdon and Croombs when Johnson hit the deck and Jack Sharp broke a con-rod, but the Aussies would not be denied. And although Joe Abbott managed to split Wilkinson and Van Praag, England fell 2 points behind. An engine failure by Grosskreutz cost him his only points of the night, as the scores were levelled again in heat twelve. When Ron Johnson fell again in the following heat, England took a 2-point lead.

The scores remained level over the next two races and the final three heats were run amid a white-hot atmosphere. Heat sixteen saw Australia enjoy a little good fortune when England's Tom Farndon suffered a puncture on his way up to the tapes and, with time running out, a 'cold' Norman Parker replaced him. The resulting 4–2 to Australia put them in the driving seat. The penultimate heat would be all about Langton and Bluey Wilkinson, but the Australian knew the fastest way around his home track and 3 points apiece meant that the visitors went into the last heat 2 points in front. Heat eighteen proved to be an anticlimax. England needed a miracle for either Abbott or Charles to beat Grosskreutz in his current form, but in the event no English rider even finished the race. Charles, who had been suffering from water on the knee, withdrew from the race and his replacement, Tiger Stevenson, was excluded for a starting infringement. When the race finally got underway, Abbott retired on the second lap leaving Grosskreutz and Case to cruise round for a 5–0 making the Aussies 7-point winners and holders of the Ashes for the first time.

Against all odds Australia fully deserved their victory, but it was a Test Series that, in reality, they should never have won. The non-selection of Jack Parker throughout the series, for whatever reason, was a flawed decision and, while it is true that one rider does not make a team, Parker had proved himself time and again to be one of the very best that England had to offer. He was certainly on a par with Eric Langdon who was England's top scorer in the series.

ENGLAND 50: E. Langdon 13, G. Lees 11, J. Abbott 9, T. Croombs 7, T. Farndon 7, F. Charles 2, T. Stevenson 1, N. Parker 0.

AUSTRALIA 57: B. Wilkinson 16, M. Grosskreutz 15, R. Johnson 10, D. Case 8, J. Sharp 5, L. Van Praag 2, W. Little 1.

AUSTRALIA v ENGLAND TEST SERIES 1934/5

1st Test	Sydney	Dec 15th	'34	Aust 35	Eng 19	L
2nd Test	Melbourne	Jan 12th	'35	Aust 30	Eng 24	L
3rd Test	Sydney	Jan 19th	'35	Aust 26	Eng 27	W
4th Test	Sydney	Feb 11th	'35	Aust 29	Eng 24	L
5th Test	Sydney	Feb 16th	'35	Aust 26½	Eng 27½	W

Australia win series 3–2

If England couldn't win in their own country, how would they be able to win in Australia? It turned out they weren't able to, but they did give a good account of themselves. Most of the squad that they took had never ridden down under before and, after an uncertain start, the final four matches were close fought affairs.

England 'exported' five regulars in Eric Langdon, Joe Abbott, Wal Phillips, Frank Varey and Harold Stevenson, who were joined by Cliff Parkinson, Arthur Atkinson, Geoff Pymar, Bill Clibbett and Dusty Haigh. Australia had Max Grosskreutz, Lionel Van Praag, Dick Case and Bluey Wilkinson. Wally Little and Frank Pearce also had Test match experience and Clem Mitchell, Bert Spencer, Mick Murphy, Tiger Lewis and Dick Sulway all made an appearance for the Aussies in their inaugural home Test Series.

Australia were without Vic Huxley and Ron Johnson, but England were without Ginger Lees, Tom Farndon and 1934 Star Champion Jack Parker.

1st Test at Sydney

AUSTRALIA 35: M. Grosskreutz 8, L. Van Praag 8, B. Wilkinson 7, D. Case 6, C. Mitchell 4, W. Little 2.

ENGLAND 19: H. Stevenson 8, E. Langton 5, J. Abbott 3, F. Varey 2, W. Phillips 1, D. Haigh 0, C. Parkinson 0.

2nd Test at Melbourne

AUSTRALIA 30: M. Grosskreutz 9, D. Case 7, B. Wilkinson 6, L.Van Praag 4, B. Spencer 4

ENGLAND 24: E. Langton 7, J.Abbott 5, H. Stevenson 4, A.Atkinson 4, W. Phillips 2, G. Pymar 1, B. Clibbett 1.

3rd Test at Sydney

AUSTRALIA 26: M. Grosskreutz 7, B. Wilkinson 6, W. Little 5, D. Case 4, L.Van Praag 2, T. Lewis 2.

ENGLAND 27: H. Stevenson 9, J.Abbott 6, A.Atkinson 4, E. Langdon 4, C. Parkinson 2, W. Phillips 1, F.Varey 1.

4th Test at Sydney

AUSTRALIA 29: W. Little 7, M. Murphy 6, M. Grosskreutz 5, C. Mitchell 5, B.Wilkinson 3, F. Pearce 3.

ENGLAND 24: J.Abbott 9, D. Haigh 6, H. Stevenson 3, E. Langdon 3, A.Atkinson 3, F.Varey 0.

5th Test at Sydney

AUSTRALIA 26½: B.Wilkinson 9, M. Grosskreutz 8, C. Mitchell 7, F. Pearce 1½, M. Murphy 1, T. Lewis 0, D. Sulway 0

ENGLAND 27½: D. Haig 8, E. Langdon 7, A.Atkinson 4, H. Stevenson 4, W. Phillips 3, F.Varey 1, C. Parkinson ½.

ENGLAND v AUSTRALIA TEST SERIES 1935

1st Test	Wembley	June 6th	'35	Eng 56	Aust 52	W
2nd Test	New Cross	June 19th	'35	Eng 59	Aust 46	W
3rd Test	Belle Vue	July 6th	'35	Eng 59	Aust 48	W
4th Test	West Ham	July 30th	'35	Eng 40	Aust 66	L
5th Test	Haringay	Aug 24th	'35	Eng 63	Aust 44	W

England win series 4-1

Abysmal rainy weather abounded in the first Test match of the season at **Wembley**. There were spills aplenty, and the first three heats took 40 minutes to complete. Huxley, Grosskreutz, Abbott and Johnson all featured in some nasty looking crashes but, fortunately, all walked away from them.

England at last welcomed Jack Parker back into the team, strangely to partner Eric Langdon and Tommy Croombs, Joe Owen and Frank Charles were all recalled. Jack Kitchen and Jack Ormston completed the England line-up. There was no change to the Aussies apart from the absent Dickie Case.

Conditions limited the action and England went into the interval, having lost Croombs, 2 points in front. Despite the efforts of Max Grosskreutz, who won all of the five races that he finished, England held Australia at bay in the second half due to a Langdon-Parker pairing that was unbeaten over the last nine heats. Kitchen was impressive for the home side, but Australian supremo Vic Huxley seemed oddly ill at ease all throughout the match.

ENGLAND 56: E. Langton 15, B. Kitchen 12, F. Charles 11, J. Parker 10, J. Ormston 5, T. Croombs 2, J. Abbott 1.

AUSTRALIA 52: M. Grosskreutz 15, B. Wilkinson 10, R. Johnson 9, L. Van Praag 8, V. Huxley 6, J. Sharp 4.

Twenty-five-year-old Tom Farndon had by now established himself as one of the very best English riders of that era. He won the Star Championship in 1933, and was the reigning British Champion. After spells with Coventry and Crystal Palace, he had ended up at New Cross where he was the undisputed darling of the terraces. However Farndon had never shown his best form for England until the second Test match of 1935 at his home track, **New Cross**.

The British Individual Champion stormed his way to 15 spectacular points in front of another packed house. With Langdon scoring 13 and Kitchen once again impressing with 10 points, England were comfortable winners by 59-46. Dickie Case returned to the Australian team and was indeed its top scorer but, apart from him and Max Grosskreutz, the Aussies were ineffectual and already looked battle-weary.

ENGLAND 59: T. Farndon 14, E. Langdon 13, B. Kitchen 10, J. Parker 8, J. Abbott 8, F. Charles 6, T. Croombs 0, G. Pymar dnr.

AUSTRALIA 46: D. Case 12, M. Grosskreutz 11, V. Huxley 8, R. Johnson 8, B. Wilkinson 5, L. Van Praag 2, J. Sharp 0, D. Smythe dnr

The third Test at **Belle Vue** had some of the best riding ever seen on a British speedway track. The English team, having already won two matches, were supremely confident and consistently outrode the Australians. Wilkinson and Johnson impressed for the Aussies but their success was kept in check by one of England's finest displays. Dickie Case got a nasty knock in his first outing and was subdued for the rest of the meeting, but even on top form he wouldn't have changed the result.

Eric Langdon was the hero for England, dropping his only point of the match to Bluey Wilkinson, but his partner Parker looked oddly out of touch. Joe Abbott put in another rock-solid performance and the Farndon-Kitchen partnership was the home side's best pairing with Kitchen staking a claim to becoming an England regular.

Australia never led in the meeting and never looked likely to and, by the end of sixteen heats, the match was already won. England raced to a 59-48 victory, and regained the Ashes with two matches still to ride.

ENGLAND 59: E. Langdon 17, J. Abbott 13, T. Farndon 11, B. Kitchen 10, T. Croombs 5, J. Parker 3, H. Stevenson dnr, R. Harrison dnr.

AUSTRALIA 48: B. Wilkinson 13, R. Johnson 11, M. Grosskreutz 9, V. Huxley 6, L. Van Praag 5, D. Case 3, J. Sharp 1, M. Murphy 0.

Even though the series had been won, 71,000 spectators turned out at **West Ham** to see the fourth Test and, to their credit, beaten Australia put on a splendid show. They were more at home on the 440-yard track and were desperate to salvage some pride. The warning signs were there for England as early as heat one, when Aussie skipper Vic Huxley set a new track record and beat Eric Langton. In heat two Van Praag finished only 0.2 seconds outside of Huxley's time and with Grosskreutz, Johnson, Van Praag and Wilkinson winning the next six heats between them, a stunned England side went into the interval 12 points adrift of the visitors.

There was no let-up in the second half, despite some spirited riding for England by Tommy Croombs on his home track. The other English West Ham rider was Harold 'Tiger' Stevenson, but he was struggling following a nasty fall at Hackney the previous night and Jack Parker looked completely out of sorts. For the Aussies, Grosskreutz was back to his very best and dropped his only point of the night to Croombs. At the end of eighteen heats, Australia were the easy winners by 66-40.

ENGLAND 40: T. Croombs 9, E. Langdon 8, T. Farndon 6, F. Charles 6, H. Stevenson 4, B. Kitchen 3, J. Abbott 2, J. Parker 2.

AUSTRALIA 66: M. Grosskreutz 17, R. Johnson 13, L. Van Praag 12, V. Huxley 9, B. Wilkinson 9, D. Case 6, Jack Sharp dnr, D. Smythe dnr.

For the final Test at **Haringay**, twenty-five-year-old Jack Ormston was recalled to ride on his home track, which proved to be an inspired move. On a rain-soaked circuit that suited the English better than the Australians, the home team took an early lead, but two 5-1's in heats eight and nine saw the Aussies draw level going into the interval. However, Wilkinson and Johnson hit the deck in subsequent races following the break and England applied the pressure. The match was effectively all over by the end of heat fifteen, after visitors Grosskreutz and Case both retired, leaving Parker and Langton to cruise to a 5-0. The following two 5-1's and a drawn last heat gave England the win by a rather flattering 63-44 scoreline.

ENGLAND 63: J. Ormston 14, E. Langton 14, F. Charles 12, T. Farndon 10, J. Parker 9, T. Croombs 2, N. Parker 2, J. Abbott 0.

AUSTRALIA 44: M. Grosskreutz 12, V. Huxley 10, L. Van Praag 8, B. Wilkinson 7, D. Case 5, R. Johnson 2, J. Sharp dnr, D. Smythe dnr.

England's celebrations were short-lived. The following week, Tom Farndon rode for his club New Cross in a match against visitors Haringay. In the scratch race final, Farndon was involved in an accident that left him with serious head injuries and, two days later, he died in hospital. It was an awful blow to England and to speedway in general. In the space of six years, Tom had enjoyed a meteoric rise to fame and, at the time of his demise, he was recognised as one of the finest riders in the world, being the current London Riders Champion and British Individual Champion.

AUSTRALIA v ENGLAND TEST SERIES 1935/36

1st Test	Sydney	Dec 21st	'35	Aust 47	Eng 25	L
2nd Test	Sydney	Jan 4th	'36	Aust 44	Eng 28	L
3rd Test	Sydney	Jan 18th	'36	Aust 44	Eng 28	L
4th Test	Sydney	Feb 1st	'36	Aust 39	Eng 33	L
5th Test	Sydney	Feb 15th	'36	Aust 32	Eng 39	W

Australia win series 4-1

Australia kept their nucleus of Huxley, Grosskreutz and Wilkinson to face England in Sydney during the winter. Clem Mitchell, Frank Pearce, Mick Murphy and Dick Sulway had all ridden in Australia's Tests the previous winter and Art Fenn and Jack Hyland had made their international debuts. For the final two Tests 'Cyclone' Billy Lamont, one of speedway's greatest pioneers was brought into the team, but he was unable to regain any of his once-stunning form.

England sent over what can only be described as the reserve team, with no sign of Langdon, Ormston, Parker, Abbott, or Charles. Tiger Stevenson led the team which included Dusty Haigh, Wal Phillips, Arthur Atkinson, Nobby Key, Cliff Parkinson and Rol Stobbart. Understandably, they fared poorly and won only the final match in the series.

1st Test at Sydney

AUSTRALIA 47: M. Grosskreutz 12, V. Huxley 9, C. Mitchell 9, F. Pearce 8, M. Murphy 5, A. Fenn 4, D. Sulway 0.

ENGLAND 25: H. Stevenson 8, D. Haigh 7, A. Atkinson 4, N. Key 3, C. Parkinson 3, W. Phillips 0, R. Stobbart 0.

2nd Test at Sydney

AUSTRALIA 44: M. Grosskreutz 12, V. Huxley 11, B. Wilkinson 10, J. Hyland 5, C. Mitchell 4, F. Pearce 1, A. Fenn 1.

ENGLAND 28: W. Phillips 7, H. Stevenson 6, A. Atkinson 6, N. Key 4, D. Haigh 4, C. Parkinson 1, R. Stobbart dnr.

3rd Test at Sydney

AUSTRALIA 44: M. Grosskreutz 12, V. Huxley 11, B. Wilkinson 11, F. Pearce 5, A. Fenn 3, C. Mitchell 2, J. Hyland 0.

ENGLAND 28: N. Key 7, W. Phillips 6, C. Parkinson 5, D. Haigh 4, H. Stevenson 3, A. Atkinson 3, R. Stobbart dnr.

4th Test at Sydney

AUSTRALIA 39: M. Grosskreutz 12, F. Pearce 8, V. Huxley 7, B. Wilkinson 6, C. Mitchell 3, A. Fenn 2, B. Lamont 1.

ENGLAND 33: W. Phillips 10, N. Key 7, D. Haigh 7, H. Stevenson 6, C. Parkinson 3, R. Stobbart 0, A. Atkinson dnr.

Empire Speedways (1935) Ltd.

present the

4th Official Test Match

ENGLAND

versus

AUSTRALIA

at

Royal Agricultural Showground, Sydney

Saturday, February 1, 1936

Souvenir Programme . . . Price 6d.

5th Test at Sydney

AUSTRALIA 32: V. Huxley 11, M. Grosskreutz 9, B. Wilkinson 5, F. Pearce 3, C. Mitchell 2, A Fenn 2, B. Lamont 0.

ENGLAND 39: W. Phillips 10, N. Key 8, C. Parkinson 6, H. Stevenson 5, D. Haigh 5, A. Atkinson 5, R. Stobbart dnr.

ENGLAND v AUSTRALIA TEST SERIES 1936

1st Test	Wembley	May 28th	'36	Eng 65	Aust 43	W
2nd Test	New Cross	June 20th	'36	Eng 49	Aust 56	L
3rd Test	Belle Vue	July 4th	'36	Eng 70	Aust 38	W
4th Test	Wimbledon	July 20th	'36	Eng 58	Aust 47	W
5th Test	West Ham	Aug 18th	'36	Eng 35	Aust 73	L

England win series 3-2

On the eve of the 1936 series England, and speedway, was dealt another sickening blow as thirty-six-year-old Dusty Haig was killed in a three-fold collision at Hackney in May.

Both teams remained virtually unchanged for the first Test at **Wembley**, England bringing Kitchen into the team proper to replace Farndon and New Cross rider George Newton making his debut at the expense of Tommy Croombs. Ginger Lees and Gus Kuhn were named as reserves. Australia stuck with the 'usual six', and selected Jack Sharp and Dick Smythe as their reserves.

New skipper Frank Charles got England off to a good start leading Australia's best pairing of Grosskreutz and Case home and Parker and Langton kept Huxley behind them in the following race. Heat three saw George Newton make a super debut, leading Bluey Wilkinson home and, two races later, he did the same to Van Praag.

Newton, in fact, proved to be the ace in England's pack, dropping his only points to Grosskreutz and Huxley. But none of the home team riders could be faulted, as England scored well throughout the team. Australia on the other hand, apart from Wilkinson and the fantastically consistent Max Grosskreutz, were disappointing.

ENGLAND 65: G. Newton 16, F. Charles 13, J. Parker 12, E. Langdon 12, B. Kitchen 5, J. Abbott 5, G. Lees 2, G. Khun 0.

AUSTRALIA 43: M. Grosskreutz 13, B. Wilkinson 11, V. Huxley 7, R. Johnson 6, L. Van Praag 4, D. Case 2. J. Sharp 0, D. Smythe dnr

Just as everyone was thinking the Aussies were down and out they bounced back. Following one of his worst Test performances at Wembley (2 points), Dickie Case topped the visitors' scorechart in the second Test at **New Cross**, and led his country to a 7-point win. The match was however marred by a controversial incident.

Australia juggled their pairings and placed Wilkinson with Grosskreutz, the leading and third-placed league points scorers. But in the early part of the match they were not as effective as expected. The man who stood between them in the league scorechart was Frank Charles of Wembley, the new England skipper, and Frank drove beautifully all night, storming to an 18-point maximum. George Newton had of course been retained and there was a new face in the England team as Russian born Stan Greatrex made his debut.

The home team faced a setback when Langton withdrew from the match after only three heats and Greatrex and Ormston were brought into play. At the interval, Australia led by 2 points. As the second half began, the Grosskreutz-Wilkinson pairing turned up the heat and scored two 5-1's. However, England staged a late revival, and by the start of heat sixteen they were only 5 points adrift.

Aussies Van Praag and Sharp lined up against Newton and Greatrex. Newton shot from the tapes ahead of Van Praag who was followed by his teammate Sharp. Sharp fell and Greatrex moved into third place and the stricken Aussie, to his credit, moved, with his machine, onto the centre green.

The riders completed another lap before the race was stopped, with the steward offering the excuse that it did not appear that the track would be safe at the time. Murphy was allowed to replace Sharp in the rerun, despite Sharp's exclusion. Not only that, but Van Praag won the rerun, with the 'illegal' Murphy taking third place. It meant of course that the original England 4-2 ended up as a 4-2 to Australia. England hit back in the penultimate heat with a 5-1 from Charles and Abbott, but Case and Huxley crossed the line first in heat eighteen to record a 56-49 win for the Aussies.

ENGLAND 49: F. Charles 18, J. Parker 8, G. Newton 7, J. Abbott 6, S. Greatrex 5, G. Lees 4, J. Ormston 1, E. Langdon 0.

AUSTRALIA 56: D. Case 16, M. Grosskreutz 12, L. Van Praag 12, B. Wilkinson 7, V. Huxley 4, R. Johnson 3, M. Murphy 2, J. Sharp 0.

For all their competitiveness, Australia were a fragile team. The senior member of the team, Vic Huxley, had a career that was now in recession. But Lionel Van Praag was at last beginning to ride to his potential at international level and Bluey Wilkinson was still a young man. But they still had only six international riders. As if to highlight the problem, Grosskreutz was absent for the third Test at **Belle Vue** and the Aussies were thrashed 70-38.

Langton made a successful return to the England team and Frank Charles was again superb. Bill Kitchen and Joe Abbott also took full advantage of the situation, as the Australians nursed the far from fit Ron Johnson and Jack Sharp in this one-sided match.

ENGLAND 70: F. Charles 16, B. Kitchen 16, J. Abbott 13, E. Langton 13, W. Phillips 7, J. Parker 5, G. Lees dnr, B. Harrison dnr.

AUSTRALIA 38: L. Van Praag 11, D. Case 8, R. Johnson 7, B. Wilkinson 6, V. Huxley 4, B. Lamont 2, J. Sharp 0, M. Murphy 0.

The Ashes were regained at **Wimbledon**, due to a determined performance by the England team who replaced Joe Abbott with Ginger Lees and named George Newton and Claude Rye as reserves. Australia were still without Grosskreutz and bought in Eric Collins as a replacement, with Murphy and Sharp filling the reserve berths. Bluey Wilkinson was carrying an unusual injury, having upset a kettle of boiling water over his foot earlier in the week and, although he must have ridden in great pain, he never let up throughout the match.

For Australia, Huxley put on a vintage performance, but their star rider was again Van Praag, who dropped just 3 points all night. Support for the top three Aussies was thin on the ground however and England had more strength in depth. Bill Kitchen, having fallen and suffered disqualification, dropped only 1 further point to Van Praag and Eric Langton was back to his very best. Jack Parker's England performances were, at that time, enigmatic. He tore around the track in his opening ride, making Van Praag and Langton look comparatively slow. But having shown what he could do, he appeared to lose interest. Wal Phillips took a nasty knock when he looped at the gate in his first appearance. But Phillips was made of tough stuff and thereafter put on an impressive display.

ENGLAND 58: E. Langton 15, F. Charles 13, B. Kitchen 11, W. Phillips 9, J. Parker 7, G. Lees 2, G. Newton 1, C. Rye dnr.

AUSTRALIA 47: L. Van Praag 15, V. Huxley 12, B. Wilkinson 9, D. Case 5, E. Collins 4, J. Sharp 2, R. Johnson 0, M. Murphy dnr.

As in 1935, with nothing to gain apart from national pride, the Aussies saved the best until last. Grosskreutz returned for the final Test at **West Ham** and formed part of a six-man attack that completely stunned England. The Australian riders frequently out-gated the English and then proceeded to give them a lesson in team riding led by skipper Bluey Wilkinson, who was unbeaten by an opponent. Losing Jack Parker with a broken wrist in the first race may have phased England. Indeed his partner Langton withdrew from the meeting after four rides having scored only 4 points and they certainly lacked the fire of their opponents.

ENGLAND 35: F. Charles 8, B. Kitchen 8, A. Atkinson 6, E. Langton 4, G. Newton 4, J. Ormston 3, T. Croombs 2, J. Parker 0.

AUSTRALIA 73: B. Wilkinson 16, L. Van Praag 15, V. Huxley 11, D. Case 11, M. Grosskreutz 10, R. Johnson 8, E. Collins 2, C. Spinks dnr.

The victory was not the end of Australia's celebrations in 1936. On September 10 Wembley Stadium staged the first ever World Championship and, although Bluey Wilkinson went through the meeting unbeaten, a complicated bonus point system that was employed in the event meant that a run-off for the title took place between Eric

Langton and Lionel Van Praag. Although Langton broke the tapes at the first attempt he was not penalised, but Van Praag kept his nerve and won the all-important race, making speedway history by becoming the first ever World Champion.

AUSTRALIA v ENGLAND TEST SERIES 1936/37

1st Test	Sydney	Dec 12th	'36	Aust 29	Eng 25	L
2nd Test	Melbourne			Aust 33	Eng 21	L
3rd Test	Sydney	Jan 13th	'37	Aust 25	Eng 28	W
4th Test	Sydney	Feb 6th	'37	Aust 26	Eng 28	W
5th Test	Sydney	Feb 20th	'37	Aust 31	Eng 22	L

Australia win series 3-2

England took a fairly good team out to Australia in the winter of 1936, comprising the Parker brothers, Jack and Norman, Wal Phillips, Tommy Croombs, Les Wotton, Jack Ormston and Cliff Parkinson. Australia only tracked three out of their six regulars – Vic Huxley, Bluey Wilkinson, and Dick Case with Wally Little, Clem Mitchell and Art Fenn making up their team for the first Test match at **Sydney**.

In front of a record crowd, estimated at 50,000, England got off to a super start as Tommy Croombs and Jack Parker collected a 5-1 after Huxley's bike had given up the ghost. In the following race the Aussies were again unfortunate as Bluey Wilkinson, having disembarked from the boat from England a few hours earlier, looped at the gate and crashed onto his back. Further misery followed for the home team as Dick Case suffered engine failure in the third heat keeping him out of the remainder of the match. However by heat six Australia were back on equal terms and it stayed that way until the final race (heat nine). Wilkinson and Mitchell shot from the gate and, despite some close attention by Wal Phillips, the Colonial pair held on to win the first Test by 4 points.

AUSTRALIA 29: W. Little 9, C. Mitchell 8, V. Huxley 6, B. Wilkinson 5, A. Fenn 1, D. Case 0.

ENGLAND 25: T. Croombs 5, N. Parker 5, J. Parker 4, L. Wotton 4, C. Parkinson 4, W. Phillips 3.

The Empire Stadium at Olympic Park, **Melbourne**, staged the second Test, but the Aussies were without Wilkinson, Fenn and Case, replacing them with Bill Rogers, Bert Spencer and Eric Bibby to ride in what were poor weather conditions. Certainly, the Roos looked weaker on paper but as so often before, when their backs were against the wall the Aussies showed all of their fighting spirit, with England providing only three race winners. Wally Little completed his second successive maximum for Australia, Clem Mitchell was also unbeaten in the match and the Roos stormed to an easy win leaving the Lions little chance of retaining the Ashes.

AUSTRALIA 33: W. Little 9, C. Mitchell 9, B. Rogers 6, V. Huxley 4, B. Spencer 3, J. Bibby 2.

ENGLAND 21: J. Parker 7, W. Phillips 6, L. Wotton 5, C. Parkinson 2, N. Parker 1, J. Ormston 0.

It was back to the **Sydney** Showground for the third Test as Wilkinson, Lamont and Case all returned to the Australian side, which had a formidable look about it. Into the bargain, the Aussies were also blooding twenty-six-year-old Vic Duggan, a rider who would have much influence in his country's speedway future. England, to their credit, rode much better than in the first two matches, with Norman Parker being vastly improved and brother Jack, the Lions skipper, winning two races after his engine had seized during his first outing. For the home side Bluey Wilkinson was unbeaten but, apart from Huxley, the rest of the team were disappointing and England took command of the match after heat four and went on to an unlikely victory.

AUSTRALIA 25: B. Wilkinson 9, V. Huxley 7, W. Little 4, D. Case 3, V. Duggan 2, B. Lamont 0.

ENGLAND 28: N. Parker 7, T. Croombs 7, J. Parker 6, C. Parkinson 3, W. Phillips 3, L. Wotton 2.

England kept their hopes alive with a 2-point win in the fourth Test at **Sydney**, in front of 40,000 captivated supporters. While Australia had the best rider on view in unbeaten Bluey Wilkinson the visitors had the better teamwork. England led as early as heat two when a machine failure for Little allowed Norman Parker and Les Wotton through and they both kept Huxley out to move into a 4-point lead which they maintained until the penultimate heat. This featured the unbeaten Wilkinson and Norman Parker. Aussie Dick Case got tangled up in the tapes and was disqualified, but Bluey made no such mistake and flew from the tapes to remain the only unbeaten rider on the night.

In the final heat, Wal Phillips faced Wally Little and Vic Huxley and, although Little was quickly away, Phillips settled into second place and held off the determined Huxley to give England a 2-point victory. However Phillips' celebrations were short-lived as, later on in the evening during the Scratch races, he crashed and suffered a compound fracture of the leg, which dealt England's chances in the final Test, a sickening blow.

AUSTRALIA 26: B. Wilkinson 9, W. Little 6, V. Duggan 5, V. Huxley 3, C. Mitchell 2, D. Case 1.

ENGLAND 28: N. Parker 8, J. Parker 6, W. Phillips 5, L. Wotton 4, T. Croombs 3, C. Parkinson 2.

Two weeks later, again at the **Sydney** Showground, following a deluge of rain England lost the Ashes on a very heavy track. They found the absence of Phillips too much to cope with and his replacement, Les Gregory, failed to score a point. Vic Huxley, in his final appearance for Australia against England, gave a vintage performance, dropping his only point to Jack Parker and only an engine failure prevented Bluey Wilkinson from again going through the card unbeaten.

AUSTRALIA 31: V. Huxley 8, W. Little 8, B. Wilkinson 6, D. Case 4, C. Mitchell 3, V. Duggan 2.

ENGLAND 22: J. Parker 7, T. Croombs 6, N. Parker 4, C. Parkinson 3, L. Wotton 2, L. Gregory 0.

It was the end of an era for Australia, as Vic Huxley retired at the end of the series. The 'Godfather of Australian Speedway' still remains one of its all time greats. In the early thirties, he won every honour on offer in the sport and was one of the few riders of his era who rose to the £5,000 per year class. His contributions and inspiration to Australia in those early days is immeasurable.

ENGLAND v AUSTRALIA TEST SERIES 1937

1st Test   Wembley   May 27th   '37   Eng 66   Aust 41   W

England win series 1-0

By 1937 Australia were a speedway nation in decline. That seems an ironic statement to make of the country that had the current World Champion Lionel Van Praag and also a rider who was considered by most to be his superior, Bluey Wilkinson. The fact of the matter was that, since the turn of the decade, the Aussies had become totally reliant on the same nucleus of riders, which had, by now, dwindled. They had lost their 'Father' Vic Huxley, they had lost the peerless Frank Arthur and now they had lost 'The Warrior' Max Grosskreutz. Although domiciled in England, having married an English girl Max announced his retirement from racing in the winter and, contrary to the public's expectations, he stuck to his guns.

However, a five-match Test Series was announced for the 1937 season. Eric Collins, Ernie Evans, Clem Mitchell (who had ridden impressively in the winter Tests in Australia) and Charlie Spinks joined Van Praag, Wilkinson, Case and Johnson. England on the other hand were getting stronger and the likes of Jack Parker, Eric Langdon, Arthur Atkinson, Jack Ormston, Bill Kitchen and Frank Charles meant that quality riders such as Ginger Lees and George Newton were in the team only as reserves.

In the first Test at **Wembley**, Wilkinson was the star with Van Praag impressive for the Aussies but they were crushed by the might of a very solid English team.

ENGLAND 66: J. Parker 13, E. Langdon 12, A. Atkinson 12, J. Ormston 11, B. Kitchen 10, F. Charles 8, G. Newton dnr, G. Lees dnr.

AUSTRALIA 41: B. Wilkinson 17, L. Van Praag 12, D. Case 5, E. Collins 3, C. Mitchell 2, R. Johnson 2, E. Evans 0, C. Spinks 0.

With the second Test arranged for June 15 at West Ham, the unthinkable happened: Bluey Wilkinson got injured. The Speedway Control Board immediately pulled the plug on the series and the remaining dates were filled with an England *v* Overseas Test Series. Could this mean the end of the most successful set of speedway matches ridden since the sport had begun? Thankfully not, but Australia had to regroup before they could fly their national flag with the pride that they had shown over the past seven seasons.

AUSTRALIA *v* ENGLAND TEST SERIES 1937/38

1st Test	Sydney	Dec 11th	'37	Aust 26	Eng 28	W
2nd Test	Sydney	Dec 26th	'37	Aust 31	Eng 23	L
3rd Test	Sydney	Jan 8th	'38	Aust 27	Eng 26	L
4th Test	Sydney	Feb 12th	'38	Aust 30	Eng 24	L
5th Test	Sydney			Aust 29	Eng 25	L

Australia win series 4-1

Australia reckoned that they could still handle England in their own backyard and so hostilities between the two nations were resumed in the winter of 1937.

Although Dickie Case had retired, the Aussies still had the 'Old Guard' of Bluey Wilkinson, Lionel Van Praag and Ron Johnson who were joined by Clem Mitchell, Vic Duggan, Charlie Spinks, Bill Rogers and Wally Little. Jack Parker again led the Lions, who comprised Les Wotton, Bill Kitchen, Tiger Stevenson, Joe Abbott, Jack Ormston, Cliff Parkinson, Arthur Atkinson and Wally Lloyd. The matches were to be run over just nine heats, a formula favoured by the home team.

When Van Praag beat Jack Parker in the opening heat, the crowd of some 30,000 immediately warmed to the match and Australia soon established a 4-point lead. However, England had the greater all-round track craft and used it to claw back the deficit. The penultimate heat proved to be the match winner for England when Joe Abbott skilfully out-manoeuvred Van Praag to take the lead and a terrific burst of speed by Bill Kitchen saw him pass both of his Aussie opponents to join partner Abbott at the front putting England 2 points ahead. The final race featured the unbeaten Australian, Bluey Wilkinson (he remained so), but with Atkinson and Wotton filling in second and third, England won the opening Test match by 2 points.

AUSTRALIA 26: B. Wilkinson 9, C. Mitchell 8, L. Van Praag 6, C. Spinks 2, B. Rogers 1, R. Johnson 0, W. Little 0.

ENGLAND 28: J. Abbott 6, L. Wotton 6, J. Parker 5, B. Kitchen 5, J. Ormston 4, A. Atkinson 2.

All of the 1937/38 Test matches took place at Sydney and the second of the series was held on Boxing Night. Australia turned the tables on England. Having taken notice of the visitor's team riding in the first Test, the home side staged an impressive exhibition of teamwork. In fact, in seven of the nine heats, the Australian pairs finished amongst the point scorers. It spelt trouble for England, who began to fall steadily behind from the first race onwards. Bluey Wilkinson was again unbeaten in the match. For England reserve Cliff Parkinson deserves a mention: when Jack Ormston's bike threw him, 'Parky' replaced him, and went out to win heat seven.

AUSTRALIA 31: B. Wilkinson 9, C. Mitchell 7, V. Duggan 5, L. Van Praag 4, C. Spinks 2, R. Johnson 2, W. Little 2.

ENGLAND 23: B. Kitchen 6, J. Parker 4, J. Abbott 4, L. Wotton 4, C. Parkinson 3, H. Stevenson 2, J. Ormston 0.

Just before the commencement of the third Test, the Australian Auto Cycle Council withdrew its instruction that the match was to be contested in heats of one mile, acceding to the riders' representation that the heats should be ¾ of a mile. Therefore each heat comprised only 3 laps.

England were at a disadvantage, being without Bill Kitchen who had been injured in the Scratch races that followed the previous Test. And, somewhat surprisingly, Australia dropped Ron Johnson. Even without Kitchen, the Lions were the better all-round team, and after four heats they led by a single point, but it was the Aussies who packed the heavier artillery. Wilkinson and Mitchell were both in scintillating form and both were unbeaten in the match. To their credit, England never gave up, but when Van Praag split Joe Abbott and Jack Ormston in the final heat, his 2 points were enough to give the home team a 1-point win.

AUSTRALIA 27: B. Wilkinson 9, C. Mitchell 9, L. Van Praag 4, B. Roger 2, V. Duggan 2, C. Spinks 1.

ENGLAND 26: J. Parker 7, L. Wotton, 7, J. Abbott 7, C. Parkinson 3, H. Stevenson 1, J. Ormston 1, A. Atkinson 0.

Australia won the Ashes in the fourth Test, but the score in no way reflected the determined riding of England, or indeed the highly competitive racing over nine electrifying heats in which every single point was contested. With Kitchen back in the side the scores were level after six heats, but when Van Praag and the reinstated Ron Johnson scored a 5-1 over Jack Parker in the next race, England were unable to reciprocate. The difference was, again, Bluey Wilkinson and Clem Mitchell who were both unbeaten and Van Praag, who dropped only 1 point to Les Wotton.

AUSTRALIA 30: B. Wilkinson 9, C. Mitchell 9, L. Van Praag 8, C. Spinks 2, R. Johnson 2, V. Duggan 0.

ENGLAND 25: J. Abbott 6, L. Wotton 5, B. Kitchen 4, C. Parkinson 4, J. Parker 3, H. Stevenson 2.

The fifth Test was almost identical to its predecessor, resulting in a 4-point win for Australia. Although England had won only one match in the series, they were far from disgraced and in fact they staged one of their better performances down under. Wilkinson set a new record by completing the whole series without dropping a point and his team-mate Mitchell dropped only 4.

AUSTRALIA 29: B. Wilkinson 9, C. Mitchell 8, L. Van Praag 4, R. Johnson 3, V. Duggan 3, C. Spinks 2.

ENGLAND 25: B. Kitchen 7, J. Parker 5, L. Wotton 4, H. Stevenson 4, C. Parkinson 3, W. Lloyd 2.

ENGLAND v AUSTRALIA TEST SERIES 1938

1st Test	Belle Vue	May 28th	'38	Eng 52	Aust 56	L
2nd Test	Wembley	June 9th	'38	Eng 63	Aust 44	W
3rd Test	New Cross	June 29th	'38	Eng 47	Aust 61	L
4th Test	West Ham	July 12th	'38	Eng 55	Aust 51	W
5th Test	Wimbledon	July 25th	'38	Eng 58	Aust 49	W

England win series 3-2

All of a sudden, in 1938, Australia found themselves with a team once again. This was due to the return of Max Grosskreutz who had found life in retirement a bit quiet for his liking. The Test matches in Britain resumed in May of that year.

England had a new look about them at **Belle Vue** in the first Test. There was no Parker and no Langdon and Frank Varey returned as skipper to partner Frank Charles. Alec Stathamm, the twenty-six-year-old Haringay rider made his international debut partnering English stalwart Bill Kitchen. George Newton and Arthur Atkinson made up England's third pair with Bob Harrison being named as the reserve.

Australia, as usual, virtually picked itself. Grosskreutz was paired with Ron Johnson, Bluey Wilkinson with Clem Mitchell and Van Praag with Charlie Spinks. Bill Rogers and Eric Collins were named as reserves.

After a year of promoting at Norwich, Grosskreutz announced his comeback in spectacular fashion when he shot from the tapes in heat one to leave Charles and Varey in his wake. And when Wilkinson and Mitchell scored a 5-1 over Bill Kitchen in the following race, England knew that they had a fight on their hands.

Lionel Van Praag had an unfortunate night, breaking a chain whilst leading his first race and then being forced towards the safety fence by Frank Varey in his next. The resulting crash put Lionel out of the rest of the meeting and left Australia with a difficult task. Heat sixteen proved to be the turning point. With three heats remaining the Aussies were 2 points ahead, but they were looking at the final race with trepidation, as the withdrawal of Van Praag had left them with a weak pairing in that particular race. The onus was on Australia not to make mistakes and Grosskreutz and Johnson rode flawlessly to keep Newton and Atkinson behind them for four laps to score the required 5-1.

In the penultimate heat, a 4-2 from Wilkinson and Mitchell over Varey secured a win for Australia. England got the expected 5-1 in the final heat, to make the score a respectable 52-56. A triumphant return by 'The Max', had seen him drop only 2 points to English riders with Bluey Wilkinson doing even better; Bill Kitchen was the only opposing rider to beat him.

ENGLAND 52: B. Kitchen 13, F. Varey 12, G. Newton 11, F. Charles 7, A. Atkinson 4, B. Harrison 3, A. Statham 2.

AUSTRALIA 56: B. Wilkinson 15, M. Grosskreutz 15, C. Mitchell 8, R. Johnson 8, C. Spinks 6, L. Van Praag 2, B. Rogers 2.

England kept their top five riders for the second Test at **Wembley**, but Tommy Croombs was recalled to replace Alec Statham and Geoff Pymar and George Wilks were brought in as the reserves. The match lacked the excitement of its predecessor and, after nine rather processional races, Australia went into the interval 1 point ahead. Even so, they looked fragile. Wilkinson and Van Praag were riding well but Grosskreutz had scored only 4 points in his first three races and he was the rider upon whom the Aussies relied. In the second half of the meeting, he deteriorated even further, and England took control, led by the impressive pairing of Kitchen and Varey who scored 24 from a possible 30 points. George Newton managed to inject some excitement into the match with his hair-raising exploits but, apart from that, there was little to enthuse about, as England levelled the series.

ENGLAND 63: F. Charles 13, F. Varey 13, B. Kitchen 11, G. Newton 11, A. Atkinson 10, T. Croombs 3, G. Pymar 1, G. Wilks 1.

AUSTRALIA 44: B. Wilkinson 15, L. Van Praag 15, M. Grosskreutz 6, C. Mitchell 5, C. Spinks 1, R. Johnson 1, B. Rogers 1, E. Collins 0.

In the third Test at **New Cross** George Newton was favourite to skipper England on his own track. But in the event an arm injury prevented him from riding at all and Stan Greatrex was brought into the side with Les Wotton replacing Pymar at reserve. Bill Longley was brought in as the Australian reserve.

Max Grosskreutz had another terrible evening and scored only 2 points. While that should have buried Australia, it didn't happen. Bluey Wilkinson and Lionel Van Praag took over and both scored immaculate 18-point maximums. So confident was Wilkinson that he had time to shepherd his partner Mitchell in most of their rides. With Ron Johnson having his best match for Australia for some time the visitors proved too much for England to handle and the home side were defeated 47-61. Whilst Greatrex made an impression for the Lions, two of the home team's most experienced riders, Frank Varey and Frank Charles, scored only 1 point between them.

ENGLAND 47: B. Kitchen 12, A. Atkinson 12, S. Greatrex 10, T. Croombs 6, G. Wilks 4, L. Wotton 2, F. Varey 1, F. Charles 0.

AUSTRALIA 61: L. Van Praag 18, B. Wilkinson 18, R. Johnson 11, C. Mitchell 7, B. Longley 3, M. Grosskreutz 2, B. Rogers 2, C. Spinks 0.

There could be no mistakes at **West Ham** if England were to stand a chance of regaining the Ashes. They stuck with Atkinson, Kitchen and Varey, included home riders Tommy Croombs and Tiger Stevenson, and gave another chance to Pymar and Statham. Over 40,000 fans packed into Custom House and England got off to a maximum start when Mitchell suffered an engine failure prior to the tapes going up and Bluey Wilkinson had an uncharacteristic fall.

Van Praag was never a lover of the West Ham track and this was reflected in his scoring, but there was compensation for the Aussies with a double figure score from Grosskreutz. In a close-fought match Geoff Pymar proved to be the trump card for the Lions, forming a formidable partnership with Arthur Atkinson and in fact it was this pair that won the match for England. In heat seventeen, with the scores level, they scored a 5-1 to give the home team a 4-point lead, duly maintained in the final heat.

ENGLAND 55: A. Atkinson 13, B. Kitchen 11, T. Croombs 10, G. Pymar 9, H. Stevenson 8, A. Statham 3, F. Varey 1.

AUSTRALIA 51: B. Wilkinson 14, M. Grosskreutz 10, C. Mitchell 8, L. Van Praag 7, R. Johnson 7, C. Spinks 5.

With the series standing at two matches each, it left everything to play for at **Wimbledon**. Some careful selection saw Atkinson, Kitchen and Croombs retained by England and the impressive Pymar given another chance on his home track. George Newton was now fit and Eric Langdon was getting back to form after a layoff due to an injury and both were included. Alec Statham and Wally Lloyd were named as the Lions' reserves.

Australia had been dealt a blow when Van Praag crashed at Manchester the previous Saturday. He arrived at Plough Lane in a great deal of pain, but after a trial run just before the start of the match, he declared himself fit. The match was a cracker, fought tooth and nail to the very end. Aussie skipper Bluey Wilkinson was the star of the night, scoring a splendid 18-point maximum and Van Praag struggled courageously for his 10 points. Grosskreutz was strangely inconsistent in netting his nine. But that was the extent of Australia's success, as their lesser lights failed to give adequate support.

For England, Geoff Pymar was the star, as he once again formed a rock-solid pairing with Arthur Atkinson. But all of the England riders were heroes. George Newton, as expected, covered every inch of the track and Kitchen and Croombs, though not so spectacular, gave their usual consistent performance. The Lions were strong throughout and they fully deserved their 9-point win to regain the Ashes.

ENGLAND 58: G. Pymar 13, G. Newton 12, T. Croombs 9, B. Kitchen 9, A. Atkinson 8, E. Langdon 7, A. Statham dnr, W. Lloyd dnr.

AUSTRALIA 49: B. Wilkinson 18, L. Van Praag 10, M. Grosskreutz 9, R. Johnson 4, B. Spencer 4, E. Collins 2, C. Mitchell 1, B. Longley 1.

The comeback series had been a huge success, drawing massive crowds, but again it showed that Australia relied too much on their top three riders, but help was on the way. Young Vic Duggan was carving himself a reputation at Bristol, and was poised to play his part in Australian Speedway history.

Bluey Wilkinson had been the best rider in the 1938 Test Series and that year he was the best rider in the world, a point which he proved by winning the World Championship from Jack Milne and Wilbur Lamoreaux at Wembley on 1 September.

AUSTRALIA V ENGLAND TEST SERIES 1938/39

1st Test	Sydney	Jan 7th	'39	Aust 22	Eng 32	W
2nd Test	Sydney	Jan 21st	'39	Aust 32	Eng 22	L
3rd Test	Sydney	Jan 28th	'39	Aust 23	Eng 31	W
4th Test	Sydney	Feb 11th	'39	Aust 28	Eng 24	L
5th Test	Sydney	Feb 18th	'39	Aust 35	Eng 18	L

Australia win series 3-2

Jack Parker once again led the Lions in Australia and England regular Arthur Atkinson agreed to join him. Parker's brother Norman had already had a successful season down under with the Lions two years earlier, so he was fully prepared and Geoff Pymar, Wally Lloyd, Alec Statham and Bob Harrison completed what was rather an inexperienced team to take to the other side of the world.

Australia were led by World Champion Bluey Wilkinson, Lionel Van Praag and Clem Mitchell. Bill Longley and Charlie Spinks had seen international action before, but Aub Lawson, Andy Menzies and Ray Taylor were making their debuts for Australia.

England got off to a great start by winning the first Test by 10 points and it was the rookies who were responsible with Pymar and Statham top scoring for the Lions. Wilkinson fought a one-man battle for the Aussies but he could do no more than win all of his races, as he desperately lacked support.

AUSTRALIA 22: B. Wilkinson 9, L. Van Praag 4, A. Menzies 3, B. Longley 3, C. Spinks 2, C. Mitchell 1, A. Lawson 0.

ENGLAND 32: A. Statham 7, G. Pymar 7, J. Parker 5, W. Lloyd 5, N. Parker 4, A. Atkinson 4.

For the second Test, Australia made the audacious move of recalling 'The Godfather' Vic Huxley who gave a fair account of himself, scoring 4 points. Van Praag found his form, Bill Longley gave an impressive performance and, although Wilkinson dropped his only point of the series, Australia were comfortable winners.

AUSTRALIA 32: B. Wilkinson 8, L. Van Praag 8, B. Longley 6, C. Mitchell 5, V. Huxley 4, C. Spinks 1, A. Menzies 0.

ENGLAND 22: A. Statham 7, A. Atkinson 6, G. Pymar 3, W. Lloyd 3, J. Parker 2, N. Parker 1, B. Harrison 0.

Alec Statham had been particularly impressive so far in the series and, in the third Test match, only Wilkinson could get the better of him as young Alec stormed to 8 points. With Pymar and Jack Parker giving good support the Lions managed to overcome another Wilkinson maximum to win the match by 8 points.

AUSTRALIA 23: B. Wilkinson 9, L. Van Praag 6, B. Longley 5, A. Menzies 1, C. Mitchell 1, A. Lawson 1, C. Spinks 0.

ENGLAND 31: A. Statham 8, J. Parker 6, G. Pymar 6, N. Parker 5, A. Atkinson 4, W. Lloyd 2.

Australia were in the position of having to win the fourth Test to stand a chance of winning the Ashes and, whereas Clem Mitchell had been the trump card twelve months earlier, it was the turn of Bill Longley in 1939. He seemed to improve every match. There was the inevitable maximum from Wilkinson and a competent display from Van Praag, but it was the 7 points scored by Longley that allowed the Roos to level the series with a 4-point win.

AUSTRALIA 28: B. Wilkinson 9, L. Van Praag 7, B. Longley 7, A. Lawson 3, R. Taylor 2, A. Menzies 0.

ENGLAND 24: J. Parker 8, A. Atkinson 7, N. Parker 3, A. Statham 2, G. Pymar 2, W. Lloyd 1, B. Harrison 1.

Unfortunately, England never stood a chance in the fifth and deciding Test match. Injuries to Pymar and Statham left them with only five riders and, although Jack Parker and Arthur Atkinson battled bravely, the task was always beyond the Lions.

AUSTRALIA 35: B. Wilkinson 9, L. Van Praag 8, B. Longley 8, A. Lawson 4, C. Spinks 3, R. Taylor 3.

ENGLAND 18: J. Parker 7, A. Atkinson 7, W. Lloyd 3, N. Parker 1, B. Harrison 0.

It had been an unjust end to the series for an England side that had done itself proud. The youngsters had come through with flying colours, but both had been the cruel recipients of fate in effect robbing England of a chance to defend the Ashes successfully in Australia.

ENGLAND v AUSTRALIA TEST SERIES 1939

1st Test	New Cross	June 7th	'39	Eng 62	Aust 46	W
2nd Test	Wimbledon	June 26th	'39	Eng 55	Aust 53	W
3rd Test	Haringay	July 15th	'39	Eng 48	Aust 58	L
4th Test	Belle Vue	Aug 12th	'39	Eng 65	Aust 42	W
5th Test	Wembley	Aug 24th	'39	Eng 71	Aust 36	W

England win series 4–1

The 1939 Test Series was ridden at a time of great unrest in Europe with Adolf Hitler seizing Czechoslovakia and setting his sights on Poland. It was a time of great uncertainty for all, but for the time being, the show went on.

For the opener at **New Cross**, Arthur Atkinson was named as the England skipper and was paired with Stan Greatrex. Eric Langdon and Bill Kitchen formed a very experienced pair and Jack Parker and Tommy Croombs had also served their country on numerous occasions. Making his debut at reserve was twenty-eight-year-old Tommy Price, with Geoff Pymar completing the squad.

Australia were up against it. Max Grosskreutz had retired (again), but there was an even bigger blow dealt to them when, at the very pinnacle of his career, World Champion Bluey Wilkinson announced his retirement from racing. Van Praag was an automatic choice for captain, and his partner was Charlie Spinks. Ron Johnson and Eric Collins formed the middle pairing, and Vic Duggan and Bill Longley made up the main body of the team with new arrival twenty-two-year-old Aub Lawson being named as reserve alongside Vic Duggan's brother Ray.

Arthur Atkinson got things underway by equalling the track record in the first heat but, to their credit, the Aussies held their own in the early heats. But a first half mishap robbed them of any chance that they may have had. In heat four, after chasing Eric Langdon for three laps, Lionel Van Praag made a big effort around the outside and damaged his ankle in the process. Van Praag withdrew from his next race, but then returned to the meeting, obviously riding in pain. England took the lead in heat six and never looked back. Atkinson was immaculate for the Lions and Ron Johnson rode his heart out for Australia, but the Aussies had a new star. Vic Duggan in his first ever Test match in England scored 15 points, in what was one of the greatest Test match debuts of all time.

ENGLAND 62: A. Atkinson 18, B. Kitchen 15, J. Parker 11, T. Croombs 8, E. Langdon 6, S. Greatrex 3, T. Price 1, G. Pymar 0.

AUSTRALIA 46: V. Duggan 15, R. Johnson 12, L. Van Praag 8, C. Spinks 4, E. Collins 3, B. Longley 3, A. Lawson 1, R. Duggan dnr.

At **Wimbledon**, Frank Charles and Joe Abbott replaced Atkinson and Greatrex, and Wally Lloyd replaced Tommy Price in the England side. For Australia, Lawson moved into the main body of the team, with Longley replacing him at reserve, and Bert Spencer took Ray Duggan's reserve place.

Australia were a completely different proposition from the first Test and a first-class match was the result. Van Praag showed what he could do when he was fully fit, dropping his only point to Bill Kitchen and Vic Duggan rode even better than he had at New Cross. After fifteen heats, Australia were only 2 points adrift, but Kitchen and Langdon showed all their experience in the next race, scoring a 5-1 over Eric Collins and Bert Spencer, leaving the Aussies a mountain to climb in the last two heats. A 4-2 to the visitors in the penultimate heat left them needing maximum points in the final heat to force a draw and, although Duggan got away, Jack Parker stayed between him and Ron Johnson to give England a 2-point win.

ENGLAND 55: B. Kitchen 14, E. Langdon 10, J. Parker 10, F. Charles 9, T. Croombs 6, J. Abbott 3, W. Lloyd 3, G. Pymar dnr.

AUSTRALIA 53: L. Van Praag 17, V. Duggan 16, E. Collins 8, B. Spencer 5, R. Johnson 5, A. Lawson 1, B. Longley 1, C. Spinks 0.

Atkinson returned for the third Test at **Haringay**, and Alec Statham made his 1939 debut for England. The Lions tried out two new reserves in the shape of Norman Parker and Bill Pitcher. Australia brought Andy Menzies in to replace Bert Spencer.

Oddly, England, who prided themselves on their team riding, sadly lacked the quality at Haringay, with only the Kitchen–Langdon pairing showing any signs of it. Australia on the other hand rode more as a team and, by the interval, the visitors led by 2 points. As the match resumed, the point was quickly brought home. Bill Pitcher had been brought in to replace the out-of-sorts Alec Statham and, when his partner Jack Parker caught his back wheel, Bill was left with a fractured rib. When Parker subsequently retired from the rerun, it left Lawson and Van Praag to collect maximum points. When Vic Duggan came to grief in the final heat, England's Atkinson and Norman Parker enjoyed the same benefits, but by then it was too late, as the Lions had been given a 10-point hiding.

ENGLAND 48: A. Atkinson 12, B. Kitchen 10, J. Parker 8, E. Langdon 8, A. Statham 5, T. Croombs 3, N. Parker 2, B. Pitcher 0.

AUSTRALIA 58: R. Johnson 16, L. Van Praag 14, V. Duggan 12, A. Lawson 8, E. Collins 7, A. Menzies 1, C. Spinks 0, B. Longley 0.

It was the last chance for the Aussies at **Belle Vue**. A win would keep them in with a chance of winning the series, but if they lost, then the Ashes returned to England.

For England, Langdon and Kitchen formed the opening partnership and Jack Parker and Arthur Atkinson were paired together. Frank Varey and Joe Abbott were both recalled forming the third pairing and Malcolm Craven and Bob Harrison were named as the reserves. The Lions had put out a very experienced side in a bid to tie up the series. The ploy worked, but not before they were hit by a series of misfortunes.

Eric Langton's bike stalled in both of his opening races, Frank Varey crashed first time out and Abbott was excluded in heat six. Even so, England were riding much better than the Australians and led by 3 points at the interval stage. There followed a complete collapse by the visitors, which saw England take maximum points in the following five heats and build up a lead that the Aussies were unable to surmount. Ron Johnson remained an Australian enigma; after top scoring with 16 points at Haringay, his return at Belle Vue was a mere 4.

ENGLAND 65: B. Kitchen 16, J. Parker 15, A. Atkinson 10, E. Langdon 8, F. Varey 8, J. Abbott 8, M. Craven dnr, B. Harrison dnr.

AUSTRALIA 42: V. Duggan 12, L. Van Praag 8, E. Collins 7, A. Lawson 6, R. Johnson 4, R. Duggan 3, E. Evans 2, A. Menzies 0.

The fifth and final Test was held at **Wembley** and, with nothing to lose, young locals Tommy Price and Malcolm Craven were drafted into the main body of the England team to join Kitchen, Langdon, Parker and Atkinson. Alec Statham and George Wilks were the named reserves.

The match turned out to be a demolition. The Australian side were pulverised. Rarely has spirit been as lacking in an Australian team as the one that rode at Wembley in 1939. Craven and Price could have hardly picked a better night to make their full debuts. They took full advantage with Price winning three races and Craven picking up 11 points.

The night itself was a very downbeat affair. There was, after all, nothing to ride for other than national pride and, in poor weather conditions, the event suffered from lack of interest. The Aussies slumped to their biggest defeat ever in front of the smallest Test crowd ever.

ENGLAND 71: B. Kitchen 15, E. Langdon 14, J. Parker 11, A. Atkinson 11, M. Craven 11, T. Price 9, A. Statham dnr, G. Wilks dnr.

AUSTRALIA 36: L. Van Praag 11, V. Duggan 11, E. Collins 7, A. Lawson 5, R. Johnson 2, R. Duggan 0, B. Longley 0, C. Spinks 0.

On the schedule of the 1939 Test Series, there were six matches programmed. The sixth was to be staged at West Ham on 19 September, but this was never ridden. On 3 September, Great Britain declared war on Germany and, along with almost everything else, speedway in Britain came to a halt.

Now the deadly rivals on track were united off it as they joined forces to battle German imperialism.

It was a pity that Australia bowed out with a whimper but they left behind a legacy of wonderful memories. Who would ever forget the majesty of Huxley, the brilliance of Van Praag, the tenacity of Grosskreutz and the sheer talent of arguably their greatest rider, Bluey Wilkinson?

And so, as Britain plunged headlong into the Second World War, we said farewell to the Australian riders. Farewell but not goodbye.

CHAPTER 2

THE FORTIES

ENGLAND v AUSTRALIA TEST SERIES 1947

1st Test	Bradford	July 5th	'47	Eng 65	Aust 43	W
2nd Test	West Ham	July 29th	'47	Eng 58	Aust 50	W
3rd Test	Wembley	Aug 14th	'47	Eng 49	Aust 57	L

England win series 2-1

With Germany surrendering in the spring of 1945, speedway resumed in Britain the following year. Even after an absence of almost seven years, most of the British speedway stars of 1939 returned to the sport. After an initial year of resolving matters, some semblance of normality began to return to British speedway the following year. So much so, that the England *v* Australia Test matches resumed.

In 1947, speedway boomed and no fewer than three divisions were operating in Britain, embracing twenty-three teams. The Australians had returned to Britain with Lionel Van Praag, Ron Johnson and Bill Longley signing for New Cross, Aub Lawson riding for West Ham and the Duggan brothers taking residence at Haringay. Even Max Grosskreutz, at forty-one years old, had returned to ride for Odsal!

The Australian team that lined up at **Odsal** for the first Test of 1947 therefore had a very familiar look about it. In fact Frank Dolan was the only new face in the side and, at twenty-nine, he was also the youngest.

There were few spring chickens in speedway at that time, because there had been little opportunity to train riders after the War. And so the majority of riders were in their thirties. This in fact was reflected by the England team, which comprised of Jack Parker (40), Norman Parker (38), Bill Kitchen (39), Tommy Price (36), Alec Statham (35), Ron Clarke (33) and Malcolm Craven (32). There is a saying that 'Speedway is a young man's game', but, in the late forties, that was not the case.

England got off to the best possible start when the Parker brothers scored a 5-1 over Longley and Van Praag, and it looked as though Price and Kitchen would enjoy the same success in the following heat. However, one of their opponents was Vic Duggan, who had already established himself as one of the very best riders in the world and he shot past Price to claim 2 points. Grosskreutz was reckoned to be the weak link in the Australian team but, after falling in his first race, he went out in his next and beat England's top pairing of Kitchen and Price and then got the better of the Parkers in his next.

Alec Statham meanwhile was going like a rocket and even won heat six with a broken fork. By the interval, the Lions led by 8 points and looked likely winners. In the second half, Bill Kitchen again beat Vic Duggan, but they were the only 2 points that the Australian dropped all night. However, apart from surprise packet Grosskreutz, Duggan severely lacked support and the 47,000 crowd saw England race to a comfortable victory.

ENGLAND 65: B. Kitchen 16, A. Statham 16, N. Parker 13, J. Parker 9, T. Price 7, R. Clarke 4, M. Craven dnr, L. Wotton dnr.

AUSTRALIA 43: V. Duggan 16, M. Grosskreutz 10, B. Longley 6, R. Johnson 5, L. Van Praag 3, F. Dolan 3, A. Lawson 0, R. Duggan 0.

For the second Test at **West Ham**, there was little change to England's side, with George Wilks replacing Ron Clarke and Wally Lloyd replacing Les Wotton at reserve. The Aussies remained unchanged.

Australia seemed much more at home on the wide open spaces of Custom House and were a more competitive team, but it was the Parker brothers who stole the show, as they dropped only 4 points between them throughout the entire match. Even so, the Aussies were always in

the match and led by 4 points at the interval. In the second half Tommy Price, who was having a quiet night, was dropped in favour of reserve George Wilks and Wilko made the most of his opportunity, winning three races. It made the difference to England who pulled away to win the match by 8 points. Jack Parker was at his very best and rolled back the years to record an 18–point maximum.

ENGLAND 58: J. Parker 18, G. Wilks 10, N. Parker 8, J. Kitchen 8, A. Statham 8, T. Price 3, M. Craven 3, W. Lloyd 0.

AUSTRALIA 50: V. Duggan 13, M. Grosskreutz 10, L. Van Praag 10, B. Longley 6, R. Johnson 6, F. Dolan 5, A. Lawson 0, R. Duggan 0.

The final Test was held appropriately at **Wembley** and, in contrast to the Aussies' miserable performance in their last visit to the Empire Stadium in 1939, they pulled out all the stops. George Wilks and Eric Langdon replaced Alec Statham and Malcolm Craven in the England team, and Australia brought in Doug McLachlan for Ray Duggan.

   Australia opened proceedings with two maximum heats wins and it was Langdon who stemmed the tide by beating his old adversary Grosskreutz in the third heat. England began to claw their way back into the match, but a 5-1 courtesy of Duggan and Lawson just before the interval put the Aussies firmly back in the driving seat. With Duggan (who was unbeaten by an opponent), Van Praag and Grosskreutz all riding spectacularly, there was no way back for England, but at least they had won the Ashes.

ENGLAND 49: J. Parker 10, G. Wilks 9, T. Price 9, B. Langdon 9, B. Kitchen 7, N. Parker 5, J. Lloyd dnr, L. Wotton dnr.

AUSTRALIA 57: V. Duggan 17, L. Van Praag 14, M. Grosskreutz 10, F. Dolan 5, B. Longley 4, R. Johnson 4, A. Lawson 3, D. McLachlan 0.

AUSTRALIA v ENGLAND TEST SERIES 1947/48

1st Test	Brisbane	Dec 6th	'47	Aust 57	Eng 47	L
2nd Test	Sydney	Dec 26th	'47	Aust 57	Eng 51	L

3rd Test	Melbourne	Jan 13th	'48	Aust 61	Eng 47	L
4th Test	Newcastle	Jan 24th	'48	Aust 79	Eng 29	L
5th Test	Sydney	Feb 7th	'48	Aust 62	Eng 46	L

Australia win series 5-0

England took a fairly good squad out to Australia in the winter. They had the experienced Parker brothers, Alec Statham and England Internationals Malcolm Craven and Bill Pitcher. Dick Harris, Odsal's top rider Oliver Hart and twenty-five-year-old Dent Olive completed the team. The English riders fared well against the top Aussie riders in the pre-Test meetings and the Lions were expected to give a good account of themselves in the Test matches.

The top Australian riders had become disenchanted regarding the oncoming Tests. Vic Duggan, Max Grosskreutz and Aub Lawson all refused to ride as they had not been consulted as to the make-up of the team and England seemed to have the first Test at **Brisbane** already in the bag. Australia still had Bill Rogers, Bill Longley, Dick Smythe, Charlie Spinks and Andy Menzies and they dug deep to come up with Ernie Brecknall, Bonnie Waddell and Dave Hynes.

Tragedy struck the Lions early on when Oliver Hart fell and damaged his arm and it all went downhill from there. For reasons known only to themselves, England decided to ride the huge Australian track as they would a comparatively small British track, broadsiding around the bends. It had been some years since the Brits had visited Australia and maybe they had forgotten the tactics that they had employed on those previous visits. The Aussies however had a less subtle but more successful method of riding – drop the clutch, open the throttle and hang on for dear life until the end of the race. In the new eighteen-heat formula Bill Rogers was robbed of a maximum only by an engine failure as England were well beaten by an inferior team 57-47.

AUSTRALIA 57: B. Rogers 15, B. Longley 13, D. Smythe 12, E. Brecknell 7, C. Spinks 6, B. Waddell 2, A. Menzies 1, D. Hynes 1.

ENGLAND 47: N. Parker 16, B. Pitcher 12, D. Oliver 7, J. Parker 6, M. Craven 3, A. Statham 2, D. Harris 1, O. Hart 0.

At **Sydney**, Australia called upon the services of young Jack Biggs. Jack had ridden at Haringay during the 1947 season but had failed to make an impression. However he turned out to be the match winner in the second Test. England did in fact get their act together but were the subject of some misfortune. Jack Parker fell in his first race and brother Norman, who had dropped only 1 point in three races, crashed in his fourth, sustaining concussion. Even so, he took part in his last programmed ride and scored 2 points. It was a much-improved performance from England, but they just had no luck on the night. As an interesting postscript, the England team met up with Malcolm Craven's brother Gil, who was to find fame with Cradley Heath the following year and the younger Craven turned out for his country at Sydney and scored his only international point.

AUSTRALIA 57: J. Biggs 13, B. Rogers 12, B. Longley 10, E. Brecknall 8, C. Spinks 8, D. Smythe 5, C. Watson 1, R. Duggan 0.

ENGLAND 51: J. Parker 13, N. Parker 10, B. Pitcher 10, A. Statham 9, D. Oliver 6, M. Craven 1, D. Harris 1, G. Craven 1.

The calvary arrived for the third Test at **Melbourne**, but unfortunately it was the Australian calvary as Vic Duggan and Max Grosskreutz, probably upset at Australia's success without them, agreed to ride. Even so, against the strongest side that they had faced so far, England did as well as they had in the first Test, as Oliver Hart made a welcome return to the team.

AUSTRALIA 61: V. Duggan 18, B. Rogers 16, B. Longley 13, E. Brecknell 6, J. Biggs 5, M. Grosskreutz 3, A. Menzies 0, F. Tracey 0.

ENGLAND 47: J. Parker 13, B. Pitcher 10, O. Hart 9, N. Parker 8, A. Statham 5, D. Oliver 1, D. Harris 1.

With Aub Lawson agreeing to return, England faced the full might of the Australians in the fourth Test at **Newcastle** and the inevitable rout followed, with only Dent Oliver offering token resistance. Vic Duggan was again unbeaten by the opposition.

AUSTRALIA 79: A. Lawson 16, V. Duggan 15, M. Grosskreutz 14, B. Rogers 11, B. Longley 11, J. Biggs 8, B. Melluish 4.

ENGLAND 29: D. Oliver 10, O. Hart 7, A. Statham 5, B. Pitcher 4, N. Parker 2, J. Parker 1, D. Harris 0.

In the final Test at **Sydney**, England put up a considerably better show against the same team. Jack Parker seemed determined to go out on a high note and collected Duggan's scalp. With proof before him that this was possible, Alec Statham did the same in a subsequent heat. By heat thirteen, a gritty performance by the Lions saw the scores tied at 33-33, but the Duggan–Grosskreutz pairing scored two maximum heat wins in the last few races and Australia pulled clear of the visitors. Poor old Norman Parker seemed to be the recipient of an Aboriginal curse. He rode three different bikes and all of them fell to pieces. In desperation, he turned to brother Jack, whose machine was working beautifully. With Norman on board, the bike roared from the tapes but after only 60 yards, the footrest broke off and, before the machine finally came to a halt, the rear chain flew off!

AUSTRALIA 62: V. Duggan 14, A. Lawson 14, M. Grosskreutz 12, J. Biggs 10, B. Roger s 4, B. Melluish 4, F. Dolan 4, B. Longley 0.

ENGLAND 46: J. Parker 15, O. Hart 13, A. Statham 9, D. Oliver 5, B. Pitcher 3, N. Parker 1, D. Harris 0.

ENGLAND v AUSTRALIA TEST SERIES 1948

1st Test	Wimbledon	May 24th	'48	Eng 61	Aust 45	W
2nd Test	Belle Vue	June 19th	'48	Eng 69	Aust 39	W
3rd Test	New Cross	June 30th	'48	Eng 57	Aust 51	W
4th Test	Haringay	Aug 13th	'48	Eng 58	Aust 50	W
5th Test	West Ham	Sept 7th	'48	Eng 45	Aust 63	L

England win series 4–1

Vengeance for their 5-0 whitewash in Australia was very much the order of the day for England in 1948 and the team that they assembled to carry out the first instalment at Wimbledon was very strong on paper, even though Bill Kitchen was injured.

Evergreen Jack Parker, brother Norman, George Wilks, Tommy Price and Alec Statham formed the top five and they were joined by one of the most charismatic characters in speedway – Squire Francis Waterman, better known as 'Split'. After only two seasons in the sport the twenty-seven-year-old Wembley rider had already made his mark and represented a new breed of rider emerging in speedway. There was another new face at reserve too, as twenty-eight-year-old Cyril Brine from Wimbledon was given a try. Malcolm Craven completed the England squad for the first Test at **Wimbledon**. There were no surprises from Australia as they fielded The Duggan brothers, Grosskreutz, Johnson, Longley, Lawson, Frank Dolan and Cliff Watson.

On this occasion, Norman Parker was mounted on a bike that didn't fall apart and he showed what he could do in the opening heat by over-taking Vic Duggan within a lap and clipping almost a second off the Plough Lane track record. In the fourth heat the English again mastered Duggan, as Statham and Wilks scored a 5-1 over the Australian skipper. The aforementioned pairing stole the show at Wimbledon, scoring 28 points from a possible 30 and Statham was unbeaten by an opposing rider in the match.

On the night, England were the much better team and the 11-point lead that they had established by the interval never looked to be in any danger. In fact the Lions had increased it after eighteen heats of racing. Tommy Price often looked ill at ease riding with the somewhat unconventional Waterman but both gave their all and any shortcomings that they may have had were compensated for by the rest of the team. So much so that the reserves, Craven and Brine, never got a look in.

ENGLAND 61: A. Statham 17, N. Parker 14, G. Wilks 11, J. Parker 7, S. Waterman 6, T. Price 6, M. Craven dnr, C. Brine dnr.

AUSTRALIA 45: V. Duggan 12, B. Longley 9, A. Lawson 7, R. Johnson 7, R. Duggan 5, M. Grosskreutz 5, F. Dolan 0, C. Watson 0.

It was on to **Belle Vue** for the second Test where home rider Dent Oliver, following his crowd-pleasing performances in Australia, was an automatic choice for the England team. The thirty-two-year-old Jeff Lloyd was given another chance, this time in the top six and Belle Vue riders Louis Lawson and Jeff's older brother Wally Lloyd were named as the Lions reserves. Jack Parker was riding for Belle Vue at that time which meant that half the England squad was made up of Aces riders. England also recalled Norman Parker, Waterman and Statham. George Wilks had unfortunately broken his hip following the first Test. For the Aussies, Jack Biggs replaced Ron Johnson who had been taken ill.

England had taken a chance on Oliver. After all he was only a novice in 1945 and the fact that he was paired with another virtual rookie, Waterman, was viewed with scepticism amongst the learned. But the move paid off in spades. The youngster was magnificent, and roared to an 18-point maximum on his international debut in Britain. Jeff Lloyd was also a great success, scoring 13 points on his debut, as England ran riot.

It must be said that Australia, who were already without Johnson, did not enjoy the best of luck. Max Grosskreutz blew his motor at the start of the opening race and missed his next two rides whilst he fought to re-equip himself. The unfortunate Australian also ended the match on his backside when he fell in his final outing. To his credit, the only two races that he completed he won, including one against Jack Parker who was in splendid form. Aub Lawson was even more unfortunate. In his opening ride, an over-ambitious manoeuvre to overtake Dent Oliver saw him leave the track, and the match, on a stretcher. From that point on, the Aussies were always up against it. But, as always, Vic Duggan never gave up, although he was forced to bow to England's 'Young Guns'.

ENGLAND 69: D. Oliver 18, J. Parker 16, J. Lloyd 13, N. Parker 9, S. Waterman 7, A. Statham 6, L. Lawson dnr, W. Lloyd dnr.

AUSTRALIA 39: V. Duggan 14, M. Grosskreutz 6, F. Dolan 6, B. Longley 4, J. Biggs 4, R. Duggan 3, C. Watson 2, A. Lawson 0.

Despite his tremendous performance, Oliver was named only as reserve for the third Test at **New Cross**, along with Tommy Price. Norman

Parker, Jeff Lloyd and Alec Statham were recalled and New Cross rider Ray Moore replaced Dent. Australia were back to full strength with the return of Lawson and Johnson.

On his own track, Ron Johnson was appointed Australian captain, but he suffered the misfortune of losing a chain when leading heat seven. Two heats later a double fall by Longley and Grosskreutz left the Aussies with a 14-point deficit at the interval. Already two matches down, the Roos had to win this one to stand any chance of retaining the Ashes and they staged a mighty comeback. In the first race of the second half, Johnson and Ray Duggan scored an unlikely 5-1 over the Parkers and further Australian successes followed in subsequent heats. However, a victory over Vic Duggan by Jack Parker and a third place from his brother Norman saved the day for England, and they reclaimed the Ashes with a 6-point win.

ENGLAND 57: J. Parker 14, S. Waterman 12, A. Statham 11, N. Parker 7, R. Moore 7, J. Lloyd 6, D. Oliver dnr, T. Price dnr.

AUSTRALIA 51: V. Duggan 15, R. Johnson 14, B. Longley 10, R. Duggan 5, F. Dolan 4, M. Grosskreutz 3, A. Lawson 0, J. Biggs 0.

England had indeed regained the Ashes but their revenge was not yet complete for the humiliation of the winter Tests in Australia. At Haringay the Parker brothers, Spilt Waterman and Alec Statham were retained. Dent Oliver was promoted into the main body of the team and, following an injury to Tommy Price, Price's Wembley team mate Bill Gilbert made his England debut. Lloyd Goffe and Jeff Lloyd were the England reserves.

Haringay was home away from home for the Aussies, as the Duggan brother, Frank Dolan and Jack Biggs all rode for the Racers, but Australia had problems. Aub Lawson was recovering from a skin graft to his leg and Max Grosskreutz, bruised and battered after the second Test at Belle Vue, had announced his retirement, this time for good. They say that every cloud has a silver lining and Max's retirement brought about an invitation for Graham Warren to join the Australian team.

Warren had arrived at Third Division Cradley Heath at the start of the season and, in an opening Challenge match, he clipped over a second off the Dudley Wood track record, scored a faultless paid maximum and won all of his second-half rides and the Scratch Race Final. Cradley promoter Les Marshall reckoned that Graham was too good for the Third Division and immediately transferred him to his other club in Division Two, Birmingham. Young, blonde and handsome Warren was an overnight sensation and soon led the Brummies' scorers. Even so, he was he entered in the Australian team only as a reserve.

As expected, the Aussies proved to be tough opposition on their 'own' track, but England were steadfast. The Parkers were a formidable pairing and Bill Gilbert was a revelation. Waterman struggled with a knee injury but, even so, he semed more comfortable than the visitor's Aub Lawson, who still looked far from fit.

Australia fell behind in the second heat, and were never able to get on terms again, although they did get to within 2 points of the Lions with five heats to go. But at this point Dent Oliver, who had been pointless thus far, produced his a scintillating ride and led the impressive Gilbert over the line for an England 5-1, which put them on the road to victory. Warren made his debut in heat eleven and, in his first time on the Haringay track, he rocketed from the tapes to win the race by a mile from his partner Bill Longley. Warren made two further appearances, but on both occasions he ended up in third place to the English riders. Even so, he had made an impressive start to his International career.

ENGLAND 58: J. Parker 15, B. Gilbert 13, A. Statham 9, N. Parker 8, S. Waterman 7, D. Oliver 3, L. Goffe 2, J. Lloyd 1.

AUSTRALIA 50: V. Duggan 15, R. Johnson 10, R. Duggan 8, B. Longley 6, G. Warren 5, J. Biggs 5, A. Lawson 1, F. Dolan 0.

Twenty-four hours before the final Test at **West Ham**, Alec Statham withdrew with an injured leg and Tommy Croombs was recalled to the England team. Oliver Hart was bought in to replace Dent Oliver, who moved down to reserve alongside Malcolm Craven. Australia made only one change, as Cliff Watson replaced Frank Dolan.

The Aussies were determined to avoid a whitewash and rode like their lives depended upon it. Warren, in the team proper, was determined to make an impression, but youthful exuberance got the better of him in

his first race and a visit to the track by his backside was the result. After winning his next race, Warren faced the Parkers in heat eight, but he got locked up with Jack and Parker senior ended up in the safety fence. Jack was getting too old to take this kind of battering and his subdued performance in the rest of the match had a significant bearing upon the result. Aub Lawson was now fully fit, and put on his best ever performance for the away team, scoring 15 points.

The likeable Bill Longley had been awarded the Australian captaincy in the final Test and he rode like a true captain, although the awesome Vic Duggan, who was in a different class from any other rider on the night, overshadowed him. By the interval, England trailed by 2 points but early in the second half, two maximum heat wins from Lawson and Warren put Australia well on their way to saving face.

ENGLAND 45: N.Parker 11, O.Hart 9, S.Waterman 7, B.Gilbert 7, J.Parker 6, M.Craven 2, T.Croombs 2, D.Oliver 1.

AUSTRALIA 63: V.Duggan 18, A.Lawson 15, B.Longley 12, G.Warren 9, R.Johnson 8, J.Biggs 1, R.Duggan 0, C.Watson 0.

It was a time of change for the Aussies. Of the old guard, only Ron Johnson remained now that Grosskreutz and Van Praag were gone forever. However, they had arguably the best rider in the world at that time in Vic Duggan, who won the British Riders Championship that year (Johnson was second) and the meteoric rise of Graham Warren indicated that Australia would still be tough opponents for England for years to come.

ENGLAND v AUSTRALIA TEST SERIES 1949

1st Test	Wembley	May 26th	'49	Eng 41	Aust 67	L
2nd Test	Birmingham	June 18th	'49	Eng 53	Aust 55	L
3rd Test	New Cross	July 13th	'49	Eng 62	Aust 46	W
4th Test	Haringay	Aug 5th	'49	Eng 53	Aust 55	L
5th Test	Odsal	Sept 3rd	'49	Eng 72	Aust 36	W

Australia win series 3-2

There was no English tour of Australia in the winter, as indecision regarding this was prevalent throughout the 1948 season and in the end it got too late to make the required arrangements.

For the first Test of 1949 at **Wembley** England stuck with their opening pairing of Jack and Norman Parker, with Bill Gilbert and Oliver Hart forming the middle pair and Alec Statham and Dent Oliver completing the third pairing. Wembley riders Split Waterman and debut boy Fred Williams were the two selected reserves. Australia kept the team that won the final Test of 1948 with one exception; twenty-five-year-old Ken Le Breton from Second Division Ashfield was called up as reserve to replace Ray Duggan.

The match turned out to be a debacle in which, on the England side, only the reserves came out with any credit. The famous Parker pairing was reduced to mediocrity, as Jack failed to win a race and Norman was withdrawn after three pointless rides. At the half-way stage, Australia had twice as many points as the Lions and a landslide victory seemed inevitable. In an attempt to stem the tide, the English reserves were called upon frequently in the second half and both Waterman and, especially, Freddie Williams showed a tenacity that was sadly lacking in their teammates.

By comparison, the Aussies were on fire. Duggan scored an immaculate maximum, but twenty-three-year-old Graham Warren, who matched him point for point, upstaged him. These two riders points tally alone almost equalled England's total.

ENGLAND 41: J. Parker 9, B. Gilbert 9, F. Williams 9, S. Waterman 5, O. Hart 3, D. Oliver 3, A. Statham 3, N. Parker 0.

AUSTRALIA 67: G. Warren 18, V. Duggan 18, R. Johnson 12, B. Longley 7, A. Lawson 6, J. Biggs 6, K. Le Breton dnr, C. Watson dnr.

Birmingham had recently been promoted into the First Division and thus became the first Midlands Club ever to stage a Test match. Perry Barr was after all, the home track of Grahame Warren and the Brummies also had Aussies Arthur Payne and Doug McLachlan. However, on the eve of the second Test, Warren had been injured and was unable to take his place in the Australian team. Therefore home riders Payne and McLachlan made their international debuts as the Aussies' opening pairing, with Johnson and Longley filling the middle spot and Vic Duggan and Watson completing the top six. Biggs and Lawson were named as the reserves.

England had had a rethink. From the main body of the team from the Wembley fiasco, they retained only Jack Parker, Bill Gilbert and Dent Oliver. Williams and Waterman were both promoted into the team, along with young Louis Lawson from Belle Vue. Cyril Roger from New Cross and Mike Erskine were the named reserves.

Arthur Payne got the Aussies off to a good start when he and McLachlan scored a 4-2 over Jack Parker after Freddie Williams fell. But Louis Lawson and Gilbert hit back with a maximum heat win in the next race. In the same race Australia's Johnson crashed and smashed his front forks, which virtually relegated him to being a passenger for the rest of the match and England began to creep ahead. By the eleventh heat, the Lions had established a 37-29 lead, but then the Roos brought reserve Aub Lawson into the match. Lawson was the catalyst for the change in Australia's fortunes.

He and Longley hit back with a 5-1 in the thirteenth heat and, two races later, Lawson teamed up with Arthur Payne for a maximum heat win. Suddenly Australia were 2 points ahead of the home team. A 4-2 by the majestic Duggan and partner Watson put the Aussies 4 points ahead for the penultimate heat, which was drawn. In the final heat Dent Oliver managed to hold back the fiery Aub Lawson, who in turn managed to keep England reserve Cyril Rogers behind him, for Australia to win a thriller by 2 points.

For England, Louis Lawson had a very impressive debut, as did Arthur Payne for the Aussies. Although the match was close, one had to remember that Australia had won without the rider who would possibly have been their greatest asset at Perry Barr – Graham Warren.

ENGLAND 53: L. Lawson 12, D. Oliver 11, J. Parker 9, B. Gilbert 8, F. Williams 7, S. Waterman 5, C. Roger 1, M. Erskine dnr.

AUSTRALIA 55: V. Duggan 18, A. Payne 13, B. Longley 10, A. Lawson 6, D. McLachlan 3, R. Johnson 2, C. Watson 2, J. Biggs 1.

For the third Test at **New Cross**, England dropped top-scoring Louis Lawson and Split Waterman and replaced them with Cyril Rogers and Tommy Price and put home rider Eric French and Cyril Brine in as reserves. For Australia there was good news – Warren was back – and some awful news –Vic Duggan was injured. Ken Le Breton was recalled for duty as reserve, but Duggan was irreplaceable.

England got off to a good start partly due to the success of the Oliver-Gilbert pairing. Oliver tended to ride the bigger tracks well and with New Cross being the smallest track in the country, some considered it folly to include him in the side at this venue, but the selectors faith proved to be justified, as, by the interval, Dent was unbeaten.

Come the interval, things looked bad for Australia. They had won only one heat and Warren did not look fully fit. With Ray Duggan failing to respond to the Roos plight, Le Breton replaced him towards the end of the first half, but Ken ran a last and, going into the break, England led 31-17. Le Breton, known as the White Ghost because of his resplendent white leathers, breathed a little fire into the Australians in the first race of the second half. He stormed past the unbeaten Parker on the first bend and led him for three laps before the cagey Lion outsmarted him on the last lap. It was not the last the crowd saw of Ken as he beat the Tommy Price-Eric French pairing to win heat sixteen. Ron Johnson, as ever, rode at his best when the Colonials were up against it, but they were unable to overcome the loss of Vic Duggan and lost the match 62-46, to keep England in with a chance of retaining the Ashes.

Jack Parker, beaten only by Bill Longley, created a new record by becoming the highest ever points scorer in Test matches; his total of 387 beating Max Grosskreutz's 375.

ENGLAND 62: J. Parker 17, D. Oliver 14, B. Gilbert 11, T. Price 11, F. Williams 6, E. French 3, C. Brine 0, C. Roger 0.

AUSTRALIA 46: R. Johnson 12, G. Warren 10, C. Watson 8, B. Longley 7, K. Le Breton 6, A. Lawson 3, A. Payne 0, R. Duggan 0.

The news on Vic Duggan was not good and he was ruled out for the rest of the series, but worse was to follow for Australia when, before the fourth Test at **Haringay**, Ron Johnson crashed at Wimbledon.

ENGLAND v AUSTRALIA

AT

NEW CROSS SPEEDWAY

Promoters	LONDON MOTOR SPORTS LTD.
Joint Managing Directors	{ CECIL L. SMITH { FRED E. MOCKFORD, G.M.

270th MEETING   1949 SEASON

WEDNESDAY, JULY 13th, 1949, at 7.45 p.m.

OFFICIALS

A.C.U. Steward
G. R. ALLEN

A.C.U. Timekeeper and Judge
A. J. GIBBONS

(Appointed by the Auto-Cycle Union)

Medical Officer
Dr. W. MITCHELL

Chief Paddock Marshal
HARRY SHEPHERD

Clerk of the Course
FRED MOCKFORD, G.M.

PRICE: ONE SHILLING

1. England, 1930. From left to right: Bob Harrison, Frank Charles, Jim Kempster, Squibb Burton, Frank Varey, Wally Hull, Jack Parker, Eric Langdon.

2. 1931 captains Colin Watson and Vic Huxley.

3. *Above:* England prior to the start of the 1931 Belle Vue Test match. From left to right: Jack Parker, Fred Wilkinson, Eric Langdon, Arthur Franklyn, Ginger Lees, Tommy Croombs, Joe Abbot, Colin Watson, Dusty Haigh, Frank Varey.

4. *Left:* Australian skipper and star of the early 1930s Vic Huxley with the team mascot.

5. *Above:* England, led by Eric Langdon, 1932. In a thrilling Test series the Lions were pushed into a last-match decider before claiming a 3-2 victory.

6. *Right:* Frank Varey, England's 'Showman Supreme' of the early 1930s.

7. Billy Lamont and Frank Arthur were two of Australia's pioneers in Test match history.

8. Rival captains, 1934. Vic Huxley paints the kangaroo and Colin Watson paints the lion at Wembley.

9. Eric Langdon, England's lynch pin of the 1930s.

10. Aussie Lionel Van Praag, speedway's first ever World Champion.

11. First-heat action at Wembley, 1936.

12. Lionel Van Praag and Stan Greatrey in the 1936 Test match at New Cross.

13. *Right:* Max Grosskreutz and Bluey Wilkinson were a constant thorn in England's side in the pre-war Test matches.

14. *Below:* Australia at Belle Vue, 1939. From left to right: Nobby Clarke (trainer), Ron Johnson, Vic Duggan, Lionel Van Praag, Andy Menzies, Ray Duggan, Arthur Simcork (team manager), Ernie Evans, Eric Collins, Aub Lawson.

15. Jeff Lloyd and older brother Wally, Belle Vue, 1948.

16. *Opposite, above:* Jack Parker leads England out onto the track for a resounding victory in the 1948 Test match at Belle Vue.

17. *Opposite, below:* Action from that match as England's Split Waterman attempts to dive under Aussie Aub Lawson.

18. *Left:* Ken Le Breton leads Dent Oliver in the 1950 Test match at Belle Vue.

19. *Below:* Graham Warren and Ken Le Breton lead Jack Parker and Dent Oliver in the 1950 Belle Vue Test.

20. *Opposite:* Merv Harding was one of the Australian top scorers in that match.

21. *Left:* In the 1950/51 tour of Australia England's Eddie Rigg was one of the riders involved in the crash at Sydney in which Aussie Ken Le Breton lost his life.

22. *Below:* Wally Green leads Jack Biggs in the 1952 Test series that saw the Lions win only one match.

23. *Opposite, above:* The 1952 Lions at Belle Vue. From left to right, back row: Arthur Forrest, Louis Lawson, Fred Mockford (team manager), Ken Sharples, Freddie Williams. Front row: Split Waterman, Bert Roger, Alan Hunt, Wally Green.

24. *Opposite, below:* Two riders who tragically lost their lives on track: Ken Le Breton (right), who died in Australia in 1951, and Alan Hunt, who lost his life in South Africa in 1957.

25. England *v*. Australia, Birmingham 1952. Arthur Payne, Alan Hunt, Ron Mountford, Graham Warren, Les Hewitt.

26. England line-up from the same meeting. From left to right, back row: Tommy Miller, Split Waterman, Derek Close, Cyril Brine. Front row: Eddie Rigg, Freddie Williams, Alan Hunt and Ron Mountford.

27. Australia's Graham Warren, c. 1952.

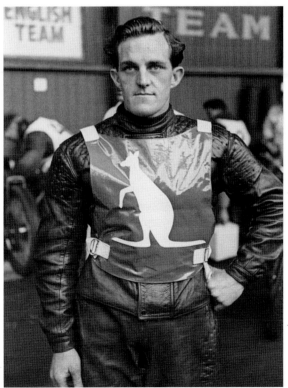

28. Arthur Payne, Australian star of the early 1950s.

29. Action from the 1950s as Aussie Graham Warren attempts to ride around the England duo of Louis Lawson and Tommy Price.

Severe head injuries ensured that he too would miss the remaining two matches. The Aussies regrouped, as Le Breton was paired with Warren, Watson with Longley and Jack Biggs and Aub Lawson formed the third pairing. Ray Duggan was given one reserve birth, whilst the second was given to twenty-three-year-old Bob Leverenz from Second Division Norwich.

England responded to Australia's dilemma by attempting to put out their strongest possible team. Norman Parker was reinstated to ride alongside brother Jack and the highly successful pairing of Oliver and Gilbert was retained, but Freddie Williams was injured so Eric French stepped in to partner Tommy Price. Louis Lawson and Cyril Brine were named as the England reserves.

What followed was a match crammed with tense excitement and a grandstand finish. It looked at the beginning as though the Lions would devour the Roos, as Jack Parker broke the track record in the first heat and Gilbert and Oliver scored a 4-2 in heat two. But Jackie Biggs won the next race and Le Breton and Warren scored a maximum heat win in the fourth as a titanic battle began.

After twelve heats, Australia were just 2 points adrift, but heat thirteen proved to be crucial. Warren led out for the Aussies followed by Dent Oliver and Ken Le Breton, who was on Dent's back wheel for most of the race. On the first bend of the final lap, Le Breton made his move and Oliver hit the deck. Although there was no contact, the packed house soundly booed the White Ghost, but the race had reversed Australia's fortunes and they now led by 2 points.

At the start of the final race, Australia led by 2 points and Jack Biggs, who was enjoying his most successful night so far for the Aussies, and local favourite Ray Duggan faced Bill Gilbert and Louis Lawson, who had been put in to replace Dent Oliver. However, the pressure got to Duggan and he broke the tapes leaving Jack on his own to face the English pairing. As the tapes went up, Biggs and Louis Lawson rode four laps of heart-stopping speedway. At the end, Parker crossed the line first to win the Ashes for Australia for the first time in fifteen years in England.

ENGLAND 53: J. Parker 16, B. Gilbert 12, T. Price 8, E. French 7, L. Lawson 5, N. Parker 4, D. Oliver 1, C. Brine 0.

AUSTRALIA 55: J. Biggs 15, G. Warren 14, C. Watson 10, K. Le Breton 8, B. Longley 5, R. Duggan 3, A. Lawson 0, B. Leverenz dnr.

For the final Test at **Odsal,** Australia were further depleted as Jack Biggs joined Vic Duggan and Ron Johnson on the sick list. Ray Duggan moved up to partner Warren, Cliff Watson was paired with Aub Lawson and Bill Longley and Ken Le Breton were the Aussies' final pairing. Bob Leverenz was named as first reserve and twenty-four-year-old Jack Young made his debut as second reserve. Young was enjoying great success at Second Division Edinburgh in his first year in Britain.

England had a reshuffle and paired Louis Lawson with Jack Parker and Tommy Price with Dent Oliver and they went for Odsal riders Oliver Hart and Ron Clarke to complete the main body of the team. Odsal's Ernie Price and Bill Gilbert were the England reserves.

On this occasion, the now legendary Aussie fighting spirit was absent, as only Warren and Aub Lawson fought to retain Australian pride. The England side made the most of the situation and completely swamped the depleted Roos winning the match 72-36, and making the overall result respectable.

ENGLAND 72: D. Oliver 18, J. Parker 15, R. Clarke 14, T. Price 10, L. Lawson 8, O. Hart 7, B. Gilbert dnr, E. Price dnr.

AUSTRALIA 36: A. Lawson 13, G. Warren 11, B. Longley 4, B. Leverenx 4, K. Le Breton 3, J. Young 1, C. Watson 0, R. Duggan 0.

Speedway showed even more signs of returning to normal as the World Championship returned to Wembley in 1949. England swept the board with Tommy Price winning the event from Jack Parker and Louis Lawson. Bill Longley and Aub Lawson were the most successful Australians finishing joint eighth.

FIFTH SPEEDWAY TEST MATCH
ENGLAND

AUSTRALIA
ODSAL, BRADFORD
Saturday, SEPTEMBER 3rd, 1949

SOUVENIR
PROGRAMME

AUSTRALIA v ENGLAND TEST SERIES 1949/50

1st Test	Sydney	Dec 17th	'49	Aust 76	Eng 32	L
2nd Test	Sydney	Jan 6th	'50	Aust 67	Eng 41	L
3rd Test	Brisbane	Jan 21st	'50	Aust 72	Eng 35	L
4th Test	Sydney	Jan 28th	'50	Aust 68	Eng 40	L
5th Test	Sydney	Feb 3rd	'50	Aust 68	Eng 40	L
6th Test	Melbourne	Feb 11th	'50	Aust 50	Eng 58	W
7th Test	Adelaide	Feb 17th	'50	Aust 70	Eng 38	L

Australia win series 6-1

England took their best ever squad to Australia in the winter of 1949, which featured no fewer than six World Finalists. Jack Parker again led the Lions and Bill Kitchen, Dent Oliver, Ron Clarke, Cyril Roger, Oliver Hart, Freddie Williams and Howdy Byford joined him. Australia's team was a shadow of former times with the Duggan brothers missing and Ron Johnson still recovering from his awful accident.

For the first Test at the **Sydney** Showground the Australians built their team around Warren, Biggs Lawson, Le Breton and Longley and added locals Norman Clay, Alec Hunter and Jack Arnfield.

Most of the English riders, especially Jack Parker, had fared well in the Open meetings prior to the first Test so, understandably, English hopes were high. But instead of the expected victory, the Lions were subjected to a humiliating defeat.

Aub Lawson and Norman Clay got the Australian ball rolling with a maximum heat win over Parker in heat one and the Aussies never looked back. The Lawson-Clay pairing were in fact split only once during the match by Bill Kitchen and Lawson and Jack Biggs were unbeaten by an opponent throughout the match. Only Bill Kitchen managed to score double figures, as the Lions were thrashed 76-32.

AUSTRALIA 76: J. Biggs 18, A. Lawson 16, G. Warren 14, N. Clay 13, K. Le Breton 10, B. Longley 5, A. Hunter 0, J. Arnfield 0.

ENGLAND 32: B. Kitchen 10, J. Parker 9, R. Clarke 6, F. Williams 5, C. Roger 2, O. Hart 0, D. Oliver 0, H. Byford 0.

England put up a better show in the second Test at the **Sydney** Sports Ground and were even in front after three heats, but Australia quickly took the reins, to assert their authority on the match. The Lions took a sickening blow when Bill Kitchen bowed out of the series in heat twelve, when he crashed and suffered concussion, broken ribs and a broken bone in his foot. On this occasion, England managed to tame Norman Clay and Parker beat Aub Lawson in the opening heat but, in truth, the English enjoyed little success and were soundly beaten 67-41.

AUSTRALIA 67: A. Lawson 16, G. Warren 15, J. Biggs 13, K. Le Breton 11, B. Longley 7, N. Clay 4, A. Hunter 1, J. Arnfield 0.

ENGLAND 41: J. Parker 11, O. Hart 7, F. Williams 6, R. Clarke 6, C. Roger 6, B. Kitchen 5, D. Oliver 0, H. Byford 0.

The 1949/50 Test Series was to be run over a marathon seven matches, so England still had time to redeem themselves. But they showed no signs of doing so in the third Test at **Brisbane**. On the eve of the match there was some terrible news. Back at the Sydney Showground on 20 January, Ray Duggan and Norman Clay were involved in a crash in which both sustained such serious head injuries, that they lost their lives.

Australia rested Bill Longley and brought Keith Gurtner into the side and Bert Spencer and Dick Smythe replaced reserves Arnfield and Hunter. England, who were without Kitchen, brought Jack's young nephew Dennis Parker into the squad. The match turned out to be another debâcle. Parker beat Warren and Oliver Hart beat Aub Lawson, but that was the extent of England's success. In a cable to the Sunday Pictorial, skipper Parker wrote that 'Our team is inferior in talent by comparison', which spoke volumes for the England team spirit on that particular tour.

AUSTRALIA 72: A. Lawson 17, G. Warren 16, J. Biggs 14, K. Gurtner 9, K. Le Breton 8, K. Cox 8, D. Smythe 0, B. Spencer 0.

ENGLAND 35: J. Parker 12, O. Hart 9, D. Oliver 5, R. Clarke 3, F. Williams 3, C. Roger 1, H. Byford 1, D. Parker 1.

All hopes of regaining the Ashes were lost with England's defeat back at the **Sydney** Showground in the fourth Test. The Lions' embarrassing performance had seen crowds dwindle and they did little to capture the imagination in this particular outing. The improving form of Oliver Hart warmed the cockles of the English hearts, but he and Jack Parker alone could not be expected to hold back the Australian onslaught as the seemingly inevitable rout again took place.

AUSTRALIA 68: A. Lawson 18, K. Le Breton 15, G. Warren 11, B. Longley 9, L. Levy 7, J. Biggs 5, K. Gurtner 3, M. Harding 0.

ENGLAND 40: J. Parker 11, O. Hart 11, D. Oliver 6, R. Clarke 5, C. Roger 4, F. Williams 3, D. Parker 0.

Oliver Hart maintained his form in the fifth Test, again at **Sydney**, being the only man to beat the flying Aub Lawson, but with Jack Parker struggling to get out of the gate, England failed to improve on their previous performance.

AUSTRALIA 68: A. Lawson 17, G. Warren 16, J. Biggs 15, B. Longley 10, B. Ryan 8, A. Hunter 1, L. Levy 1, M. Harding 0, T. Argall 0.

ENGLAND 40: O. Hart 11, J. Parker 9, R. Clarke 8, D. Oliver 7, C. Roger 3, F. Williams 2, D. Parker 0, H. Byford 0.

For the sixth Test at **Melbourne**, England had to face the ignominy of riding against a diluted Australian team in order to make racing competitive. Warren, Biggs and Le Breton were all rested and Merv Harding, Norman Lindsay, Jack Bibby, Andy Menzies, Ken Walsh and Jack Down all joined Aub Lawson and Bill Longley. As if nothing would go right for England, they had to face their opponents without Freddie Williams who had a poisoned jaw.

At least England were able to save face and win against their mediocre opponents, thanks to an unfortunate incident in heat seventeen when the scores were locked at 48-48. As the result of a first bend pile-up, Jack Bibby was left with a broken leg and Oliver Hart was badly shaken. Substitutes were allowed in the rerun and, with Ron Clarke leading from the start, young Dennis Parker held Bill Longley at bay to give England a 5-1 and a 4-point lead. A maximum heat win in the final race gave the Lions an overdue but hollow victory.

AUSTRALIA 50: A. Lawson 18, B. Longley 12, M. Harding 12, N. Lindsay 4, J. Bibby 4, A. Menzies 0, J. Down 0, K. Walsh 0.

ENGLAND 58: J. Parker 14, R. Clarke 14, O. Hart 9, C. Roger 6, D. Oliver 6, H. Byford 5, D. Parker 4.

Australia decided to give the next generation a run in the seventh and final Test at **Adelaide**, and Jack Young, Frank Young, Bob Leverenz, Lindsay Mitchell and John Williams were brought in to join Lawson, Longley and Merv Harding and, once again, it spelled disaster for England. Jack Young gave England a look into the future as he stormed to 17 points. In fact he and partner Merv Harding scored 26 points out of a possible 30, as the Lions went out of the ill-fated series with a whimper.

AUSTRALIA 70: J. Young 17, B. Longley 16, A. Lawson 15, M. Harding 9, L. Mitchell 8, F. Young 3, B. Leverenz 2, J. Williams 0.

ENGLAND 38: J. Parker 14, R. Clarke 10, O. Hart 6, C. Roger 3, D. Oliver 2, H. Byford 2, D. Parker 1.

CHAPTER 3

THE FIFTIES

ENGLAND v AUSTRALIA TEST SERIES 1950

1st Test	West Ham	June 6th	'50	Eng 47	Aust 60	L
2nd Test	Belle Vue	June 24th	'50	Eng 58	Aust 50	W
3rd Test	New Cross	July 12th	'50	Eng 63	Aust 45	W
4th Test	Wimbledon	July 31st	'50	Eng 62	Aust 46	W
5th Test	Wembley	Aug 31st	'50	Eng 53	Aust 55	L

England win series 3-2

England must have looked upon the 1950 Test Series against Australia with trepidation. After being thrashed unmercifully down under in the winter by a series of watered-down Australian teams, they now faced the full might of the Aussies in England. Vic Duggan returned, to partner the vastly improved Jack Biggs, Graham Warren was paired with Ken Le Breton and Aub Lawson's pairing with Bill Longley completed a fearsome Australian top six. Jack Young and Dick Seers were the impressive reserves named for the opening Test at **West Ham**.

England seemed bereft of ideas and their selected squad consisted entirely of riders who had already been capped. It was difficult to criticise the selection of Jack Parker. Even at forty-three, he remained one of England's top riders and this time he was given Cyril Rogers as a partner. The middle pairing had a fresh look about it as Eric French teamed up with home rider Malcolm Craven and Tommy Price and Freddie

Williams completed the main body of the team. (Williams was in fact Welsh so, technically, he was not eligible to ride for England but, over the years, speedway can be seen to have been quite flexible regarding eligibility). Louis Lawson and Split Waterman were named as the Lions reserves.

The spirits of the 50,000 crowd were raised when Parker and Roger scored a 5-1 over Duggan in the opening heat and French beat Warren in the next race. The Aussies immediately hit back but they were dealt a blow when Warren blew his motor in heat five. Warren withdrew from heat eight, to be replaced by Jack Young which meant that, with Le Breton already being in the race, Australia were fielding two Second Division riders against the experienced Parker and Roger. The resulting 5-1 to the visitors stunned England and another maximum heat win in the following race saw the Roos go into the interval 2 points ahead.

In effect Australia had lost Warren. But what a replacement Jack Young proved to be as he and Le Breton scored another two maximum heat wins in the second half of the meeting. With Duggan springing to life and Aub Lawson being effective throughout, England began to totter and the Aussies took command and cruised to a 13-point win. Jack Young had been undefeated by an opponent in his three outings.

ENGLAND 47: T. Price 10, J. Parker 8, C. Roger 6, E. French 6, L. Lawson 6, F. Williams 5, M. Craven 4, S. Waterman 2.

AUSTRALIA 60: A. Lawson 12, V. Duggan 12, K. Le Breton 11, B. Longley 10, J. Young 7, J. Biggs 6, G. Warren 2, D. Seers dnr.

Williams, Roger, Craven and Waterman were all dropped from the England team for the second Test at **Belle Vue**. Dent Oliver was recalled on his home track to partner Parker, Louis Lawson was an obvious choice to move into the main body of the team and thirty-year-old Eddie Rigg from Odsal was making his England debut. Another debutante was Bert Roger, the younger brother of Cyril and Alec Statham joined him at reserve.

The Roos meanwhile had been having a mini injury crisis and nonstarters were Bill Longley (fractured rib) and Jack Biggs (fractured toe). Once again Australia looked to the Second Division and brought in

Bob Leverenz and Ashfield's red-leathered Merv Harding. So not only did they have the White Ghost in their team they also had the Red Devil! Finally, Arthur Payne replaced Dick Seers.

It was not the Aussies' night. Aub Lawson turned up at Hyde Road a very sick man, but still rode in the match and Vic Duggan had his worst match ever for his country, scoring only 1 point from his first three outings and being replaced in his others. With fourteen heats gone, England led by 12 points and seemingly had the match sewn up, but there followed two maximum heat wins from Warren and Le Breton and Harding and Leverenz, that left the England fans blanching. As it happens, England won the final two heats to clinch the match by 8 points, but they certainly made heavy weather of it.

If Jack Young was the sensation at West Ham, then Merv Harding proved to be so at Belle Vue, belying his Second Division status to score 14 points in his first international in England, on a track that he had never seen before. For England, Eddie Rigg had a wonderful debut and Louis Lawson certainly did the job he was brought in to do on his home track, but Dent Oliver was just as disappointing as his counterpart Vic Duggan.

ENGLAND 58: L. Lawson 14, E. Rigg 12, T. Price 10, J. Parker 8, E. French 8, A. Statham 5, D. Oliver 1, B. Roger dnr.

AUSTRALIA 50: G. Warren 15, M. Harding 14, K. Le Breton 7, A. Lawson 5, J. Young 5, B. Leverenz 3, V. Duggan 1, A. Payne 0.

The big news that preceded the third Test at **New Cross** was that Jack Parker had been replaced by his brother Norman, who took over the captaincy of the England team. Cyril Brine was brought in to partner the new skipper and Bert Roger moved up into the full team to ride with Eric French. Cyril Roger was recalled to pair up with Tommy Price and Louis Lawson and Alan Hunt were the named reserves. England had taken a leaf out of Australia's book and looked to the Second Division where twenty-six-year-old Alan Hunt of Cradley Heath, was one of the outstanding riders.

The Australians were expected to struggle on the tight New Cross track, but help was at hand as Biggs, Longley and even Ron Johnson returned to the side. However they did so, rather surprisingly, at the expense of the young fliers Harding and Young.

One week before the match took place, England received the devastating news that one of her greatest servants Joe Abbott had been killed whilst riding in a match at his home team Odsal. Joe was forty-seven years old.

In the first half, the opening England pairing of Parker and Brine, after an indifferent first race, scored two tactical maximum heat wins. On both occasions Brine shot from the tapes and Norman sat behind him to nurse Cyril for the four laps. By the interval England led by 8 points. The start of the second half spelled disaster for Vic Duggan. He had scored only 2 points from his first three rides, but in heat ten he lost control of his machine and the resulting crash saw him jar his spine and retire from the meeting.

With the failure of Ron Johnson to make an impact, Graham Warren was the only Australian to make any impression on a solid England team. He dropped only 1 point to Cyril Roger, in what was a magnificent display of riding. But one man does not make a team and the Roos were soundly beaten.

For England, both of the Roger brothers rode brilliantly, but even they were somewhat overshadowed by debutante Alan Hunt who produced four electrifying rides ending with a heat win in the final race.

ENGLAND 63: B. Roger 14, C. Roger 14, C. Brine 11, T. Price 10, N. Parker 7, A. Hunt 7, E. French 0, L. Lawson 0.

AUSTRALIA 45: G. Warren 17, J. Biggs 7, A. Lawson 6, K. Le Breton 6, B. Longley 4, V. Duggan 2, R. Johnson 2, C. Watson 1.

Internal trouble kept Cyril Roger out of the England team at **Wimbledon**, and the Lions made the bold step of moving Alan Hunt into the top six. No doubt influenced by the Cradley rider's success, the selectors once again looked to the Second Division and came up with Vic Emms from Halifax to fill one of the reserve berths, while Ron Clarke claimed the other.

Australia reverted back to their youth policy and recalled Young and Harding. In fact they went one further and conscripted the seventeen-year-old wonderboy from Wimbledon, Ronnie Moore. Moore had

been an overnight sensation in his first year in British speedway and his international debut, on his home track, put him in the record books as the youngest rider ever to appear in a Test match. Ronnie actually came from New Zealand, but he was in fact born in Australia, which made him eligible for selection. Sadly, Vic Duggan had requested to be omitted from the team and Graham Warren was his natural successor as captain of the Kangaroos. Aub Lawson and Ken Le Breton joined the youngsters in the main body of the team and Bill Longley was dropped to reserve alongside Junior Bainbridge from Second Division White City. The omission of Jack Biggs was somewhat of a surprise.

The Australian plan was to pair each of its less experienced riders with one of its long-term men, but this fell apart when Ronnie Moore's partner Aub Lawson crashed out of the meeting in heat five. Left to his own devices, young Ronnie struggled, although he did win heat eleven, from Eric French and World Champion Tommy Price. Australia seemed to have over-invested in youth, as the more experienced English riders gave them a lesson in tactical speedway. But even so the Aussie young-sters were a lively bunch and the old hands of England must have known that it was only a matter of time before they would be looking up the exhaust pipes of these precocious Colonials.

Graham Warren was the best rider on view with five wins and an inexplicable last place, but once again it was Alan Hunt who was the most talked-about rider on the night.

Alan had a horrendous journey to Plough Lane when his van broke down en route. The hired vehicle that he acquired had five punctures during the last 50 miles to Wimbledon and he arrived as a very frus-trated man. But that never showed in his performance. He won his first two races and added another win in the second half of the match, to be second highest scorer for the Lions.

Jack Young may have been equally as successful for the Aussies, as he took 5 points from his first two rides, but when his forks collapsed in his third, he was a virtual passenger for the remainder of the match. England had regained the Ashes in what was a splendid performance. Australia's hopes went out of the window when Aub Lawson made his exit.

ENGLAND 62: C. Brine 13, A. Hunt 12, T. Price 10, E. French 9, B. Roger 9, N. Parker 9, R. Clarke dnr, V. Emms dnr.

AUSTRALIA 46: G. Warren 15, K. Le Breton 8, J. Young 7, M. Harding 6, R. Moore 5, A. Lawson 3, B. Longley 1, J. Bainbridge 1.

For the fifth and final Test at **Wembley**, England recalled Jack Parker in place of Bert Roger and Freddie Williams re-emerged as reserve alongside Halifax's Arthur Forrest. Australia had a rethink, and dropped Ronnie Moore, Junior Bainbridge and Bill Longley. They called up Arthur Payne to ride with Birmingham teammate Warren and paired Jack Biggs with Ken Le Breton. Jack Young was retained and partnered Aub Lawson and Merv Harding was named as reserve along with Vic Duggan, who had been showing improvement in his form.

The match was ridden under treacherous conditions, but even so, Warren equalled the track record in the opening heat. After seventeen thrilling heats, England were 2 points adrift and Hunt and Williams faced Young and Lawson in the final race. Hunt shot past a surprised Lawson on the first lap but, try as he may, Freddie Williams could not catch third-placed Jack Young and the drawn heat gave the Aussies a 2-point win.

ENGLAND 53: C. Brine 16, T. Price 15, F. Williams 8, E. French 5, A. Hunt 5, J. Parker 2, N. Parker 2, A. Forrest 0.

AUSTRALIA 55: G. Warren 15, K. Le Breton 12, A. Lawson 9, J. Young 6, J. Biggs 6, V. Duggan 5, A. Payne 2, M. Harding 0.

AUSTRALIA v ENGLAND TEST SERIES 1950/51

1st Test	Sydney	Dec 16th	'50	Aust 63	Eng 45	L
2nd Test	Sydney	Jan 5th	'51	Aust 65	Eng 42	L
3rd Test	Sydney	Jan 27th	'51	Aust 60	Eng 48	L
4th Test	Bathurst	Feb 3rd	'51	Aust 67	Eng 40	L
5th Test	Adelaide	Feb 7th	'51	Aust 58½	Eng 49½	L
6th Test	Brisbane	Feb 9th	'51	Aust 60	Eng 48	L
7th Test	Sydney	Feb 10th	'51	Aust 60	Eng 48	L

Australia win series 7-0

The 1950/51 winter tour of Australia was an ill-fated event to say the least. First there was a decision by the Control Board not to send an official team and then there was torrential rain which washed out so many meetings that it meant that the last four matches had to be ridden in just over a week. There were restrictions on the use of electricity for night meetings and then there was a complete ban on electricity for evening sport, which necessitated the matches being ridden in daylight, which just didn't attract the crowds. All small fry compared to the fact that, for the first time ever, a rider lost his life in a Test match.

Following the Board's decision, Jack Parker took matters into his own hands and, just eight days before setting sail, he began forming the 'England' team. Deservedly, Jack had his best ever season in Australia as, apart from his tremendous performances in the Test Series, he won the Australian 3- and 4-lap Championship, the Champion of Champions and the Jubilee Championship. However, the only other England International that Jack managed to enlist was Eddie Rigg. The rest of the team comprised new World Champion Freddie Williams' younger brother Eric, Coventry's Bob Fletcher and Derrick Tailby, Glasgow's Tommy Miller (his Scottish ancestry was conveniently overlooked) and West Ham's youngster Reg Fearman. It was a thoroughly makeshift side and the Australian promoters were most unimpressed with the attitude of the British Speedway Control Board.

Lionel Van Praag made his return to the Australian team for the first Test at **Sydney**, and he joined Aub Lawson, Graham Warren and Ken Le Breton as the Aussie strikeforce. Buck Ryan, Bill Melluish, Noel Watson and Alan Quinn completed the line-up.

Freelancing Fred Yates had to be called up to make up England's full complement, but he did little to influence the result. A rather ill tempered match saw Le Breton cautioned after an on-track skirmish with Eddie Rigg and, mid-match, England manager Harry Tovey put in a protest regarding the Aussies 'creeping' at the tapes. This was upheld and the home team was given an official caution. Aub Lawson was untroubled throughout the match and scored a peerless 18-point maximum, and only Jack Parker beat Warren, but Van Praag showed that he had not weathered as well as Parker, as he scored only 7 points in a comfortable Australian victory.

AUSTRALIA 63: A. Lawson 18, G. Warren 17, K. Le Breton 10, L.Van Praag 7, B. Ryan 6, B. Melluish 4, N.Watson 1, A. Quinn 0.

ENGLAND 45: J. Parker 14, E. Williams 10, E. Rigg 10, T. Miller 5, B. Fletcher 3, D.Tailby 3, R. Fearman 0, F.Yates 0.

The second Test at the **Sydney** Sports Ground was marred by a fatal accident. Australia retained only Lawson, Le Breton, Van Praag and Ryan for this match and added Jack Gates, Dick Seers, Jack Arnfield and Lionel Levy. Derrick Tailby's tour ended in heat four, when he fell and broke a thumb. Lawson, Gates and Ryan were the stars for the home team as they built up a steady lead, but Jack Parker was just as impressive for England. On the last corner of the final heat, Eddie Rigg was nursing Bob Fletcher round for an England 5-1, when Le Breton ran into the back of him. The resulting crash left the White Ghost with a fractured skull and he died the next day in hospital.

AUSTRALIA 65: Aub Lawson 15, J. Gates 15, B. Ryan 13, K. Le Breton 7, D. Seers 5, J. Arnfield 5, L.Van Praag 5, L. Levy 0.

ENGLAND 42: J. Parker 16, E. Williams 10, E. Rigg 8, B. Fletcher 5, T. Miller 2, R. Fearman 1, D.Tailby 0, F.Yates dnr.

There were more changes in the Australian side for the third Test at **Sydney**, when Arthur Payne and Jack Chigwell replaced Van Praag and Levy and Jack Biggs replaced the unfortunate Le Breton. By that time Ron Clarke of Odsal had transferred from Perth and joined the England squad to replace Tailby. Ron would have made the squad competitive, but the tragedy of the second Test was weighing heavily on Eddie Rigg and he became a passenger for the remainder of the tour.

England seemed fated not to win a match in the series as, on the eve of the third Test, Eric Williams went down with a bout of tonsillitis. Jack Parker rolled back the years to score a brilliant maximum and Tommy Miller burst to life with a 13-point return, but support was sadly lacking from the bottom half of the Lions team.

AUSTRALIA 60: A. Lawson 16, B. Ryan 14, J. Biggs 11, J. Gates 6, D. Seers 5, A. Payne 5, J. Chignall 2, A. Hunter 1.

ENGLAND 48: J. Parker 18, T. Miller 13, R. Clarke 10, B. Fletcher 4, E. Rigg 3, R. Fearman 0, F. Yates 0.

Australia regained the Ashes at **Bathurst**, as they secured the fourth win of the series. England's bad luck continued as four of their bikes were damaged in an accident en route and they suffered machine failures throughout the match. The nightmare continued for Eddie Rigg as he was pushed against the windscreen of the vehicle in the accident and suffered concussion and a gashed leg, which forced him to retire from the meeting after only one outing. Jack Parker was once again master of all that he surveyed, but again sadly lacked support.

AUSTRALIA 67: J. Gates 13, B. Ryan 12, A. Lawson 11, J. Arnfield 11, A. Hunter 10, D. Seers 9, D. Lawson 1.

ENGLAND 40: J. Parker 18, R. Clarke 8, R. Fearman 5, T. Miller 3, E. Williams 3, B. Fletcher 2, E. Rigg 1.

Meanwhile, following the Le Breton tragedy, Australia received another devastating blow. Graham Warren, who was racing in New Zealand, had been involved in a near-fatal track accident, which had left him with three fractures of the skull and, although he was making a remarkable recovery after lying unconscious for eight days, doctors advised that his racing days were over.

Eddie Rigg withdrew from the team at **Adelaide**, but with Eric Williams regaining his health, England gave Australia a fight in the fifth Test, with only a six-man team. Bob Leverenz stepped in for Australia and, but for him, the Lions would have won the match.

AUSTRALIA 58½: B. Leverenz 17, A. Lawson 16, B. Ryan 13½, F. Young 6, J. Gates 3, J. Williams 2, F. Woodroffe 1, L. Van Praag 0.

ENGLAND 49½: J. Parker 13, E. Williams 12, R. Clarke 12, T. Miller 7½, B. Fletcher 4, R. Fearman 1.

Ron Clarke was contractually obliged to return to Perth and missed the sixth Test at **Brisbane** and, with Rigg out also, England lost to an

Australian team laced with local talent. Keith Gurtner, Charlie Spinks and Keith Cox were brought into the home side, but once again Jack Parker was the star of the match.

AUSTRALIA 60: A. Lawson 12, K. Gurtner 12, B. Ryan 10, C. Spinks 10, J. Gates 8, K. Cox 8.

ENGLAND 48: J. Parker 16, T. Miller 16, E. Williams 11, B. Fletcher 3, R. Fearman 2, F. Yates 0.

Only 4,000 spectators turned out to see the seventh and final Test at **Sydney** and the match went the way of most of the others. Fletcher had never got the hang of the Australian tracks and it had all been too much for young Fearman at that stage of his career. However Tommy Miller and Eric Williams had done themselves proud, and Jack Parker had defied all logic to become master of Australia.

AUSTRALIA 60: A. Lawson 17, B. Ryan 11, L. Levy 11, D. Seers 9, A. Hunter 7, J. Gates 3, J. Chignall 2, J. Arnfield 0.

ENGLAND 48: J. Parker 16, T. Miller 13, E. Williams 12, B. Fletcher 4, R. Fearman 2, F. Yates 1.

So Jack Parker had beaten the rain, the injuries, the lack of electricity and the Speedway Control Board, to complete the winter tour of Australia, against all odds, but England were now lacking credibility down under and the Australian promoters felt that they had been short-changed. This was certainly not the fault of Parker, who had enlisted the best riders who were available and had ridden at his best throughout the tour, as the results showed, but the problem was lack of volunteers.

To be fair, it was different for the Australians. They already had their best riders competing in Britain, so the Test matches in England were easy to organise by comparison. But when asking for a show of hands to travel halfway around the world to ride, where facilities, especially for bike maintenance, were notoriously poor, the hands of the top riders stayed down.

This meant that the Test matches in Australia were becoming farcical and there was a real danger of them being scrapped. 'Parker's Lions' were undoubtedly the poorest squad of riders ever to be assembled as an England team, but that is no reflection on the effort that they put into their riding. Parker and Eddie Rigg aside, there was Eric Williams, who was a second string at Wembley, Tommy Miller, who was one of the best riders in Division Two, Bob Fletcher and Derrick Tailby from Division Two's Coventry, neither boasting a 7-point average in the lower division and Reg Fearman, who was a West Ham reserve with less than a 3-point average. Under awful circumstances, the team did well, but as an England team they lacked credibility and the Australian promoters knew it.

The Australians of course looked to be in trouble, as they had been robbed of almost half of the national team. Ken Le Breton obviously had so much more to give before he was cruelly snatched away. Perhaps the same could not be said of Vic Duggan, who had decided to retire, but he would remain a legend.

After having the best season of his career, Graham Warren now, having narrowly escaped death, lay in a hospital bed with a big question mark over his future. Warren was arguably the best rider in the world at that time. A fall in the 1950 World Championship may well have cost him the title as he was unbeaten in his other four rides, but as it was Graham had to settle for third place behind Freddie Williams and Wally Green.

The Aussies did of course have their clutch of impressive young riders. In fact Jack Young and Ronnie Moore already had one World Final under their belts, but the likes of Bob Leverenz and Junior Bainbridge would have to mature quickly in order to keep Australia competitive in Britain.

ENGLAND v AUSTRALIA TEST SERIES 1951

1st Test	Haringay	June 1st	'51	Eng 48	Aust 60	L
2nd Test	Odsal	June 30th	'51	Eng 59	Aust 49	W
3rd Test	Wembley	July 19th	'51	Eng 49	Aust 58	L
4th Test	Birmingham	Aug 4th	'51	Eng 46	Aust 62	L
5th Test	West Ham	Aug 28th	'51	Eng 49	Aust 58	L

Australia win series 4–1

Due to his phenomenal success in Australia in the winter, Jack Parker was reinstated as England's captain and number one for the first 1951 Test match at **Haringay** and his partner was to be Cyril Brine. Split Waterman was recalled to ride with World Champion Freddie Williams and Alan Hunt, who had moved to First Division Birmingham, was paired with England's hard man Cyril Roger. Norman Parker and Eddie Rigg were the England reserves.

Australia received a boost when Graham Warren made an unexpected return to British speedway at Birmingham a few days before the match and declared himself available. His offer was taken up and he was placed at reserve with Junior Bainbridge. Skipper Aub Lawson was paired with Cliff Watson, while Jack Young and Ronnie Moore filled in the middle, with Bob Leverenz and Jackie Biggs forming the last pairing.

England, who were reckoned to be the perfect team, began as red-hot favourites and 27,000 spectators turned out to be treated to some thrilling races in a classic match. The Lions got off to a bad start when Jack Parker fell in the opening heat and they suffered further misfortune in the following race. Split Waterman and Ronnie Moore both tore into the first bend in heat two, and with neither willing to give an inch, both fell heavily. Moore returned to the pits, minus a few teeth but able to carry on, but Waterman was a spent force after the crash.

Even so, England led by 8 points after six heats, but the Aussies fought back and levelled the scores at the interval stage. Graham Warren was brought into play in the early stages, but he looked ill at ease and in heat ten, unable to correct an overslide, he was struck under the chin by his own handlebars. But the famous Australian fighting spirit had returned and Ronnie Moore picked himself up to score three maximum heat wins with partner Jack Young as the visitors began to forge in front. Young was incredible. He had travelled from Ireland overnight and was mounted on a bike that had not been stripped for four matches. After running a third in his first race, he broke the Haringay track record and was unbeaten in his other five outings. For England, Norman Parker was a valuable reserve and Freddie Williams put on a good show, but they were well beaten by the end, as the 'perfect team' lacked the enthusiasm of their opponents.

ENGLAND 48: F. Williams 11, J. Parker 9, C. Brine 8, N. Parker 8, C. Roger 7, A. Hunt 5, S. Waterman 0, E. Rigg 0.

AUSTRALIA 60: J. Young 16, A. Lawson 15, J. Biggs 9, R. Moore 8, B. Leverenz 6, J. Bainbridge 4, C. Watson 2, G. Warren 0.

At **Odsal** for the second Test, home rider Eddie Rigg was named as England's number one, and Norman Parker was promoted to partner him. Wembley's Bob Oakley made his international debut as a partner to teammate Freddie Williams, while Jack Parker and Cyril Rogers formed the third Lions pairing. Arthur Forrest and Alan Hunt were the English reserves. Watson and Warren were excluded from an Australian team which saw Bainbridge join Lawson as the opening pairing, with the other two pairings being unchanged. Arthur Payne and Merv Harding were the Roos reserves.

It proved to be a short and painful debut for Oakley who, unable to avoid partner Williams in his first ride, crashed into the fence and was unable to continue in the remainder of the match. His replacements, Forrest and Hunt, were lively reserves, as were Payne and Harding for the visitors, but England were the much better team on the day, with Norman Parker being the only weak link. Jack Young, once again, stole the limelight with another breathtaking performance. Young was quickly establishing himself as the best rider in the sport, but he was viewed with some scepticism because he still rode in the Second Division with Edinburgh. Unfortunately for Australia, on this occasion, apart from Jack Biggs, Young lacked support from his teammates, as even the great Aub Lawson failed to shine.

ENGLAND 59: F. Williams 13, E. Rigg 12, J. Parker 12, C. Roger 8, A. Hunt 6, N. Parker 4, A. Forrest 4, B. Oakley 0.

AUSTRALIA 49: J. Young 16, J. Biggs 11, A. Lawson 6, A. Payne 6, R. Moore 4, M. Harding 3, J. Bainbridge 2, B. Leverenz 1.

There were changes on both sides for the third Test at **Wembley**. Williams and Norman Parker were England's opening pair, with skipper Jack Parker and Cyril Roger taking the middle and Hunt and Waterman completing the third pairing. George Wilks and Tommy Price made their 1951 debut as reserves. Australia dropped Leverenz and Bainbridge to reserves and promoted Payne to ride with Warren as

1951 SERIES
SECOND SPEEDWAY
TEST MATCH

ENGLAND

AUSTRALIA

AT

ODSAL STADIUM, BRADFORD

SATURDAY, JUNE 30th, 1951

SOUVENIR

PROGRAMME

SECOND TEST MATCH

ENGLAND
v.
AUSTRALIA

SATURDAY, 30th JUNE, 1951, at 7.0 p.m.

Official Programme - - - - 1/-

their middle pairing. The Young-Moore pairing was retained and Jack Biggs partnered Lawson.

In front of 54,000 spectators, England put on a rather jaded performance in contrast to the polished performance of their rivals. Jack Young uncharacteristically fell in the opening heat, but in heat four he and Ronnie Moore scored a maximum heat win to put Australia in front for the first time. There was an unlikely hero for the Aussies in the form of Arthur Payne who dropped only 1 point in the first half as the visitors went into the interval leading the home side 31-23.

The second half was a similar tale with the Roos showing much more determination than England, who were served well by only Williams and Waterman, although Wilks proved to be an effective reserve. Payne had an equally successful second half for Australia, but partner Warren looked sadly out of touch. However, with Aub Lawson back on top form, Australia were comfortable winners by 58-49. Lawson was unbeaten by an opponent throughout the match.

ENGLAND 49: S. Waterman 13, F. Williams 12, G. Wilks 7, N. Parker 6, A. Hunt 4, J. Parker 3, C. Roger 3, T. Price 1.

AUSTRALIA 58: A. Lawson 17, A. Payne 16, J. Young 10, J. Biggs 9, R. Moore 6, J. Bainbridge 0, G. Warren 0, B. Leverenz 0.

England's chances of regaining the Ashes were slipping away and a victory in the fourth Test at **Birmingham** was now essential. The selectors chose a team made up entirely of post-war riders, for the first time ever bringing the average age of the squad being down to only twenty-six. The twenty-three-year-old Scot Tommy Miller was brought in to ride with Freddie Williams, Hunt and Rigg were paired together and Split Waterman was joined by twenty-four-year-old Derek Close from Division Two's Newcastle. Cyril Brine and twenty-four-year-old Birmingham rider Ron Mountford were the reserves. Australia made only one change, as Coventry's Les Hewitt replaced Junior Bainbridge at reserve.

Tommy Miller got England off to a great start with a sensational win in the opening heat, but after scoring 1 point from his next two rides, he was dropped by team manager Les Marshall. These were strange

Official Souvenir Programme — One Shilling

ENGLAND v. AUSTRALIA

FOURTH SPEEDWAY TEST MATCH

(1951 Series)

ON

SATURDAY, 4th AUGUST, 1951

AT 6–30 p.m.

AT

BIRMINGHAM SPEEDWAY

BIRCHFIELD HARRIERS ALEXANDER SPORTS
GROUND, PERRY BARR, BIRMINGHAM

THE RIVAL CAPTAINS

tactics from Marshall who decided to stick with Williams, who had scored only 1 point from his first three outings. The World Champion continued to have his worst ever match for England before he was replaced in his last ride, but by then the damage had been done. Conversely, Miller was reinstated for his last ride, which he won. Eddie Rigg was the best English rider on view, but of the 'new blood' only Miller impressed. Alan Hunt was disappointing on his home track, and the Australians took full advantage.

Jack Young helped himself to an immaculate maximum. Jack Biggs was beaten only by Rigg and Warren rode well until he tired in his last two races. It all spelled big trouble for England, as Rigg and Miller were their only race winners. By the end of the match, Australia had easily retained the Ashes with an impressive 62-46 win. The youth policy plan had not worked for England. Perhaps it was not younger riders that they needed – maybe it was more determined ones

ENGLAND 46: E. Rigg 13, S. Waterman 10, T. Miller 9, A. Hunt 6, R. Mountford 3, D. Close 2, F. Williams 2, C. Brine 1.

AUSTRALIA 62: J. Young 18, J. Biggs 16, G. Warren 8, R. Moore 7, A. Payne 7, A. Lawson 6, B. Leverenz 0, L. Hewitt dnr.

Split Waterman was named as the England skipper for the final Test at **West Ham,** to be partnered by George Wilks. Local rider Malcolm Craven was recalled to the team and was paired with Eric Williams, who was rewarded for his valiant efforts for his country during the winter in Australia. Eddie Rigg was an automatic choice to be in the team and Cyril Roger was recalled to join him Tommy Miller and Dennis Gray were named as reserves as the England selectors desperately searched for a combination to restrain the visitors.

The Aussies switched things around, pairing Warren with Lawson, Young with Leverenz, Biggs with Moore and calling in Keith Gurtner at reserve with Les Hewitt.

Young and Leverenz put Australia ahead in the second heat, and they never looked back, although Young enjoyed mixed fortunes all night. With Ronnie Moore having his best Test so far and Graham Warren looking something like his old self, England were never in it. Split

Waterman played a superb captain's role both on and off the track and was the best rider of either team on the night, as he dropped only 1 point to Ronnie Moore.

ENGLAND 49: S. Waterman 17, E. Rigg 14, E. Williams 9, C. Roger 3, M. Craven 3, D. Gray 2, G. Wilks 1, T. Miller 0.

AUSTRALIA 58: G. Warren 12, R. Moore 11, A. Lawson 10, B. Leverenz 10, J. Young 9, J. Biggs 6, L. Hewitt 0, K. Gurtner 0.

Australia were going through a renaissance and, while England couldn't seem to get it right, the Aussies couldn't put a foot wrong. They had unearthed a star of the highest calibre in Jack Young. To prove the point he won the World Championship that year after a run-off with Split Waterman and fellow countryman Jack Biggs. In doing so, he became the first ever Second Division rider to win the title. With young Ronnie Moore finishing in fourth place and Bob Leverenz finishing ninth, Australia were well established as the top speedway nation in the world in 1951.

AUSTRALIA v ENGLAND TEST SERIES 1951/52

1st Test	Sydney	Jan 5th	'52	Aust 69	Eng 37	L
2nd Test	Sydney	Jan 11th	'52	Aust 49	Eng 59	W
3rd Test	Sydney	Jan 19th	'52	Aust 76	Eng 32	L
4th Test	Brisbane	Feb 2nd	'52	Aust 66	Eng 41	L
5th Test	Sydney	Feb 8th	'52	Aust 64	Eng 44	L

Australia win series 4-1

The prickly subject of who was to tour Australia for the 1951/52 winter season began as 1951 came to a close in Britain. Alan Hunt expressed a desire to be included in the squad but, when arrangements could not be made for his wife and child, he withdrew. Eddie Rigg could not be persuaded as he had calculated that the last winter tour cost him in the region of £200.

Jack Parker once again assumed the role of tour manager, knowing that the Australian promoters would not tolerate another mediocre England line-up. To his credit, Parker did improve on the previous year's team. Cyril Roger and Malcolm Craven were genuine England Internationals who had both ridden in Australia previously and Bert Roger and Ron Mountford also had England caps. Arthur Bush of Bradford and Wembley's Jimmy Gooch were both First Division riders of a limited success and Gordon McGregor was the top rider in Motherwell's Second Division side.

Before embarking on the Test Series, England rode three challenge matches against State sides, drawing one and losing two. At the Sydney Royale, a few days before the opening Test, Jack Parker successfully retained the New South Wales Championship. But in the same meeting Ron Mountford lay down his bike to miss fellow countryman Gooch and was hit in the chin by the footrest of the following rider and was taken to hospital.

The Australian side for the first Test at the **Sydney** Showground had a strange look about it. Aub Lawson and Arthur Payne were the only riders to have ridden in the British Tests, although Keith 'Buck' Ryan, Jack Chignall and Lionel Levy had all faced England in Australia before. The rest of the team comprised Don Lawson, Alan Wall and Noel Watson.

With Malcolm Craven getting injured in a car crash and Ron Mountford still unfit, England could only field six riders for the match and with only Parker and Bert Roger performing, England were slaughtered.

AUSTRALIA 69: B. Ryan 16, L. Levy 14, A. Lawson 13, A. Payne 10, D. Lawson 9, N. Watson 7, J. Chignall 0, A. Wall 0.

ENGLAND 37: J. Parker 14, B. Roger 11, J. Gooch 5, C. Roger 4, A. Bush 2, G. McGregor 1.

The second Test took place at the **Sydney** Sports Ground and Australia were strengthened by the inclusion of Bob Leverenz and Cliff Watson. But England were back to full strength and gained a surprise victory, the first one in Sydney for over twelve years. The English riders had begun to sort their bikes out, but the main reason for the visitor's success was an 18-point maximum from Jack Parker. Now aged forty-seven, Parker always seemed to shed half his years when crossing to the other side of the world.

AUSTRALIA 49: B. Ryan 14, A. Lawson 13, A. Payne 6, C. Watson 6, J. Chignall 6, B. Leverenz 2, N. Watson 1, L. Levy 1.

ENGLAND 59: J. Parker 18, B. Roger 9, J. Gooch 8, C. Roger 8, R. Mountford 7, G. McGregor 6, A. Bush 3, M. Craven 0.

In the third Test, at the **Sydney** Showground, England imploded. Cyril Roger had only one ride before retiring from the meeting with a sick bike and, after breaking the track record in the first heat, Jack Parker faded. The result was that the Aussies ran riot and equalled their largest ever points haul against England. The inclusion of Jack Biggs was obviously detrimental to England and Parker and Gooch were the only two visitors to win a race.

AUSTRALIA 76: A. Payne 18, A. Lawson 16, B. Ryan 15, L. Levy 9, N. Watson 8, J. Biggs 8, J. Chignall 2, D. Lawson 0.

ENGLAND 32: J. Parker 9, R. Mountford 8, B. Roger 7, J. Gooch 4, G. McGregor 2, M. Craven 2, C. Roger 0, A. Bush 0.

By the time of the fourth Test at **Brisbane** it had all begun to go wrong for Jack Parker. In heat five, a tussle with main rival Aub Lawson saw him hurtle into the fence at 60 miles per hour. He was left with a gashed leg and a completely wrecked bike, but that was not to be the end of his problems on this particular tour. Cyril Rogers and Malcolm Craven gave much improved displays, but Australia retained the Ashes.

AUSTRALIA 66: A. Lawson 17, K. Gurtner 15, L. Levy 12, B. Ryan 10, K. Cox 8, J. Chignall 3, B. Waddell 1, S. Langdon 0.

ENGLAND 41: C. Roger 11, M. Craven 10, J. Parker 9, B. Roger 6, J. Gooch 3, G. McGregor 2, R. Mountford 0, A. Bush 0.

The final Test match at the **Sydney** Sports Ground was a close-run event and at the end of the first half Australia led by only 2 points. Parker had dropped only 1 point at that time but, in the interval, he was taken ill and withdrew from the meeting, leaving the rest of the team at the mercy of the Australians, who romped home.

AUSTRALIA 64: K. Gurtner 18, C. Watson 15, A. Lawson 13, N. Watson 8, A. Hunter 6, B. Ryan 3, J. Chignall 1, L. Levy 0.

ENGLAND 44: C. Roger 9, J. Parker 8, M. Craven 8, B. Roger 7, G. McGregor 6, R. Mountford 4, J. Gooch 2, A. Bush 0.

Five days later at the Sydney Showground, Jack Parker was practising in a speed-car for a special match race against Sydney Show Ground promoter Bill Renolds, when his car hit the fence. It rolled over three times and finished up upside down, a total wreck. The unconscious Parker was rushed to hospital and was placed on the critical list, where he eventually recovered with severe concussion and a broken arm. This was his twelfth visit to Australia and he left it with his career in jeopardy.

ENGLAND v AUSTRALIA TEST SERIES 1952

1st Test	Wimbledon	June 9th	'52	Eng 52	Aust 56	L
2nd Test	Wembley	June 26th	'52	Eng 52	Aust 56	L
3rd Test	Belle Vue	July 19th	'52	Eng 50	Aust 58	L
4th Test	New Cross	Aug 20th	'52	Eng 46	Aust 62	L
5th Test	Haringay	Sept 12th	'52	Eng 55	Aust 53	W

Australia win series 4-1

As the first Test match of 1952 approached, the England selectors had two of their chosen riders on the injured list. Norman Parker had an injured left foot and Split Waterman had a damaged ankle and jarred spine. Both were expected to be fit for the opener but, in the event, Parker made it and Waterman didn't. In fact, Parker was named as skipper, and number one for the Lions, the first Test being at his home track **Wimbledon**, where he was also skipper and number one rider. Another Wimbledon rider, Cyril Brine, was paired with the captain, with Tommy Price and Bert Roger forming the middle partnership. Alan Hunt and Freddie Williams completed the main body of the team with Tommy Miller and Wally Green of West Ham being the reserves.

Even though Aub Lawson did not ride in Britain that year, the Aussies still looked strong, with Young and Merv Harding as the opening pair, followed by Ronnie Moore and Graham Warren, with Jack Biggs and Arthur Payne being the final pairing. Bob Leverenz and Junior Bainbridge were the reserves.

Disaster hit England as early as heat one when Jack Young dived between Parker and Brine. Parker, trying to recover, hit Young's back wheel and was flung awkwardly towards the fence, which resulted in a trip to hospital for the England skipper and a robust round of boos for the Australian captain. To their credit the Lions took the loss in their stride and, by the interval, they led by 4 points. But as the second half began, Young and Harding began with their second maximum heat win for the Roos, and the battle was on.

Heat eleven saw an alarming crash that put Graham Warren out of the remainder of the meeting, but another couple of 5-1's from Young and Harding clinched the match for Australia. Bert Roger was the only English rider to beat Young in the match, but nobody beat Ronnie Moore who, by then, was reckoned to be the second best rider in the world.

Fewer than 20,000 spectators had turned up at Wimbledon which, in those days, was disappointing for a Test match, but that was a sign of the times. A decline in British speedway had begun that would see it near extinction by the end of the decade.

ENGLAND 52: C. Brine 13, B. Roger 12, A. Hunt 9, F. Williams 7, W. Green 6, T. Price 5, T. Miller 0, N. Parker 0.

AUSTRALIA 56: R. Moore 18, J. Young 16, M. Harding 10, J. Biggs 10, G. Warren 1, A. Payne 1, B. Leverenz 0, J. Bainbridge 0.

Split Waterman was fit for the second Test at **Wembley** and duly took his place as England captain to be partnered by Wally Green. Alan Hunt was paired with Bert Roger and Freddie Williams and Cyril Brine formed the third pairing. Injuries to Tommy Price gave Tommy Miller another chance at reserve, where George Wilks joined him. The only change to the Australian side was at reserve, with Leverenz asking to be relieved of duty. He was replaced by Cliff Watson, with Lionel Benson filling the second reserve spot.

The first shock came as early as heat one, when Wally Green beat the formidable Young-Harding pairing, but the Australian pairing had their revenge when they scored a maximum heat win in heat seven, to turn the Aussies 2-point deficit into a 2-point lead, which they retained up until the interval. Although the scores were close, racing wasn't and the match was thoroughly unexciting. With Cyril Brine scoring only 1 point from three outings, Tommy Miller was brought in to replace him and the fiery Scot breathed some life into the match, winning his first race and finishing second to Ronnie Moore in his next. But by the final heat, England needed a 5-1 to draw the match, and Arthur Payne crossed the line first to secure another Australian victory at Wembley. After finishing third in his first race, Jack Young was unbeaten. Young Ronnie Moore went one better, scoring his second successive Test maximum.

ENGLAND 52: W. Green 12, B. Roger 11, F. Williams 10, S. Waterman 7, A. Hunt 5, T. Miller 5, G. Wilks 1, C. Brine 1.

AUSTRALIA 56: R. Moore 18, J. Young 16, A. Payne 8, M. Harding 6, J. Biggs 5, L. Benson 2, G. Warren 1, C. Watson 0.

After Tommy Miller's fighting display at the Empire Stadium, the England selectors promptly dropped him for the third Test at **Belle Vue**. Hyde Road was the home track of Jack Parker, who had now returned to racing. But Parker was overlooked and home riders Louis Lawson and Ken Sharples were given the nod instead. Although Split Waterman was retained, the England captaincy was taken over by Bert Roger. Alan Hunt, Wally Green, Freddie Williams and Arthur Forrest completed the squad.

The Roos were a man short as Young's partner Merv Harding had been injured and Leverenz had returned home. So Cliff Watson was brought in to partner the Aussie skipper. The top five remained the same and Bainbridge was recalled at reserve with Lionel Benson.

The match began without Moore and Benson, who had not yet arrived. Benson turned up in time to replace the absent Moore in heat two, but this resulted in a 5-1 to debutante Sharples and partner Waterman, who repeated the dose over no less a rider than Jack Young in heat four to put England 6 points ahead. Moore arrived in time to take his place in heat five and immediately stopped the rot by scoring a 5-1 with Arthur Payne. But the Lions knew that they had to win this match to be in with a chance of winning the Ashes and they fought doggedly to go into the interval with a 4-point lead.

The second half got off to a cracking start when Young suffered his second 5-1 reversal, at the hands of Hunt and Roger. At this point fortunes turned against England. Young was thereafter unbeaten, Warren rode like the Warren of old and Moore and Payne dropped only 1 point between them in the entire second half, as the Aussies steamrollered their way to an 8-point win and retained the Ashes. It was the first time that Australia had won at Belle Vue for fourteen years.

ENGLAND 50: K. Sharples 12, A. Hunt 11, W. Green 11, S. Waterman 8, B. Roger 6, F. Williams 1, L. Lawson 1, A. Forrest 0.

AUSTRALIA 58: J. Young 14, J. Biggs 12, A. Payne 12, R. Moore 11, G. Warren 8, C. Watson 1, J. Bainbridge 0, L. Benson 0.

England were running out of ideas. For the fourth Test at **New Cross**, they recalled Eric French to ride with Bert Roger and Ron Mountford to ride with Waterman and they paired Hunt and Fred Williams together, naming Wally Green and Cyril Brine as the reserves. The Aussies moved Benson up to partner Young and left the other two pairings as they were. Bill Longley and Keith Gurtner were both recalled as reserves.

England were accused of lacking spirit at New Cross, as French, Waterman and Williams all faded out of the match. French, especially, was a disappointment as, paired with his own skipper Roger, on his own track, he was expected to be a stumbling block for the Aussies. Where

Belle Vue Speedway
BULLETIN AND PROGRAMME

THIRD OFFICIAL TEST

ENGLAND
v
AUSTRALIA

Vol. 25. No. 17.

807th Meeting

SATURDAY JULY 19th 1952

1/.

Roger was the best of the English, French offered him little support. Ron Mountford had a rough deal, being replaced after two outings in which he fell and ran a third, but with options running out for manager Mockford, Ron was reinstated for his final two rides in both of which he came second. Young and Moore proved yet again that they were the two finest riders in the world as both recorded maximums, which, along with another impressive display from Graham Warren, buried England.

ENGLAND 46: B. Roger 11, A. Hunt 9, F. Williams 8, S. Waterman 8, E. French 5, R. Mountford 5, W. Green 0, C. Brine 0.

AUSTRALIA 62: R. Moore 18, J. Young 18, G. Warren 10, J. Biggs 8, A. Payne 6, B. Longley 2, L. Benson 0, K. Gurtner dnr.

England found themselves looking at a whitewash for the first time in their own country, and the selectors threw caution to the wind. Of the team that lost at New Cross, only Freddie Williams and Alan Hunt were retained (Split Waterman and Bert Roger were injured). Jeff Lloyd made his first England appearance for four years, this time as skipper, and he was partnered by twenty-three-year-old Haringay rider Ron How. Derek Close was given another chance, riding with Williams and Hunt's new partner was Eddie Rigg. Both the reserves were making their debuts for their country, as Brian Crutcher from Poole and twenty-eight-year-old Dick Bradley from Bristol were chosen in a desperate bid to save face in the final Test at **Haringay**. With the return of Harding, Australia were back at full strength and named Cliff Watson and Ken Walsh as their reserves.

In the event both teams had bad luck, but the difference was that England's bad luck probably won the match for them. It all began as early as heat one when the Lions skipper Jeff Lloyd crashed and aggravated a knee injury that put him out of the match. This brought the reserves into play. Crutcher was the first to be introduced in heat six, as a strange England pairing of Crutcher and Ron How lined up against Moore and Payne. Payne was well away, but How tucked into second place, and held Ronnie Moore at bay, while Crutcher snapped at the Australian wonderboy's heels for four laps to no avail. The result put Australia 6 points ahead. Dick Bradley was given his chance in heat eight and seized the opportunity with both hands, as he and How kept Warren and Biggs behind them to begin an England revival.

England returned from the interval 6 points down but the first race of the second half proved to be the turning point. Bradley was leading the field when How, Young and Harding all disappeared amongst a jumble of machines. Harding was stretchered from the track and Young's bike was written off – a crucial point, as he scored only 3 points in his next three outings on a spare bike. Bradley won the rerun from Aussie reserve Ken Walsh while How held Young at the back. The match became a test of stamina for the Bradley boy as he was called up just two races later to face Ronnie Moore. He had already beaten the world's number one, so it stood to reason that he could beat the world's number two – and he did, although Moore had his revenge in heat fifteen, inflicting Dick's first defeat of the match. Bradley was given only one race respite before he was on track again and, along with Ron How, he again inflicted a 5-1 upon Warren and Biggs to put England ahead for the first time, by 2 points.

With one race left, Williams and Close were due to meet Moore and Payne and the roof was raised when the announcement was made that Dick Bradley was to replace Derek Close. Bradley made the gate, but it was his sixth outing in ten races and it took its toll as the comparatively fresh Ronnie Moore overtook him. However Fred Williams held Arthur Payne at the back and the match was England's. It had been the high point of Bradley's career and was to remain so.

ENGLAND 55: D. Bradley 16, F. Williams 12, R. How 9, E. Rigg 8, D. Close 5, A. Hunt 4, B. Crutcher 1, J. Lloyd 0.

AUSTRALIA 53: R. Moore 15, J. Young 11, J. Biggs 10, A. Payne 7, G. Warren 6, M. Harding 2, K. Walsh 2, C. Watson dnr.

It had been a tremendously successful night for both Bradley and How. Although they were both acknowledged as accomplished riders, neither had been regarded as being part of England's hierarchy. In reality, Ron How had only been selected because the match was held at his home track and Dick Bradley was only given his chance because of injuries to other riders. But maybe they had shown their contemporaries the way forward. Young and Moore were held in such high regard by their peers, that maybe other riders faced them thinking that they would do well to finish in second place. These two young firebrands went into the match with nothing to lose, fearing no reputations and they earned England an unlikely victory.

Six days later, Jack Young, who was now a Division One rider with West Ham, retained the World Championship from Fred Williams and Bob Oakley with Ronnie Moore again finishing in fourth place, and Arthur Payne taking fifth.

AUSTRALIA v ENGLAND TEST SERIES 1952/53

1st Test	Sydney	Aust 86	Eng 22	L
2nd Test	Sydney	Aust 77	Eng 31	L
3rd Test	Brisbane	Aust 73	Eng 35	L

Australia win series 3-0

Once again, the winter in Australia took on farcical elements, as Jack Parker struggled to put together an England side to take on the Roos. The best that he could muster was a clutch of Second Division riders led by Scots Tommy Miller and Ken McKinlay from White City. Rayleigh's Gerry Jackson and Maurie McDermott were persuaded to make the trip (although Jackson had to return to England before the first Test) and Ron Mason, Ted Stevens and Val Morton completed the squad. On paper, they wouldn't have beaten a decent Southern League side and the Board of Control refused to recognise them. Thus all the Tests were unofficial. Part of Parker's problems was that another 'England' team was touring New Zealand. And frankly, on paper, they were a better side than Parker's.

With Gerry Jackson unable to take his place in the team, England were loaned Hugh Geddes but even so the first Test at the **Sydney** Showground was a fiasco, as the Australian riders ran riot.

AUSTRALIA 86: G. Warren 18, L. Levy 16, A. Quinn 15, A. Lawson 14, B. Ryan 14, D. Lawson 9.

ENGLAND 22: J. Parker 6, R. Mason 5, K. McKinlay 4, T. Miller 3, M. McDermott 2, T. Stevens 2, V. Morton 0, H. Geddes 0.

The shorter **Sydney** Sports Ground had traditionally suited the English riders better and indeed they did improve in the second Test. But it was marginal and mainly due to Ken McKinlay's improved performance.

AUSTRALIA 77: G. Warren 16, A. Lawson 15, L. Levy 13, B. Ryan 13, K. Gurtner 11, A. Quinn 7, K. Walsh 2, D. Lawson 0.

ENGLAND 31: K. McKinlay 10, McDermott 6, T. Miller 6, V. Morton 3, T. Stevens 3, J. Parker 2, H. Geddes 1.

The third and final Test at **Brisbane** was to be Jack Parker's last and appropriately he went out with a fine performance. However Tommy Miller was already on his way back home and, apart from Parker and McKinlay, England had nothing to offer.

AUSTRALIA 73: A. Lawson 17, L. Levy 16, B. Ryan 12, K. Gurtner 11, K. Cox 10, C. Watson 7, S. Littlewood 0, B. Spencer 0.

ENGLAND 35: J. Parker 15, K. McKinlay 10, R. Mason 4, V. Morton 3, M. McDermott 2, T. Stevens 1.

It was all over for England in Australia for what proved to be five years. Although the Ashes was still a popular tournament in England, it had become rather pointless in Australia and things had not been helped by Parker's latest touring side. There had been no other rider before, or since, that had done as much for British speedway in Australia as Jack Parker did, but now approaching fifty, he was in danger of losing credibility in the land where he had become a legend.

ENGLAND v AUSTRALIA TEST SERIES 1953

1st Test	Norwich	June 20th	'53	Eng 46	Aust 62	L
2nd Test	Wembley	Aug 13th	'53	Eng 57	Aust 51	W
3rd Test	Birmingham	Aug 29th	'53	Eng 61	Aust 47	W

England win series 2-1

The Test Series against Australia in 1953 was reduced to three in number, with **Norwich** staging their first ever Test match as the opener. Despite the heroics of Bradley and How in England's last domestic outing in 1952, neither were included in one of the youngest teams that had ever represented the Lions. The oldest member of the side was skipper Split Waterman and he was barely thirty-one. Ken Sharples and Freddie Williams were the opening pairing with home rider Billy Bales part-nering Waterman and Alan Hunt, who was just recovering from a bout of flu partnering Arthur Forrest. Another Norwich rider, Fred Rogers, was named as reserve along with Brian Crutcher.

Aub Lawson had returned to Britain to ride for Norwich and he was selected for the Aussies at number one, to ride with Arthur Payne. Jack Young was paired with a new face, twenty-four-year-old Peter Moore, who was building himself a reputation of one of the fastest gaters in the country at Wimbledon. Their third pairing looked dangerous with Biggs and Moore being linked together. The ever-improving Keith Gurtner was named as first reserve and their number eight was some-thing of a surprise as Johnny Chamberlain of Yarmouth made his debut and Graham Warren was designated as the number nine rider.

The gates at the Firs Stadium had to be closed after 27,000 specta-tors turned up for their first taste of Test speedway. The match had captured the imagination of the Norwich public to such an extent that the first punters turned up at 6.00 a.m. complete with a dart-board to help them pass away the long twelve-hour wait! And it was worth the wait.

Australia won the match 62-46 but that flattering scoreline belied the action that led to the result. As was expected, Australia's Young, Moore and Lawson were the match winners, but local lad Billy Bales was the hero. After being beaten by Jack Young in his first outing, with England

NORWICH SPEEDWAY

HOLT ROAD, NORWICH

'Phone: Norwich 26002

First

Official Test Match

ENGLAND

— *versus* —

AUSTRALIA

Saturday, 20th June,

1953

Meeting No.

12

9ᴰ SOUVENIR PROGRAMME 9ᴰ

Nº 21140

The right of admission to this Stadium is reserved.

trailing 6-12 after three heats, Billy teamed up with Split Waterman in heat four for a maximum heat win that put the Lions back in the match. Ronnie Moore won the last heat of the first half ahead of Waterman and Bales to put Australia 6 points ahead at the interval and England were never able to recover.

In the second half of the match, Bales cut loose. In heat eleven, he streaked away from the tapes to blow away Jack Young and beat the World Champion by six lengths with the crowd erupting. Next on the list was his club captain Aub Lawson two heats later. After four pulsating laps, Billy pulled away from Lawson on the last bend to win the race and equal the Norwich track record. As good as Bales was, he could not master Ronnie Moore in his last race. Indeed, no one could as young Ronnie clocked up his third Test maximum.

Disappointments on the England side were Alan Hunt and Freddie Williams. Hunt flew in from the Channel Isles on the morning of the match and looked jaded. Williams led Jack Young for over three laps before being overtaken in heat eight and England manager Fred Evans did not replace him for that reason, but Freddie scored only 1 point in his other three outings. Even though they lost, it was considered to be an encouraging display by the England team.

ENGLAND 46: B. Bales 13, K. Sharples 9, S. Waterman 8, A. Forrest 7, F. Williams 3, A. Hunt 3, F. Rogers 2, B. Crutcher 1.

AUSTRALIA 62: R. Moore 18, J. Young 17, A. Lawson 13, A. Payne 7, J. Biggs 3, J. Chamberlain 3, P. Moore 1, K. Gurtner dnr

There were changes to the England side for the second Test at **Wembley**, the graveyard of so many England performances. Tommy Miller, who was now the leading rider in Division Two with an almost 11-point average, was brought in to partner skipper Waterman. Freddie Williams was retained, on his home track and was paired with West Ham's Pat Clarke and Dick Bradley was recalled to partner Brian Crutcher as the Lions third pairing. Eric Williams and Tommy Price were probably England's strongest ever reserves. Australia recalled Warren to ride with Young, put Payne with Moore, paired Biggs with Lawson and dropped Peter Moore to reserve with Gurtner.

For the first time, Coventry supremo Charles Ochiltree was managing England. And he was totally ruthless. England got off to a good start when Waterman beat Young in the opening race but Ronnie Moore won heat two and Biggs and Lawson scored a 5-1 over Crutcher and Bradley in heat three to put Australia 4 points ahead.

After suffering a 4-2 defeat in the next race, Ochiltree dropped Bradley from heat five and installed Eric Williams to ride with Crutcher. When Ronnie Moore's bike packed up, the England pair scored a 5-1 over Arthur Payne. Two heats later, Eric again replaced Dick Bradley and this time he beat Jack Young, with partner Crutcher finishing third. Ochiltree then replaced Tommy Miller, who had scored only 1 point in two outings, with Tommy Price for heat eight to partner Waterman. Again Moore's bike failed and the result was another 5-1 to England to put them 2 points ahead. A 4-2 to the Roos in heat nine levelled the scores at the interval stage.

England came out for the second half with their tails up. Eric Williams had again been brought in and he and partner Waterman, who had already broken the Wembley track record, scored an unlikely 5-1 over Jack Young in heat ten.

There seemed to be no end to the miracles that the English riders could perform on this night, as Price came in for Pat Clarke in the next race and beat Ronnie Moore. Eric Williams again replaced Bradley in the next race and suffered his first defeat of the night at the hands of Aub Lawson. But when Price replaced Clarke in heat thirteen, he combined with Eric's brother Fred to score another England 5-1 over Young and England stretched for home. The Lions won an incredible match by 6 points; the first win at Wembley for fourteen years. Manager Ochiltree was hailed as a tactical genius, but in effect his job was made easy by having the two best reserves ever seen in a Test match. The selectors basked in the knowledge that the British public thought that they were very clever, but they had merely looked at the situation logically. The match was being held at Wembley, Wembley were the best team in the country and so half of the England team comprised of Wembley riders. They put their best and fourth best in the main body of the team, and placed numbers two and three as reserves. Straightforward. That presupposes that every rider rides to his potential – and, on this occasion, they did.

ENGLAND 57: E. Williams 15, T. Price 12, S. Waterman 12, F. Williams 8, B. Crutcher 6, P. Clarke 3, T. Miller 1, D. Bradley 0.

AUSTRALIA 51: J. Biggs 13, J. Young 12, A. Lawson 11, R. Moore 10, A. Payne 3, K. Gurtner 1, G. Warren 1, P. Moore 0.

For the all-important third and deciding Test at Birmingham, the England selectors made sweeping changes. Out went Freddie Williams, Crutcher, Miller, Clarke and Bradley. Eric Williams and Tommy Price were elevated into the main body of the team and Eddie Rigg was recalled to join Arthur Forrest, Alan Hunt and Split Waterman. Home rider Eric Boothroyd was a surprise choice at reserve, as was Leicester's Len Williams.

Australia called up Exeter's Jack Geran in place of Gurtner, but the match turned into a nightmare for the visitors before racing even commenced. Ronnie Moore, who was unfit and on holiday in the Channel Isles, failed to arrive and the Aussies were down to seven riders with Dick Seers and Grahame Warren being the reserves. Seers was Moore's replacement in the opening ride and with his partner, Roo's skipper Arthur Payne, struggling with a sick motor, the pair were beaten into last place in the opening race. Australia pulled back in the next two heats, but in Moore's next programmed ride, heat four, Payne fell and reserve Warren could not get past Price and Hunt. There was a big hole in the Aussie team, that they were not able to fill and, although Young and Biggs were on top form, the visitors began to totter and they trailed by 6 points at the halfway stage. Arthur Payne's misfortunes carried over to the second half of the match and, when he blew his motor in heat ten, he retired from the meeting. It meant that one complete pairing was now the two Australian reserves and neither was making an impression. In fact in their two remaining races, they were the victims of maximum heat wins for England. As the match wore on, the Australians became demoralised and even Jack Young dropped 3 points, as England stormed ahead to win the match 61-47, and regain the Ashes.

ENGLAND 61: T. Price 14, S. Waterman 11, E. Rigg 11, A. Hunt 10, E. Williams 8, A. Forrest 7, E. Boothroyd dnr, I. Williams dnr.

AUSTRALIA 47: J. Young 15, J. Biggs 13, A. Lawson 7, D. Seers 5, G. Warren 3, A. Payne 2, J. Geran 2. Ronnie Moore – non arrival.

A hastily arranged Test Series was arranged between England and New Zealand in late September 1953. It was the first full-blooded meeting between the two countries and acknowledged the Kiwis' arrival on the international scene. It was time for Ronnie Moore to choose his nationality and he opted to ride for New Zealand. By doing so, he lost his eligibility to ride for Australia and, in effect, it ended the Test matches in Britain between the old rivals.

New Zealand lost all three Test matches. The irony was that without Moore, Australia were seen as not being strong enough and with Moore, New Zealand were also not strong enough.

Apart from Moore, the Kiwis had the precocious eighteen-year-old Barry Briggs, who was in only his second season in Britain with Wimbledon, but he was already causing a stir. Barry was quite big for a speedway rider, even in those days and he had quite a physical approach to his speedway. This made him unpopular with some of his contemporaries but, in those days, he lacked the finesse that he would later acquire and most of his early misdemeanours were down to inexperience and overenthusiasm.

Geoff Mardon was another Wimbledon rider with undoubted class, as was Trevor Redmond, the twenty-six-year-old Wembley rider. Ron Johnson from Belle Vue was another classy Kiwi rider, who in fact was the 1950/51 New Zealand Champion.

ENGLAND v AUSTRALASIA TEST SERIES 1954

1st Test	West Ham	Aug 10th	'54	Eng 60	Aust 48	W
2nd Test	Belle Vue	Sept 4th	'54	Eng 64	Aust 44	W
3rd Test	Bradford	Sept 25th	'54	Eng 56	Aust 52	W

England win series 3-0

Attendances at Speedway meetings continued to fall in 1954 and clubs continued to close. Stock cars had taken over as the major spectator sport at many venues and generally the damn things left the tracks in a poor state for speedway racing. The First Division had been depleted to only eight teams, but the general public still wanted to see Test matches. Ronnie Moore, having ridden for New Zealand the previous year, was now allied to the Kiwis, which left a hole in the Australian team that they were unable to fill. Although New Zealand had given a good account of themselves the previous year, it was decided, as late as July, to combine the teams under the name of Australasia, to face England in three Test matches.

Ronnie Moore was at that time hobbling around on crutches, so he was a non-starter for the Colonials, and therefore took over as team manager with the team for the first Test at **West Ham** being made up from three Aussies and five Kiwis. Barry Briggs opened with Jack Young, Aub Lawson partnered Trevor Redmond and Ron Johnson was paired with Geoff Mardon. The reserves were Jack Biggs and Merv Neil. England had a very familiar and compact look about them in Waterman Rigg, Forrest, Crutcher, Wally Green and Freddie Williams. Freddie's brother Eric was first reserve and the spectacular twenty-year-old Peter Craven from Belle Vue was making his England debut as second reserve.

The more fancied riders came unstuck and it was left to the lesser lights to provide the thrills in this exciting battle. Geoff Mardon in particular suffered misfortune, but the visitors' cause was not helped by manager Ronnie Moore's reluctance to use his reserves earlier. Jack Young was beaten by Wally Green in his first outing, Brian Crutcher headed him home in his second, and he was on the wrong end of a 5-1 courtesy of Rigg and Forrest in his third. As Jack crossed the line behind the Bradford pair, his handlebars snapped clean off and he was dumped on the track while his machine careered into the fence. Moore replaced Lawson with Biggs in heat 8, and this resulted in a maximum heat win for Australasia, but in the following heat, Mardon dropped a chain for the second race in succession and England went into the interval 16 points in front, with Brian Crutcher unbeaten so far.

The visitors fought back tenaciously in the second half, with Briggs, Mardon, Lawson and Young all winning races. In fact one of Jack's wins spoilt Brian Crutcher's maximum, but England had matters in hand, and never looked like being beaten.

ENGLAND 60: B. Crutcher 17, A. Forrest 15, E. Rigg 9, S. Waterman 7, W. Green 7, F. Williams 5, E. Williams 1, P. Craven 0.

AUSTRALASIA 48: J. Young 12, T. Redmond 10, G. Mardon 8, J. Biggs 7, B. Briggs 5, A. Lawson 4, R. Johnson 1, M. Neil 1.

Freddie Williams and Wally Green were both dropped from the England team for the second Test at **Belle Vue**, being replaced by Eric Williams and Peter Craven, and Derek Close and Birmingham's Arthur Payne were named as reserves. Ronnie Moore was back in the saddle and paired up with Trevor Redmond for the Australasians, with Young and Ron Johnson forming the opening partnership. Mardon and Biggs completed the main body of the team, with Merv Neil and Barry Briggs filling the reserve berths.

Young and Johnson proved a potent opening pairing when they took maximum points from Forrest and Rigg, and a fall by Rigg in his second outing and a machine failure by Craven saw England struggle to pull back the points. They finally did this, ironically through Forrest and Rigg in heat 8, and finished the first half with the scores level. In fact the Forrest-Rigg pairing was the dominant feature of the match, and went through the second half of the meeting unbeaten, as all of the England riders began to improve. Young Peter Craven featured in a maximum heat win over Ronnie Moore, with his Belle Vue teammate Ken Sharples in heat 14, as England completely took over the match to beat the visitors by 20 points.

ENGLAND 64: A. Forrest 13, K. Sharples 12, E. Williams 11, E. Rigg 11, B. Crutcher 10, P. Craven 7. A. Wright dnr, D. Close dnr.

AUSTRALASIA 44: J. Young 15, G. Mardon 13, R. Moore 7, R. Johnson 6, M. Neil 1, J. Biggs 1, T. Redmond 1, B. Briggs 0.

Ronnie Moore turned up for the final Test match at **Bradford** as World Champion after scoring a peerless 15-point maximum at Wembley the week before to take the title ahead of Brian Crutcher and Swede Olle Nygren. Jack Young finished in fourth place and young Barry Briggs surprised many people by finishing joint fifth in his World Final debut.

England retained the prolific pairing of skipper Forrest and Rigg, and Arthur Wright was promoted into the team to try his luck with Eric Williams. Brian Crutcher's new partner was Peter Craven, and the Lion's reserves were Ron How and Bradford's Keith Milner. The visitors faced a huge setback when Jack Young was taken ill, and could not take his place in the team, so Barry Briggs joined the top five of Redmond, Moore, Johnson, and Lawson, and Dick Seers joined Jack Biggs at reserve.

The Aussies got off to a great start in heat 1 when a last bend surge by Briggs, to overtake Forrest, saw him join partner Redmond at the front for a maximum heat win. Arthur Wright seemed a likely winner of heat 2 but his engine failed and Moore and Johnson shot past him for another 5-1 to the visitors putting them 8 points ahead after only 2 heats. As both Arthur Forrest and partner Eddie Rigg struggled with their bikes, the Lions did little to improve matters, and remained 6 points adrift at the halfway stage. In the interval, mechanical problems were resolved, and England began to get back into the match; in fact a Rigg-Forrest 5-1 over Lawson and Mardon in heat 15 levelled the scores.

With Peter Craven struggling, Ron How had been brought in, and, in heat 16, he powered around three riders on the first bend to take the lead from Barry Briggs. When partner Crutcher held off Redmond for four laps, the resulting 4-2 gave England a 2-point lead. The following heat again saw Rigg and Forrest at their best and a 5-1 against Moore won the match for the Lions.

A crowd of almost 11,000 watched the match, which didn't seem high in those days, but track conditions, due to rain, were bad and the weather was cold and windy. The series had been a success, and Australasia looked likely to be England's Test match rivals for some years to come.

ENGLAND 56: B. Crutcher 15, E. Rigg 10, A. Forrest 10, E. Williams 9, A. Wright 6, R. How 4, P. Craven 1, K. Milner 1.

AUSTRALASIA 52: G. Mardon 13, R. Moore 11, B. Briggs 10, T. Redmond 7, A. Lawson 5, R. Johnson 4, D. Seers 2, J. Biggs 0.

ENGLAND v AUSTRALASIA TEST SERIES 1955

1st Test	Wimbledon	June 13th	'55	Eng 39	Aust 67	L
2nd Test	Wembley	June 23rd	'55	Eng 67	Aust 41	W
3rd Test	West Ham	July 5th	'55	Eng 42	Aust 66	L
4th Test	Bradford	July 20th	'55	Eng 66	Aust 42	W
5th Test	Birmingham	July 27th	'55	Eng 61	Aust 46	W
6th Test	Norwich	Aug 5th	'55	Eng 57	Aust 51	W

England win series 4-2

The winter of 1954/55 was another winter of discontent. The closure of Haringay sent a shudder down speedway's spine, as it left a mere seven clubs in Division One. Speedway continued to dig itself deeper into a hole as promoters and riders blamed one another for the sport's predicament. To top it all, World Champion Ronnie Moore threatened not to return, as he was now more interested in motor racing. In the event, Moore did come back, but it was another unhappy year for British speedway.

Once things settled down and riders had returned, the number of Test matches against the Colonials was increased to six. England were thought to be on a hiding to nothing, and the reason was Barry Briggs. He had begun the season like an express train and currently led the Division One points scorers, from Ronnie Moore and Jack Young. This meant that the English riders would be up against one of the top three riders in the country, in every race.

For the opening Test at **Wimbledon**, Peter Moore, Aub Lawson and Bob Duckworth were selected as partners for the 'terrible trio', and Jack Biggs was named as reserve along with Rayleigh's Peter Clarke. Peter Moore was a much-improved rider, currently seventh in the Division One point scorers, and along with Briggs and Ronnie Moore (no relation), he formed a trio of Wimbledon riders. As the first Test was being held on their own track, things did indeed look grim for England.

Captain Tommy Price, who partnered Brian Crutcher, led the Lions. Eddie Rigg was riding with Arthur Wright, and Ken Sharples and Ron Mountford formed the last England pairing with Ron How and Phil Clarke as reserves. It wasn't a bad team, but there wasn't a rider in it as good as Ronnie Moore, Young, or Briggs.

TEST MATCH

Speedway

ENGLAND v. AUSTRALASIA

1955

WIMBLEDON STADIUM
N°. 2001

MONDAY, 13th JUNE

Official Souvenir Programme

1/-

England began to fall apart prior to the match however. Crutcher failed a late fitness test on an injured foot, and Arthur Wright and Eddie Rigg were both involved in separate car accidents on the way to Plough Lane. Rigg was badly shaken, and Wright's bike was written off and he had to borrow a machine. Phil Clarke moved up to replace Crutcher, and Freddie Williams came in at reserve.

Ronnie Moore and Peter Moore got the visitors off to a good start, with a 5-1 victory, and were unbeaten during the first half of the match. Rigg, Mountford and How were all fallers in that half, as the Lions began to take a pounding, but it looked as though there might be a modicum of success in heat 8 when Williams, who replaced Price, shot from the tapes followed by partner Clarke, and Aub Lawson. However, Briggs, who was stuck at the back, swept past all three riders on the inside of the next bend, and Lawson overtook Clarke, to chalk up another heat win for Australasia.

Wright and Clarke were the only English riders to win a race in the first half; at the break, the visitors led 36-17. There was little or no improvement in the second half, when Freddie Williams was England's only race winner (twice), and thereby ended the Moores' chance of scoring maximum points in all of their six outings. Aub Lawson received a badly gashed hand in a heat-14 crash. When he came out for the re-run, his hand was so heavily bandaged that he was forced to ride the rest of the meeting with no glove on, and he still won two subsequent races. Barry Briggs had an expensive night. He had six rides on five different bikes (and bent three of them) but he still won four races. It was indeed a sad night for England.

ENGLAND 39: A. Wright 10, F. Williams 10, P. Clarke 9, R. How 4, T. Price 2, R. Mountford 2, E. Rigg 1, K. Sharples 1.

AUSTRALASIA 67: R. Moore 18, J. Young 15, B. Briggs 12, P. Moore 11, A. Lawson 9, P. Clark 2, B. Duckworth 0, J. Biggs 0.

Brian Crutcher returned to skipper the home side at **Wembley** for the second Test. Together with the Williams brothers and Tommy Price, Brian made four Wembley riders in England's top six, as they strove to make the most of the home track advantage. Arthur Wright and Phil

Clarke joined them, with Ron Mountford and Ken McKinlay named as the reserves, and Billy Bales as ninth man. The Aussies promoted Peter Clark to ride alongside Young and Bob Duckworth dropped to reserve with Jack Geran.

The match began promisingly enough when Crutcher and Price split the Moores, and Eric Williams headed Briggs home in heat 2, with Wright picking up the odd point. Freddie Williams and Phil Clarke held Peter Clarke at the back in heat 3, while Jack Young flew away. There seemed to be a plan afoot here. If England could fill in the middle placings until one of the big three Aussies cracked, they could strike, and take the advantage. Ronnie Moore won heat 4, but when Peter Moore fell, the England plan again worked, and they retained their 2-point lead. Things quickly began to go wrong for Australasia over the next few heats, as Briggs' bike let him down, and a cracked frame caused Ronnie Moore to crash, and, come the interval, England were looking good with an 8-point lead.

The Lions began the second half with their tails up. Conversely, the visitors, with Briggs struggling and Moore on borrowed equipment, began to lose heart. In heat 13, the impressive Freddie Williams headed home Jack Young, who had been unbeaten in the first half, and in his next outing, Crutcher and Price also showed Young maximum England power. Both Freddie Williams and Brian Crutcher were magnificent for England and Ron Mountford proved to be a superb reserve, stepping in to record two maximum heat wins with Freddie, in a thoroughly deserved England win.

ENGLAND 67: F. Williams 17, B. Crutcher 16, E. Williams 11, A. Wright 9, T. Price 7, R. Mountford 4, P. Clarke 3, K. McKinlay dnr.

AUSTRALASIA 41: J. Young 15, R. Moore 9, J. Geran 7, B. Briggs 5, A. Lawson 3, P. Moore 2, P. Clark 0, B. Duckworth 0.

By the time the third Test at **West Ham** came around, the series had begun to capture the imagination of, not only the public, but the riders too, and Australasia were desperate to make amends for their poor showing in the previous match. The visitors won at Custom House by 66-42 but the scoreline bore no relation to the brilliant speedway that

was enjoyed by the West Ham crowd, or indeed, the heroic perform-
ances of the England riders in a classic encounter. Australasia promoted
Jack Geran into the top six and put Peter Clark back at reserve with
Jack Biggs. England also had a reshuffle, putting Crutcher with Freddie
Williams, Wright with leading Division Two rider Ken McKinlay, and
they recalled Alan Hunt to ride with Ron Mountford. Eric Williams
was dropped to reserve, and Jack Young's West Ham teammate, Gerry
Hussey, made his debut at number eight.

The facts of the match were that Jack Young and Ronnie Moore went
through the card unbeaten and Ken McKinlay was England's only race
winner in 18 heats, but that gives the impression that the Lions rode
like lambs which was simply not the case. McKinlay was outstanding for
the home side and his heat win was at the expense of many determined
efforts from Barry Briggs. Mac was worth more points than he scored,
as was Alan Hunt, who proved that he was still competitive at international level.

However, the Colonials' top three were again brilliant, and England,
who were now 2-1 down, were looking to the next Test, waiting for
one of them to crack.

ENGLAND 42: K. McKinlay 11, B. Crutcher 10, A. Hunt 9, A. Wright
6, F. Williams 4, E. Williams 2, R. Mountford 0, G. Hussey 0.

AUSTRALASIA 66: R. Moore 18, J. Young 18, B. Briggs 14, J. Biggs
9, J. Geran 4, P. Moore 2, A. Lawson 1, P. Clark 0.

In a 'horses for courses' policy, England's opening pairing at **Bradford**
were both Bradford riders – Arthur Forrest and Arthur Wright.
McKinlay and Hunt were paired together and Ron How was recalled
to ride with Brian Crutcher. Ken Sharples and Phil Clarke were the
Lions reserves. Australasia paired Biggs with Moore, Geran with Young
and Duckworth with Briggs. Aub Lawson was dropped to reserve,
where Ron Johnson made his first appearance of the series. After such
an impressive start, Peter Moore was dropped from the side.

It must be said that the visitors were unfortunate in the fourth Test.
Ronnie Moore's chain snapped when he was leading heat 1, presenting
5 points to the Bradford pairing, but there was no fluke in the following

race when McKinlay made a mockery of his Second Division status, leading Jack Young all the way to the finishing line. Moore was his next victim, in heat 4, as England began to establish a lead. They began to pull away as Young ran an unusual last place in heat 5, and when Briggs pulled out of the next race with machine problems, England set sail for victory. Arthur Forrest completed an unbeaten first half with a victory over Jack Young and England began the second half with a 12-point lead.

Barry Briggs rode the second half on the Bradford track spare. Ken Sharples was bought in by England, to great effect, and Forrest stormed his way to an 18-point maximum, which put the writing on the wall for the Antipodeans. The chink in the Australasian armour was once again exposed as the Lions romped to a 66-42 win to level the series. Arthur Wright may have been disappointed with his 6-point return as he captained the England side for the first time, but at least he captained the winning side.

ENGLAND 66: A. Forrest 18, B. Crutcher 14, K. Sharples 10, K. McKinlay 9, A. Wright 6, A. Hunt 4, R. How 4, P. Clarke dnr.

AUSTRALASIA 42: R. Moore 12, J. Young 9, B. Duckworth 8, B. Briggs 6, J. Biggs 3, J. Geran 3, R. Johnson 1, A. Lawson 0.

The myth had now been exposed. Australasia had the three best riders in the world, but they lacked the strength in depth of England. Before the series had begun, there was talk of an Aussie whitewash, but now they looked vulnerable – ripe for the taking in fact.

The visitors were up against it in the fifth Test at **Birmingham**. Ronnie Moore had been injured in a midget car crash at Wimbledon, and Jack Biggs had been rushed to hospital with appendicitis. They did a quick shuffle round and paired Geran with Young, Peter Moore with Ron Johnson and Duckworth with Briggs. Lawson and Clark were the reserves. Ken Middleditch made his debut for England in the opening pairing with Alan Hunt. Middleditch was one of the top riders in Division Two with Poole and his inclusion was no doubt influenced by the success of his Division Two colleague Ken McKinlay in the England team. Mountford and Crutcher were the middle pairing, and Forrest

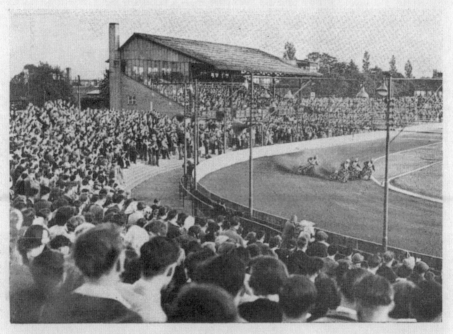

Birmingham Speedway

FIFTH OFFICIAL TEST MATCH
(1955 SERIES)

ENGLAND
v.
AUSTRALASIA

Wednesday, July 27th, 1955, at 7-45 p.m.

Official Souvenir Programme - One Shilling

and McKinlay completed an unusual line-up with Billy Bales and Ken Sharples named as the reserves.

Middleditch got off to a dream start, beating Jack Young in the opening heat and he held Briggs off for three laps in his next race, before being pipped at the post. A win in his third race made Ken the most successful rider, apart from Briggs, on either side in the first half of the meeting. The visitors struggled, and, even though they fought hard, they trailed by 6 points at the interval. Luck was against them in the later heats as Arthur Forrest knocked off the impressive Ron Johnson and got away with it, and in the following heat – heat 15 – a torrid battle developed between Middleditch and Briggs. Barry attempted to go through a fictitious outside gap and brushed against the fence, jostling the Poole Pirate and on went Briggs's exclusion light. It ended all Australasian hopes and the Lions romped home 61-46, to take the lead for the first time in the series.

ENGLAND 61: K. Middleditch 13, A. Forrest 12, B. Crutcher 11, R. Mountford 10, A. Hunt 8, K. McKinlay 7, B. Bales 0, K. Sharples dnr.

AUSTRALASIA 46: B. Briggs 15, R. Johnson 12, J. Young 9, P. Clark 4, A. Lawson 4, P. Moore 1, B. Duckworth 1, J. Geran 0.

For the final Test at **Norwich**, Ronnie Moore was still missing, so Australasia had another reshuffle, retaining the Young-Geran pairing, but partnering Duckworth with Briggs, and pairing the Norwich skipper Aub Lawson with Ron Johnson. Peter Moore and Peter Clarke were the visitor's reserves. England too went for the home track advantage and selected Billy Bales to ride with Middleditch and Phil Clarke to partner Forrest, with Crutcher and Ron How forming the final pairing. Cyril Roger, another Norwich rider, and Arthur Wright were the Lions reserves.

The match was another thriller with every point being fought for tooth and nail. Young and Geran looked set for a 5-1 in the opening heat, but the diminutive Billy Bales powered through to split them on the last bend, and when Crutcher took Briggs' scalp in heat 2, the scores were level. Crutcher came to grief in his next outing which left Geran and Young free to score maximum points. A fall in heat 5 saw

Duckworth injure his ankle and retire from the meeting, to be replaced by the ineffectual Australasian reserves, but even so, as the match swung one way and then the other there were rarely more than 2 points separating the teams. Middleditch and Bales scored a memorable 5-1 over Briggs in heat 8. Indeed Bales provided most of the thrills on the night. England were holding a 2-point lead going into the penultimate heat and, when Briggs led Bales and Middleditch was stuck behind Peter Moore, it looked as though the scores would be levelled, but as Billy shot past Briggo on the line, the Lions retained their 2-point advantage.

In the final heat Cyril Roger teamed up with Crutcher, as a replacement for Ron How, and Peter Moore replaced Aub Lawson, to partner Ron Johnson. In an anti-climactic race, Johnson was excluded for unfair riding and Moore was excluded for falling. Aub Lawson was allowed in the rerun, but the out-of-sorts Norwich skipper trailed in last behind the victorious England pairing.

ENGLAND 57: B. Bales 13, A. Forrest 12, B. Crutcher 10, P. Clarke 7, K. Middleditch 5, C. Roger 5, A. Wright 3, R. How 2.

AUSTRALASIA 51: J. Young 17, B. Briggs 13, R. Johnson 10, J. Geran 6, A. Lawson 4, P. Moore 1, B. Duckworth 0, P. Clark 0.

England won the series with a team that was significantly short of the old guard. No Price, no Hunt, no Rigg and no Williams brothers. New riders were emerging, taking the Lions into another era. There were two factors that had a significant bearing on the outcome of the series – the injury to Ronnie Moore and the failure of Peter Moore to reproduce anything like his awesome performance in the first Test at Wimbledon.

For some reason, young Peter Craven had not been selected for the series, but ironically, one month later, it was he who stood on the podium at Wembley as World Champion, ahead of Ronnie Moore and Barry Briggs.

ENGLAND v AUSTRALASIA TEST SERIES 1956

1st Test	Bradford	July 11th	'56	Eng 55	Aust 53	W
2nd Test	Birmingham	Aug 10th	'56	Eng 65	Aust 43	W
3rd Test	Poole	Aug 28th	'56	Eng 57	Aust 51	W

England win series 3-0

When Jack Young announced that he was not returning to Britain for the 1956 season, it effectively closed down his club West Ham, who had been suffering from diminishing crowds for some time. Poole moved up to save Division One, but who would save Australasia, who had lost a third of their strike force? There were three matches only in the 1956 Test Series, England having completed a Test Series against Sweden only one week prior to the opening Test against the Antipodeans at Bradford.

There were no surprises in the Colonial team, with Briggs, Moore, Biggs, Johnson, Duckworth, Lawson and Peter Moore virtually picking themselves. England selected Crutcher, McKinlay, Waterman, Hunt, Wright, How, Mountford and Bert Edwards; Forrest was unable to ride on his home track due to injuries.

The match was the most exciting and enthralling Test match ever seen at Odsal, with both teams fighting like tigers throughout. Ken McKinlay was trembling and sweating with flu but he insisted upon riding, and collected 5 points from his first two outings before he was forced to withdraw. However, when England began to lose their grip he returned to the match to score another 5 points from a further 2 outings, and was in fact the only rider to beat Barry Briggs on the night. At no stage did England have more than a 6-point lead, and a maximum heat win from Briggs and Johnson put Australasia in front for the first time. But the Lions clawed their way back and held a 2-point advantage going into the final heat. Ronnie Moore shot from the tapes, hotly pursued by Split Waterman, but Duckworth was holding Hunt at the back, to force the draw. On the third lap Hunt 'grabbed a handful' and shot past his Kiwi opponent to secure victory for England.

In truth, the visitors were a three-man team; the fact was that they always had been. The previous year they lost Geoff Mardon to

ODSAL SPEEDWAYS LTD
PRESENT

ENGLAND

versus

AUSTRALASIA

FIRST TEST MATCH

at

Odsal Stadium, Bradford
Wednesday, July 11th, 1956

at 7-30 p.m.

THIRTEENTH MEETING   TWELFTH SEASON

SOUVENIR PROGRAMME 1/-

retirement, and this year there was no Jack Young. They couldn't possibly suffer any further losses and remain competitive.

ENGLAND 55: B. Crutcher 16, S. Waterman 11, K. McKinlay 10, A. Hunt 8, B. Edwards 4, A. Wright 3, R. Mountford 2, R. How 1.

AUSTRALASIA 53: B. Briggs 17, R. Moore 16, J. Biggs 10, R. Johnson 3, P. Moore 3, B. Duckworth 3, A. Lawson 1.

For the second Test at **Birmingham**, Australasia added twenty-eight-year-old Aussie Ray Cresp from Wembley, and England replaced How, Mountford and Wright with Phil Clarke, Eric Boothroyd and Ken Middleditch. Good old Bert Edwards was retained as his career was undergoing something of a renaissance.

Australasia suffered some bad luck when Ron Johnson seized his motor in his first race, and was ineffective for the remainder of the match. But it is doubtful if this had a significant bearing on the result. England's performance was described as 'the best by an England side since the war'. Briggs and Ronnie Moore were neutralised by the English onslaught that was led by three brilliant heat leaders in Hunt, McKinlay and Crutcher. Hunt was in his element on his own track at Perry Barr, and stormed to an 18-point maximum, but this was a great all-round England performance in which all of their riders were heroes.

ENGLAND 65: A. Hunt 18, K. McKinlay 14, B. Crutcher 13, E. Boothroyd 8, B. Edwards 7, P. Clarke 3, S. Waterman 1, K. Middleditch 1.

AUSTRALASIA 43: R. Moore 14, B. Briggs 10, J. Biggs 8, A. Lawson 7, P. Moore 1, B. Duckworth 1, R. Cresp 1, R. Johnson 1.

England had already won the series of course before the third Test at **Poole**, but you would never have guessed it, as the two teams served up one of the best matches ever seen at Wimbourne Road. The Aussies brought in Jack Geran and Ray Cresp was dropped. England released Waterman and Boothroyd and finally bought in World Champion Peter Craven with Cyril Roger occupying a reserve berth.

POOLE SPEEDWAY

FINAL OFFICIAL TEST MATCH
(1956 SERIES)

ENGLAND

v.

AUSTRALASIA

Tuesday, August 28th, 1956, at 7.45 p.m.

OFFICIAL PROGRAMME 6ᴰ

Australasia fired a warning shot across the English bows with a 5-1 in the opening heat, but England quickly retaliated in the following race, when Craven and McKinlay held Ronnie Moore at bay. There was another 5-1 to the visitors in heat 5, but again retaliation was swift as reserve Bert Edwards and Crutcher immediately scored an unlikely maximum heat win over Barry Briggs.

There followed a patch of misfortune for England when Hunt had engine failure in the seventh heat, and Clarke fell in the eighth and it was not until heat 13 before The Lions took the lead for the first time in the match. After some breathtaking racing, England led by 2 points after seventeen heats, and in the final race, they had their best pairing of Craven and McKinlay. Craven had dropped only 1 point to the opposition up until then (Aub Lawson) but in that last race, there were no mistakes as England's most successful pairing (27 points out of a possible 30), powered home for another maximum heat win in a first-class match.

ENGLAND 57: P. Craven 15, B. Crutcher 13, K. McKinlay 12, K. Middleditch 6, B. Edwards 5, A. Hunt 5, C. Roger 1, P. Clarke.

AUSTRALASIA 51: R. Moore 11, J. Biggs 9, J. Geran 9, A. Lawson 9, B. Briggs 7, B. Duckworth 4, R. Johnson 2, P. Moore 0.

ENGLAND v AUSTRALASIA TEST SERIES 1958

1st Test	Swindon	June 11th	'58	Eng 51	Aust 57	L
2nd Test	Oxford	June 18th	'58	Eng 44	Aust 64	L
3rd Test	Coventry	July 23rd	'58	Eng 65	Aust 43	W
4th Test	Belle Vue	Aug 20th	'58	Eng 58	Aust 50	W
5th Test	Southampton	Sept 9th	'58	Eng 63	Aust 45	W

England win series 3-2

Having easily disposed of the Poles, England were under no illusions that Australasia would be anything like as easy to handle. Besides anything else, Jack was back. Promoter Charles Ochiltree had persuaded

Jack Young to end his two-year sabbatical in Australia and return to Britain to ride for him as captain of Coventry. Young was not the perpetual scoring machine of five years earlier, but he had quickly re-established himself as one of the very top riders in the country. The visitors were still missing one of their top riders however, as Ronnie Moore had decided not to return to England (he did actually return, but not until July).

For the first Test at **Swindon,** Young was paired with twenty-seven-year-old home rider Neil Street, and Peter Moore partnered Jack Geran, now from Leicester. World Champion Barry Briggs was paired with Aub Lawson, and Jack Biggs and Ray Cresp were the Australasian reserves. This meant that Briggs was the only New Zealand rider in the team, but they were hardly likely to chuck him out and call themselves Australia!

England kept the nucleus of the team that beat the Poles, with Craven, McKinlay, Bradley and How, and home riders White and Williams. Swindon had another rider at reserve as twenty-three-year-old Mike Broadbanks made his England debut. Gerry Jackson was second reserve.

Although England led the Colonials by 2 points at the halfway stage, they looked precariously balanced. George White had damaged his foot in his third ride, McKinlay and How were not working as a pairing, and Ian Williams was struggling on his own track. On the other side, Briggs was unbeaten, and Young and Neil Street were proving to be a handful. It all spelled trouble for The Lions in the second half. Sure enough, the Australasians began to claw their way back into the match and by heat 16 they had established a 6-point lead that they retained until the end. Briggs went through the card unbeaten and was the only rider to beat Peter Craven. But the highlight of the match was the performance of England reserve Broadbanks. In three outings, he scored 7 points and, had he been bought in sooner, the result may have gone the other way.

ENGLAND 51: P. Craven 16, G. White 8, M. Broadbanks 7, D. Bradley 6, K. McKinlay 6, I. Williams 4, R. How 4, G. Jackson 0.

AUSTRALASIA 57: B. Briggs 18, N. Street 12, P. Moore 12, J. Young 11, J. Geran 3, J. Biggs 1, A. Lawson 0, R. Cresp 0.

The visitors dropped reserve Ray Cresp and replaced him with Southampton's thirty-one-year-old Aussie, Chum Taylor, for the Second Test at **Oxford**. England, who were still without Brian Crutcher who was nursing a damaged shoulder, made one change to the top six, bringing in the home rider, Gordon McGregor of Scotland, in place of Ian Williams. Arthur Forrest and the twenty-eight-year-old home rider Ronnie Genz replaced the two reserves.

Although Australasia were without the services of Ronnie Moore and Jack Young was scoring 4 or 5 points fewer than he used to, they were compensated by the form of skipper Neil Street and Peter Moore. Street was incredible at Oxford, scoring a paid maximum, as he and partner Young stormed to four maximum heat wins. With only five heats gone, the visitors had established an 8-point lead and never looked like losing it. Peter Craven struggled to get out of the gate, but even so he was the only rider to beat Barry Briggs on the night. Unfortunately England manager Gordon Parkins did not have Mike Broadbanks to call upon as both of the England reserves were lacking. That made the difference, as the Lions were beaten by 20 points.

ENGLAND 44: P. Craven 13, G. White 10, K. McKinlay 10, D. Bradley 5, R. How 4, G. McGregor 2, R. Genz 0, A. Forrest 0.

AUSTRALASIA 64: B. Briggs 17, N. Street 15, P. Moore 12, J. Young 11, J. Geran 5, J. Biggs 2, C. Taylor 2, A. Lawson dnr.

The third Test at **Coventry** saw the return of Ronnie Moore who replaced Chum Taylor as the Australasians' reserve. It also saw the return of Brian Crutcher to an England side that underwent some changes. Coventry's Jim Lightfoot came in to partner Craven, McKinlay and How were retained, and Forrest, who was now a Coventry rider himself, was paired with Crutcher. Broadbanks was recalled as reserve with Billy Bales.

With both Neil Street and Peter Moore completely adrift, it was left to Briggs and Young to keep the Australasians afloat, and nobody could have done any better as they scored all but twelve of their team's points between them, Briggs scoring a maximum. Ronnie Moore, who had only just arrived back in Britain, was given five outings and, although he demonstrated all of his old skills, the speed had not yet returned and he scored only 5 points.

England were outstandingly good, with not a weak link amongst them. So much so, that the reserves never got a look in. By the interval they led by ten points and only looked like increasing that – which they did, to keep the series alive.

ENGLAND 65: K. McKinlay 15, P. Craven 14, B. Crutcher 14, J. Lightfoot 8, R. How 7, A. Forrest 7, B. Bales dnr, M. Broadbanks dnr.

AUSTRALASIA 43: B. Briggs 18, J. Young 13, J. Geran 5, P. Moore 4, R. Moore 3, N. Street 0, J. Biggs 0, A. Lawson 0.

The antipodeans began as favourites at **Belle Vue,** where they drafted the home side skipper Ron Johnson into the team to ride with Jack Biggs. Ronnie Moore and Barry Briggs were a formidable middle pairing, with Jack Young and Peter Moore completing the top six. Chum Taylor and Aub Lawson were the reserves.

England had been having a problem with Brian Crutcher. He had already gone on record in saying that speedway was more or less a hobby for him and that his business was his main interest, as that was where his long-term future lay. It was hard to argue against, but it was not what the speedway public wanted to hear, and the Board of Control and the speedway press took a dim view of this. Matters took a turn, when it was announced that England would be making a post-season tour of Sweden and Poland and, as Mr Crutcher was undoubtedly one of England's two finest riders, he would be expected to represent his country. Brian said that this would affect his business and flatly refused to be considered for either visit. With tempers frayed on both sides, on the eve of the Belle Vue Test, he withdrew from the England team.

England gave Mike Broadbanks a chance in the main body of the team to ride with Craven and Billy Bales was brought in as McKinlay's partner. Gordon McGregor was recalled to pair up with Ron How, and Eddie Rigg and Arthur Forrest were named as the Lions' reserves.

Craven got the show on the road with a win over his club captain Johnson, and when Briggs' machine failed in the following heat, McKinley beat Ronnie Moore to put the home side 2 points ahead.

Briggs pulled out of his next ride, and Craven beat him in heat 8, as Briggo failed to win a race in the first half, by which time England led by 4 points. Two heat wins after the interval put the Lions in a commanding lead that was unchallenged until heat 16 when Johnson and Lawson had a maximum heat win for the Australasians. But the unbeaten Craven beat Ronnie Moore and Briggs in the penultimate race, and McKinlay's victory in the last race was enough to win the match for England. Briggo was dogged by engine troubles all night and the home team took full advantage of the situation to level the series.

ENGLAND 58: P. Craven 18, K. McKinlay 14, R. How 12, G. McGregor 4, B. Bales 4, A. Forrest 3, M. Broadbanks 2, E. Rigg 1.

AUSTRALASIA 50: R. Johnson 15, R. Moore 10, J. Young 10, P. Moore 6, B. Briggs 4, A. Lawson 2, C. Taylor 2, J. Biggs 1.

A good crowd, fine weather and a perfect track set the scene for the fifth and deciding Test at **Southampton**. England were back at full strength with Crutcher riding at number one, paired with fellow Saints rider Dick Bradley. Broadbanks and Craven remained and How and McKinley paired up, with Forrest and Bales at reserve.

The Australasians, for some reason, had omitted Ron Johnson; Briggs and Ronnie Moore were now their opening pairing. Young and Peter Moore filled in the middle partnership and Chum Taylor was paired with Jack Geran. Neil Street and Aub Lawson were the reserves.

In the battle of the number ones, Briggs beat Crutcher in the first heat. The following race had an unexpected result, when Broadbanks beat Young but Craven trailed in third. There was another surprise in heat 3, when Geran beat McKinlay to level the scores, but England scored 2 maximum heat wins in heats 5 and 6 to leap ahead, and they led by 8 points at the interval. A good all-round performance by the Lions saw them romp home by 63–45. Broadbanks was the lowest scorer with 6 points and he would certainly have improved upon that had his motor not blown when he was leading heat 9. Briggs was back to his brilliant best, dropping only 1 point to Craven but, apart from Geran, he lacked support, and consequently England won the Ashes.

SOUTHAMPTON STADIUM
COURT ROAD, SOUTHAMPTON   PHONE 24426

SPEEDWAY RACING

Tuesday, September 9th, 1958

The Sports Arena of the South of England

The FIFTH, FINAL & DECIDING TEST MATCH

★ # ENGLAND ★

VERSUS

AUSTRALASIA

Official Programme — — 6d.

ENGLAND 63: B. Crutcher 15, P. Craven 12, K. McKinlay 12, D. Bradley 10, R. How 8, M. Broadbanks 6, A. Forrest 0, B. Bales dnr.

AUSTRALASIA 45: B. Briggs 17, J. Geran 12, J. Young 5, R. Moore 4, N. Street 3, A. Lawson 3, P. Moore 1, C. Taylor 0.

Briggs maintained his superiority throughout the year, retaining the World Championship from Ove Fundin and Aub Lawson.

AUSTRALIA v ENGLAND TEST SERIES 1958/9

1st Test	Queensland	Dec 27th	'58	Aust 39	Eng 31	L
2nd Test	Sydney	Jan 10th	'59	Aust 44	Eng 16	L
3rd Test	Sydney	Jan 7th	'59	Aust 32	Eng 28	L
4th Test	Melbourne	Feb 3rd	'59	Aust 36	Eng 24	L
5th Test	Adelaide	Feb 13th	'59	Aust 21	Eng 39	W

Australia win series 4-1

Test matches in Australia, in 1958/9, were ridden by five riders from each team, and over 10 heats. England were a team of varying talents, led by Ken McKinlay. Ron Mountford and Gordon McGregor had represented England in Australia before, but for Coventry's Nick Nicholls and McKinlay's Leicester teammate Alf Hagon, it was a new experience. For the first Test in **Queensland**, the Australian team consisted of Keith Gurtner, Lionel Levy, Merv Andrews, Bob Sharp, and Peter Dykes. The match was ridden in appalling weather conditions, McKinlay commenting that it would have been called off in England. With the England riders usually missing the gate, they quickly got 'filled in', and the Aussies had the match won by the eighth heat, but England restored some pride with maximum heat wins in the last two races to pull back to within 2 points of their hosts.

AUSTRALIA 31: K. Gurtner 12, L. Levy 7, B. Sharp 6, M. Andrews 4, P. Dykes 2.

ENGLAND 29: K. McKinlay 10, R. Mountford 8, G. McGregor 6, A. Hagon 5, N. Nicholls 0.

There was bad news for England at the **Sydney Showground** when Peter Moore and Aub Lawson showed up to ride for Australia. They joined Gurtner, Levy and Sharp to make the Aussies twice as strong as in the first Test, with disastrous results for England. The Lions were a disgrace as McKinlay scored all but 5 of his team's total in one of the worst England displays abroad. And there had been some bad ones over the years. Once again we were told that the English riders were used to the smaller tracks, but both Mountford and McGregor had ridden the Showground before, and they scored only 4 points between them in this farcical match.

AUSTRALIA 44: L. Levy 10, K. Gurtner 10, P. Moore 10, A. Lawson 8, B. Sharp 6.

ENGLAND 16: K. McKinlay 9, G. McGregor 3, N. Nicholls 2, R. Mountford 1, A. Hagon 1.

England returned to the **Sydney Showground** the following week to try to make amends, which they almost did. In fact on the night they were the better team. The Aussies dropped Aub Lawson and almost paid for it. Nick Nicholls crashed heavily in his first ride and was taken to hospital, but, led by the unbeaten McKinlay, the Lions kept plugging away. Nicholls returned to take his final ride, and beat Levy and Gurtner and, but for an engine failure to Mountford, England may well have won the match.

AUSTRALIA 32: P. Moore 10, B. Bryden 8, L. Levy 7, K. Gurtner 5, B. Sharp 2.

ENGLAND 28: K. McKinlay 12, G. McGregor 7, R. Mountford 3, A. Hagon 3, N. Nicholls 3.

Melbourne saw the introduction of mighty Jack Young to an Aussie team, which retained Peter Moore and added old favourite Junior Bainbridge and local hero Jack Scott. Mick Simmons completed a strong looking Colonial side. However, it was McKinlay who stole the thunder again as he roared to his second successive maximum. Unfortunately, apart from Gordon McGregor, support for Ken was thin on the ground, and it resulted in another defeat for England.

AUSTRALIA 36: P. Moore 10, J. Bainbridge 10, J. Young 9, J. Scott 5, M. Simmonds 2.

ENGLAND 24: K. McKinlay 12, G. McGregor 6, R. Mountford 3, N. Nicholls 2, A. Hagon 1.

For the final Test at **Adelaide**, the Aussies kept their top four, and were joined by Ted Hamlyn and Don Pettijohn. England were delighted to receive a visit from Leicester's young whizz-kid Gerry Hussey, who completely transformed the team. This time it was the Aussies who were on the run as they crumbled before the rejuvenated England team. McKinlay completed an immensely successful season down under with another maximum.

AUSTRALIA 21: J. Young 10, J. Scott 7, P. Moore 3, J. Bainbridge 1, D. Pettijohn 0, T. Hamlyn dnr.

ENGLAND 39: K. McKinlay 12, G. Hussey 10, R. Mountford 9, G. McGregor 5, N. Nicholls 3, A. Hagon dnr.

It all came a bit too late of course, but it did highlight the fact that, given a half-decent side, England could compete successfully in Australia. Of course, it should be added that, in those days, all but a handful of riders were part-time, and therefore had to hold jobs down, making the Australian tour impossible for most.

ENGLAND v AUSTRALASIA TEST SERIES 1959

1st Test	Southampton	Sept 8th	'59	Eng 52	Aust 56	L
2nd Test	Norwich	Sept 12th	'59	Eng 62	Aust 46	W
3rd Test	Swindon	Sept 26th	'59	Eng 63	Aust 45	W

England win series 2-1

Jack Young had, once again stayed in Australia for the 1959 British speedway season, as had Barry Briggs in New Zealand, following a dispute with the Wimbledon management. But at the time of the Test Series, Briggo was in England to defend his World Championship and made himself available to the visitors. Geoff Mardon had made a return, riding for **Southampton**, who featured no fewer than five riders in the opening Test at their home track. Chum Taylor was in the Australasian team, courtesy of Jack Geran being injured, and he partnered Aub Lawson. Briggs and Ronnie Moore were again an awesome opening pair and Peter Moore and Geoff Mardon completed the visitors' team with Jack Scott and Bob Duckworth as the reserves. England had a strong opening pairing too in Crutcher and How, who were followed by Craven and Broadbanks and McKinlay and George White, with Ian Williams and Dick Bradley at reserve.

Ron How beat World Champion Briggs in the first race, and with Crutcher keeping Ronnie Moore at the back, it was a good start for the Lions. However, with the scores level, they were the recipients of a bad refereeing decision in heat 9, that had a significant bearing on the result of the match. Broadbanks had the front wheel of his machine jammed in the tapes when the referee released them and consequently the tapes rode lopsided, completely boxing Peter Craven in. Craven made no attempt to start, reasonably expecting a re-start. No such order was given and, after some hesitation, Broadbanks pulled away in a futile attempt to catch Lawson and Taylor, but to no avail. The resulting 5-1, and a 4-point Australasian lead caused bedlam in the pits, and it was some time before order was restored.

The second half opened with more refereeing lunacy. Crutcher made his only gate of the night and when Briggs tried to come underneath him, the champion came to grief. Barry struggled to free himself from his machine, but was unable to do so quickly and the red lights came on. To everyone's amazement it was announced that the race would be re-run because of an unsatisfactory start. Briggs made no such mistake the second time around and a 4-2 to the visitors, under somewhat dubious circumstances, put them 6 points ahead. England doggedly fought back to level the scores, but an unexpected 5-1 by Peter Moore and Mardon over the previously unbeaten Ken McKinlay once again put the Aussies in the driving seat, and they held on for the win.

ENGLAND 52: R. How 16, P. Craven 11, K. McKinlay 11, M. Broadbanks 6, I. Williams 6, B. Crutcher 2, G. White 0, D. Bradley 0.

AUSTRALASIA 56: P. Moore 12, A. Lawson 12, B. Briggs 11, R. Moore 8, G. Mardon 8, C. Taylor 5, B. Duckworth 0, J. Scott dnr.

Australasia made few changes to the team for the second Test at **Norwich**. Bob Duckworth was promoted into the top six, and Chum Taylor was dropped to reserve along with home rider Johnny Chamberlain who replaced Jack Scott. England followed suit, replacing George White with Cyril Roger, and placing Reg Trott and Jack Unstead at reserve. England were dealt a blow when Brian Crutcher didn't show which meant an early call up for reserves Trott and Unstead. However, things evened out when Barry Briggs, who had limped home last on a sick motor in his first two races, withdrew from the meeting, It left the door open for the Lions, who provided the race winner in fourteen of the eighteen heats, and romped home to a 16-point victory.

ENGLAND 62: P. Craven 16, R. How 16, K. McKinlay 12, M. Broadbanks 9, R. Trott 6, C. Roger 3, J. Unstead 0.

AUSTRALASIA 46: A. Lawson 13, R. Moore 13, G. Mardon 9, P. Moore 4, B. Duckworth 4, C. Taylor 3, J. Chamberlain 0, B. Briggs 0.

The third and final Test, at **Swindon**, was staged the week after the 1959 World Championship, and the Australasians still had the World Champion in their team. But it was not Barry Briggs, who had finished third, after a run off with Olle Nygren and the perennial Aub Lawson – it was Ronnie Moore. Ronnie strung together five wins to regain the title ahead of second placed Ove Fundin.

The Aussies split the world numbers one and three up, pairing Peter Moore with Briggs, and Lawson with Ronnie Moore (the world's number one with the number five). Jack Geran returned to partner Neil Street, and Geoff Mardon moved down to reserve with Chum Taylor.

England fielded only a seven-man team and, with Bradley at reserve, Gordon McGregor and Ian Williams joined Craven, McKinlay, How, and Broadbanks. With the destination of the Ashes at stake, the first half of the meeting was a very lacklustre affair, and the Lions seemed to be coasting to a comfortable win with a 10-point advantage over their rivals. However, three successive heat wins by the antipodeans slashed England's lead, and changed the match into a supercharged battle that went to a last heat decider.

With the riders on two minutes, Aub Lawson returned to the pits with his clutch burned out and Mardon stepped in to partner Ronnie Moore against How and Williams. The World Champion shot from the tapes and, after 2 laps, overtook Williams, but Ron How kept between the two Australasians to ensure a 2-point win for England to win the Ashes. Barry Briggs was the man of the match, and only a fall prevented him from scoring a maximum, but Briggo did remount to take a point in that race.

ENGLAND 55: P. Craven 13, M. Broadbanks 11, R. How 11, I. Williams 8, G. McGregor 6, K. McKinlay 5, D. Bradley 1.

AUSTRALASIA 53: B. Briggs 16, R. Moore 14, G. Mardon 7, P. Moore 6, A. Lawson 5, N. Street 3, J. Geran 2, C. Taylor dnr.

AUSTRALIA v ENGLAND TEST SERIES 1959/60

1st Test	Melbourne	Jan 16th	'60	Aust 21	Eng 38	W
2nd Test	Sydney	Jan 30th	'60	Aust 26	Eng 34	W
3rd Test	Sydney	Feb 6th	'60	Aust 16	Eng 44	W
4th Test	Queensland	Feb 20th	'60	Aust 17	Eng 43	W
5th Test	Brisbane	Feb 13th	'60	Aust 18	Eng 42	W

England win series 5-0

To their credit, England did take an improved side to Australia for the winter Tests of 1959/60. McKinlay, Broadbanks and McGregor were all experienced internationals and Gerry Jackson had done service too. The only rider to be making his international debut was twenty-five-year-old Bob Andrews, but the Wimbledon rider seemed poised on the verge of stardom, and was expected to do well.

On the other hand, Australia put out a strange team to face the Lions in the first Test at **Melbourne**. Jack Young was making his only appearance in the series and was joined by Jack Scott, Junior Bainbridge, Ken Cameron, Jack Board and home rider Mick Simmonds.

McKinlay began where he had finished the previous year and scored a superb maximum, but what brilliant support he gained from the other English riders, as they stormed to a 17-point win over ten races. Only the super-Scot beat Bainbridge, but Jack Young struggled on a sick machine, and the other Aussies just couldn't handle the Lions.

AUSTRALIA 21: J. Bainbridge 11, M. Simmonds 4, J. Scott 3, J. Young 3, J. Board 0, K. Cameron 0.

ENGLAND 38: K. McKinlay 12, G. McGregor 9, G. Jackson 7, B. Andrews 6, M. Broadbanks 4.

It was Bob Andrews' turn to take the spotlight at the **Sydney Showground**, so often the graveyard of the England team. One point dropped to Bill Bryden in his opening ride was the only blemish on Bob's otherwise perfect scorecard. Australia fielded a completely different team that featured Bryden, Keith Gurtner, Bob Sharp, Des Simon and Brian Collins, but they achieved little success against the rampant Lions.

AUSTRALIA 26: B. Bryden 8, K. Gurtner 6, B. Collins 5, B. Sharp 4, D. Simon 3.

ENGLAND 34: B. Andrews 11, M. Broadbanks 10, K. McKinlay 9, G. Jackson 3, G. McGregor 1.

In a desperate effort to stop the landslide, the Aussies talked Lionel Levy out of retirement to stop the rot at **Sydney**, as he joined up with Gurtner, Sharp, Collins and Bryden, but he, along with the rest of the Australian team, was outclassed. Maybe, following the previous year's debâcle, the Aussies had taken England too lightly as there was a distinct lack of 'British Aussies' such as Peter Moore and Aub Lawson on show, and they paid for it with the biggest defeat ever suffered by Australia on their own turf. McKinlay and Broadbanks were unbeaten by the opposition, as England retained the Ashes.

AUSTRALIA 16: B. Bryden 7, B. Sharp 5, B. Collins 2, K. Gurtner 2, L. Levy 0.

ENGLAND 44: K. McKinlay 12, M. Broadbanks 10, G. Jackson 10, B. Andrews 6, G. McGregor 6.

Out of the 10 heats raced at **Queensland**, England scored six 5-1's, as again no Aussie got the better of McKinlay and Broadbanks, as the rout continued.

AUSTRALIA 17: B. Bryden 6, K. Gurtner 5, D. Simon 3, B. Sharp 3, J. Scott 0.

ENGLAND 43: K. McKinlay 12, M. Broadbanks 11, G. Jackson 8, B. Andrews 7, G. McGregor 5.

Another McKinlay maximum completed the whitewash at **Brisbane**, in what had been England's most successful winter tour of Australia. Not only had they won the series for the first time in Oz, but they had not lost a single match in doing so.

AUSTRALIA 18: B. Bryden 6, B. Sharp 4, L. Levy 3, D. Simon 3, K. Gurtner 2.

ENGLAND 42: K. McKinlay 12, M. Broadbanks 10, B. Andrews 9, G. McGregor 6, G. Jackson 5.

It had been a fantastic result for England, but to put things in perspective, the Australian promoters, in an effort to cut costs, had used local riders, and it had backfired on them, in fact Australia's performance had been more abysmal than England's had been twelve months earlier.

It was obviously difficult to get things right for a tour of Australia. Usually, due to a number of reasons, England had been too weak in the past, but now it had been the turn of the host nation to be so, but that should not detract from England's performance. Too often in the past, we had seen riders who were stars in the British League, unable to perform on the sprawling Australian tracks. But this year had seen the Lions represented by five real battlers, who didn't go down there expecting to lose.

It all revolved around Ken McKinlay of course, he had been Jack Parker's successor, and was now the 'Godfather' of England in Australia, and only Parker had been more successful than Ken in Australia.

CHAPTER 4

THE SIXTIES

ENGLAND v AUSTRALASIA TEST SERIES 1960

1st Test	Coventry	June 1st	'60	Eng 49	Aust 59	L
2nd Test	Norwich	June 15th	'60	Eng 54	Aust 54	D
3rd Test	Ipswich	June 30th	'60	Eng 51	Aust 57	L
4th Test	Leicester	Aug 19th	'60	Eng 52	Aust 56	L
5th Test	New Cross	Sept 7th	'60	Eng 47	Aust 61	L
6th Test	Southampton	Sept 20th	'60	Eng 41	Aust 67	L

Australasia win series 5-0 with 1 match drawn

At the turn of the decade, the outlook of British speedway was considerably brighter with the formation of the Provincial League. This was a form of Division Two but was intended to act as a breeding ground for potential National League riders. Some National League riders dropped down into the PL to offer their experience to the youngsters and add some stability to the new league, but they were, in respect, the lesser lights, and all of the top riders remained in the NL.

Charles Ochiltree had again persuaded Jack Young to return to Brandon, and **Coventry** was indeed the venue for the first Test of the 1960 season. Barry Briggs looked as though he would miss out on the 1960 season, but when he was granted a transfer to New Cross, who were making a return to the NL, Briggo set sail for Britain. However, with New Cross riding at home against Ipswich on the same night as the opening Test match, Barry was missing at Coventry, and so was Peter Moore, who was now the number one rider with the Witches. On current form however, the Australasians still had a strong heat leader trio in Ronnie Moore, Jack Young and Ron Johnson, and Geran, Duckworth and Lawson were three able second strings. Johnnie Chamberlain was given another outing at reserve and Graham Warren, who had made a comeback to Britain for Coventry, was his fellow reserve.

Young Nigel Boocock had joined Coventry the previous season and, as one of the brightest prospects in the sport, he formed England's middle pairing with Peter Craven. Ken McKinlay and George White were the openers and Bob Andrews, following his successful tour of Australia, formed an all-Wimbledon pairing with Ron How to complete the team. Mike Broadbanks was a strong reserve and was joined by Ronnie Genz. Brian Crutcher had indeed retired to concentrate on his business full-time. Thus, England had lost one of their greatest post-war riders.

In a match that had little about which to enthuse, England were beaten 59-49, but they could count themselves unfortunate. George White crashed out of the match in heat 6 with facial cuts and abrasions and Ron How fell in the same place in the following race. Ken McKinlay was well ahead in the next heat when his bike packed up, and this trilogy of disasters possibly cost the Lions the match. The Aussies failed to score a single point from the back, but their gating was so superior, that they didn't need to on this occasion. Peter Craven was the only rider to head Ronnie Moore home, when he won heat 2.

ENGLAND 49: P. Craven 14, K. McKinlay 11, R. How 8, M. Broadbanks 6, N. Boocock 6, R. Genz 3, B. Andrews 1, G. White 0.

AUSTRALASIA 59: R. Moore 17, R. Johnson 15, J. Young 13, J. Geran 7, B. Duckworth 3, A. Lawson 2, J. Chamberlain 2, G. Warren 0.

New Cross were riding again on the night of the second Test at **Norwich**, but at least Peter Moore was able to join his Dominion team mates, who dropped Bob Duckworth. Ray Cresp and Jack Biggs replaced the reserves. England retained their three heat leaders, Craven, McKinlay and How, recalled George White, promoted Broadbanks and

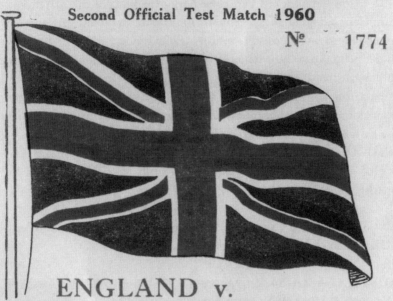

brought in local rider Billy Bales. Boocock and Andrews both dropped to reserve.

As a spectacle, the match was much better than its predecessor, and both teams were locked in a close battle for most of the match with Australasia nudging ahead, only for England to draw level. After establishing a lead once more, the visitors seemed to have the match tied up in the penultimate heat when Peter Moore and Ron Johnson shot out of the gate, but Craven, the most spectacular rider in speedway, showed great daring as he stormed from the back to win the race and complete his maximum. It still left England needing a 5-1 in the final heat to draw the match. This time it was the England pairing of How and Andrews who led from the tapes, and Ronnie Moore was too tired to catch them as How too completed his maximum to ensure that England drew the match.

ENGLAND 54: P. Craven 18, R. How 18, K. McKinlay 7, B. Bales 6, M. Broadbanks 2, B. Andrews 2, G. White 1, N. Boocock 0.

AUSTRALASIA 54: R. Moore 13, R. Johnson 12, A. Lawson 9, J. Young 9, P. Moore 9, J. Geran 2, R. Cresp 0, J. Biggs dnr.

The third Test, at **Ipswich**, saw the return of Briggs, who was riding as well as ever. The Lions did not only have him to worry about however, as he lined up with World Champion Ronnie Moore, the home side skipper Peter Moore, the legendary Jack Young, the evergreen Aub Lawson and Ron Johnson, who was having his best season ever in British speedway. It was a formidable task for the England team, and it proved to be beyond them.

There was an old familiar face in the England team. Eric Williams had emigrated to New Zealand in the fifties, but Johnnie Hoskins had talked him out of retirement to ride alongside Briggs at New Cross, and Eric was riding as well as ever. He lined up with Craven, How, McKinlay, White and Nigel Boocock, with Broadbanks and Andrews as reserves.

Once again, the Australasians were the superior gaters and the English riders seemed unable to come from the back. The visitors were the better team on the night, and established an early lead, which they never

IPSWICH SPEEDWAY
FOXHALL HEATH

THURSDAY, JUNE 30TH, 1960
at 8 p.m.

MEETING No. 16   1960 SEASON

THIRD OFFICIAL TEST MATCH

ENGLAND
versus
AUSTRALASIA

SPECIAL SOUVENIR PROGRAMME 9d

relinquished. The English pairing of McKinlay and White were plagued by machine troubles, and Broadbanks, who was only given one outing, led his race until his engine let him down on the very last lap, condemning him to a last-place finish. What a return Briggs made to the Dominions, scoring 17 points and dropping his only point to Peter Craven in heat 2. Australasia were now in an impregnable situation being two matches up with one drawn.

ENGLAND 51: P. Craven 15, R. How 9, N. Boocock 9, E. Williams 9, G. White 3, K. McKinlay 2, B. Andrews 4, M. Broadbanks 0.

AUSTRALASIA 57: B. Briggs 17, R. Moore 14, P. Moore 12, J. Young 7, R. Johnson 5, A. Lawson 2, R. Cresp 0.

The fourth Test, at **Leicester**, was a cut and thrust affair, with the lead changing hands on five occasions. England basically kept the team that failed in the third Test, with home rider Bryan Elliot stepping in at reserve to replace Mike Broadbanks. Australasia also retained the same team, but added Chum Taylor to the main body of it. The Lions had the advantage that Briggs appeared to be riding a sick bike, but they failed to make it pay. Their three top riders – Craven, How, and McKinlay – all performed commendably, but Andrews, Boocock, and Williams scored only 4 points between them, and so lay the story of the match. By comparison, the visitors' second string was much more successful and, by the end of 18 heats, Australasia had won the series.

ENGLAND 52: P. Craven 17, K. McKinlay 15, R. How 11, G. White 5, B. Andrews 2, N. Boocock 1, E. Williams 1, B. Elliott 0.

AUSTRALASIA 56: R. Moore 16, J. Young 10, B. Briggs 9, C. Taylor 8, R. Johnson 8, J. Geran 5. R. Cresp dnr, A. Lawson dnr.

There were changes made to the England team for the final Test, at **New Cross**, and, with Ron How being injured, Split Waterman made his return after some three years. Split had retired, but he too was persuaded to make a comeback for New Cross, and he joined Craven, McKinlay and Boocock from the previous Test. Thirty-year-old Les McGillivray,

LEICESTER SPEEDWAY

— Has Pride in Presenting —

FOURTH INTERNATIONAL SPEEDWAY TEST MATCH
(6th Series - Season 1960)

ENGLAND v. AUSTRALASIA

Friday, 19th August, 1960 at 7.45 p.m.

19th Meeting   *12th Season*

Official Souvenir Programme - One Shilling

the Ipswich skipper, was a new face and Ian Williams was given another run, ahead of reserves Bobby Andrews and Ronnie Genz.

On paper, the visitors looked the stronger of the two teams, featuring the ominous opening pairing of Briggs and Young. Ronnie Moore and Ron Johnson were another impressive partnership, with Peter Moore and Chum Taylor likely to be the Australasians' achilles heel. Cresp and Lawson were the reserves. Craven and Waterman were the victims of a Briggs-Young 5-1 in the opening heat, as the Commonwealth team paved the way for a whitewash.

Ian Williams had his finest ever match for the Lions, but any advantage that England may have gained from this was negated by the perform-ance of Peter Craven who looked hopelessly out of touch. Despite the 61-47 score, the Aussies didn't have it all their own way, and one by one they were all picked off at some time or another during the match, but England missed How and carried too many passengers to threaten the Dominions seriously.

ENGLAND 47: K. McKinlay 12, I. Williams 11, S. Waterman 10, N. Boocock 6, P. Craven 5, B. Andrews 3, L. McGillivray 0, R. Genz 0.

AUSTRALASIA 61: R. Moore 16, J. Young 15, P. Moore 15, B. Briggs 9, R. Johnson 5, C. Taylor 1, R. Cresp 0, A. Lawson 0.

The following night at Wembley, the Australasians took four places out of the top six in the World Championship without providing the win-ner. That particular honour, in 1960, went to the Swede, Ove Fundin, who won the title after a three-man run-off with Ronnie Moore and Peter Craven. Peter Moore was the fourth-placed man from Ron Johnson and Barry Briggs.

The final Test, at **Southampton**, was almost a carbon copy of its predecessor, as the Australasians finished in great style. Briggo dropped his only point to Peter Craven, and Ronnie Moore and Jack Young put on world-class displays. With nothing to ride for, the Lions, apart from Peter Craven looked a beaten team from the outset. And they subse-quently were.

ENGLAND 41: P. Craven 14, K. McKinlay 7, M. Broadbanks 5, R. Genz 5, B. Andrews 5, N. Boocock 3, B. Elliott 2, D. Bradley 0.

AUSTRALASIA 67: B. Briggs 17, R. Moore 16, J. Young 14, C. Taylor 9, A. Lawson 7, P. Moore 4, R. Cresp 0, N. Street 0.

The times were changing. Sweden were quickly emerging as a world power in speedway. They had audaciously challenged England, back in 1958, and had shocked the speedway world by winning a three-match Test Series in Britain, and, in a way, it brought about the demise of Australasia. Australasia were, at present, too good for England, but, after all was said and done, they were not a country, and were only conceived as a speedway team to give England some serious Test opposition. Being a hybrid, they were never welcomed with the same enthusiasm as the Australians had been. However, the Swedes were thoroughbreds, and were destined to be England's next opponents, but England knew that they had to get properly prepared for the task, and so the Great Britain team evolved.

As Great Britain, the new team had access to all of the colonial riders (ironically, the Australasian team could have been the Great Britain team) so England's 'deadly rivals' now became their allies. It meant the disbanding of the Australasian team, which would not resurface for many years.

The National League continued to struggle in the early sixties, and, by the end of 1964, it was on its knees and facing extinction. Although the highly successful Provincial League strongly opposed the idea for some time, amalgamation took place in 1965, and the hugely successful British League was formed, thus saving the sport in Britain. Within twelve months, the BL boasted no fewer than nineteen teams, and, two years on, a Division Two was formed with a further ten teams, as speedway, at last, began to boom again in Britain.

Our tale resumes in the winter of 1967. But by then there had been many changes. Peter Craven had been tragically killed in a racing accident at Edinburgh in September 1963. By that time, Craven had won another World Championship and was recognised as one of the all-time greats of speedway. The nature of this book does not even begin to represent what Peter Craven achieved in world speedway. He was a speedway genius, years ahead of his time, and he was the forerunner of today's speedway riders. Often called the 'Wizard of Balance', Peter rarely put his foot down, as he balanced the bike perfectly, while broadsiding around the bends. Commonplace nowadays, certainly, but over forty years ago it was a phenomenon, and it made him the most spectacular rider of his generation.

Jack Young had long since gone and Ronnie Moore had also retired. Ove Fundin had become a legend, winning the World Championship an incredible five times. Although past his best, Ove was still a formidable opponent. Briggo was chasing him hard, having claimed the title four times and, since the formation of the British League, had ruled the roost in Britain. He looked certain, at least, to equal Fundin's record of World Championship wins, but there was a new kid on the block. There had been a massive influx of European riders into the British League, especially in the last year, and the old Provincial League had produced its own crop of stars, with none burning brighter than New Zealander Ivan Mauger, who was quickly becoming the number one threat to Briggo's superiority in the BL.

Other speedway nations had also risen to prominence, as Great Britain took part in Test matches against Poland, the USSR, and of course Sweden, who were arguably the top speedway nation at that time, churning out a seemingly endless number of world-class riders. There was also a resurgence of Australian riders in Britain, a young breed, who did not fancy their chances in Britain, but were quite content to try in their own backyard, and so, in the winter of 1967, the Australia *v* England matches recommenced.

AUSTRALIA *v* ENGLAND TEST SERIES 1967/68

1st Test	Sydney	Nov 11th	'67	Aust 53	Eng 54	W
2nd Test	Brisbane	Nov 25th	'67	Aust 62	Eng 46	L
3rd Test	Sydney	Dec 2nd	'67	Aust 43	Eng 64	W
4th Test	Sydney	Dec 16th	'67	Aust 68	Eng 40	L
5th Test	Adelaide	Jan 5th	'68	Aust 46	Eng 62	W

England win series 3-2

Of the pre-British League era, only a few riders remained, notably McKinley, Boocock and Broadbanks. However, a fresh crop of young English riders had developed, and names that were virtually unheard of at the time of the last Test match, were now stars in the British League.

England took a fine squad over to Australia for the first time in nearly a decade managed and mentored by Ken McKinlay. Nigel Boocock had emerged as the top English rider by the mid-sixties, and the Coventry Bee had finished third in the BL riders' averages in 1967. At thirty years of age, Nigel was the elder brother of twenty-two-year-old Eric Boocock, who had finished only one place behind him in the averages. Terry Betts was the popular skipper of King's Lynn and, at twenty-four-years-old, was one of the most spectacular riders in the BL. A great mate and neighbour of Betts was twenty-nine-year-old Colin Pratt. Colin was the skipper of the Hackney Hawks, and made his first visit to Australia as the current London Riders Champion. A teammate of Pratt's at Hackney had been twenty-four-year-old Roy Trigg, another Londoner, and the dynamic twenty-year-old from Long Eaton, Ray Wilson, completed the England squad. As an England team, it didn't come much better, and, for once, the visitors had put together their best team, and a young one to boot, to take on the Aussies in Australia.

The Aussies had a couple of old faces such as Keith Gurtner, Chum Taylor and Bill Bryden, but, in the main, they were a new crop too, led by twenty-six-year-old Wolves rider Jim Airey. Twenty-seven-year-old Gordon Guasco had been a teammate of Airey's in 1966, but he had remained down under for the 1967 season. Twenty-two-year-old John Boulger had only one British season under his belt with Long Eaton, but he was already being talked of as a tremendous prospect and Greg Kentwell was another Australian who had tasted British speedway in 1967 with Halifax.

For the first Test, at the **Sydney Showground**, Australia fielded Airey, Guasco, Kentwell, Bill Bryden, Kevin Torpie, Jack White and Trevor Harding. On paper, they didn't look as strong as the Lions, but strange things had been known to happen in Test Series in Australia.

The series got under way with 30,000 spectators treated to a humdinger of a match. There were never more than 3 points separating the sides. England lost McKinlay early on when his bike gave up the ghost, but reserve Terry Betts was in good form and proved to be a more than adequate replacement. It was the night of the English young guns, as Eric Boocock, Roy Trigg and Betts were equal to anything that the Roos threw at them. However, by the last heat, the Lions trailed by a single point. Trigg and Nigel Boocock shot from the gate and, although Greg Kentwell passed Nigel, Triggy roared home in front, for England to win a thriller by a single point.

The English riders were requested to do a post-match lap of honour on their bikes. Terry Betts led the parade, with Colin Pratt as a passenger. As Bettsy turned around to see the whereabouts of his teammates, he was treated to some Australian hospitality, as he was struck on the head and knocked out by a beer bottle, as pandemonium broke out. Terry was taken to hospital and received eight stitches in a deep cut above his left eye, along with other facial and scalp lacerations. Meanwhile, the lout who had launched the bottle was himself treated to some Australian hospitality, or should that be hospitalisation, as he received a broken nose, ribs and jaw from his fellow countrymen before the police got to him. Welcome to Australia boys!

AUSTRALIA 53: J. Airey 15, G. Guasco 14, G. Kentwell 12, J. White 5, T. Harding 4, B. Bryden 3, K. Torpie 1.

ENGLAND 54: E. Boocock 14, R. Trigg 13, T. Betts 10, N. Boocock 8, C. Pratt 4, R. Wilson 3, K. McKinlay 2.

John Boulger, Keith Gurtner and Peter Ingram replaced Bill Bryden, Kevin Torpie, and Trevor Harding for the second Test, at **Brisbane**, and the Aussies looked stronger for it. The lead changed hands frequently in the early heats, and McKinlay broke the track record in heat 6. But after heat 8, Australia had moved 4 points ahead.

In heat 9, a little needle crept into the match. Up to that point, McKinlay and Gordon Guasco were unbeaten, and Greg Kentwell and Ray Wilson joined them in the next race. At the first attempt, Kentwell broke the tapes and, in the restart, did the same again. Ray Wilson dismounted and complained to the officials, while Mac was having words with Guasco and Kentwell. Order was eventually restored and McKinlay won the race from Guasco and Wilson, for the Lions to pull back to within 2 points of their hosts.

Early in the second half of the match, Airey and Boulger scored the first 5-1, which set Australia on their way. Colin Pratt was brought in to replace Nigel Boocock, who was having mechanical problems, but he failed to make an impact, and England began to drop behind. They did maintain an interest in the meeting as McKinlay tried for a maximum in the very last heat. But he was denied by a fall and the Aussies levelled the series.

AUSTRALIA 62: G. Guasco 14, K. Gurtner 14, J. Airey 13, J. Boulger 8, P. Ingram 8, J. White 4, G. Kentwell 1.

ENGLAND 46: K. McKinlay 15, E. Boocock 10, R. Trigg 8, R. Wilson 7, T. Betts 4, N. Boocock 2, C. Pratt 0.

Following the meeting, due to the mechanical problems being suffered by England, it was agreed that both sides could call upon eight riders for the remainder of the matches and the visitors could add a locally-based Brit. England enlisted Bill Landels for the third Test, at **Sydney**, but he saw no action. Australia replaced Jack White with Chum Taylor and also topped up their team with Bill Bryden.

The Roos had their fair share of mechanical trouble all night, and, by the halfway stage, Gurtner withdrew with magneto problems. Even so, this did not detract from a superb England performance. Eric Boocock scored the first maximum of the series, and brother Nigel was in stunning form also. Betts still seemed a little under the weather; which was understandable. Reserve Pratt was only given one outing, from which he was pointless. Guasco and Boulger were disappointing for the home side, and reserve Greg Kentwell stepped in to great effect when called upon. However, England were in charge from the start, and slowly increased their lead to win by 21 points.

AUSTRALIA 43: J. Airey 13, G. Kentwell 10, C. Taylor 7, G. Guasco 6, J. Boulger 4, B. Bryden 3, K. Gurtner 0, P. Ingram 0.

ENGLAND 64: E. Boocock 18, N. Boocock 15, K. McKinlay 13, R. Wilson 9, R. Trigg 5, T. Betts 4, C. Pratt 0. B. Landels dnr.

Apart from the Test matches, the English riders were enjoying great success in the open meetings in which they competed, and, although Jim Airey was the winner in the Australian Solo Championship, he was chased home hard by Nigel Boocock, Eric Boocock and Ken McKinlay, who occupied the next three places.

Sydney also played host to the fourth Test, and Australia needed to win it to be in with a chance of winning the series. They put on their best display so far, to blow England away with a powerful performance that left the Lions reeling. The Aussies had an unlikely hero in Greg Kentwell, who had enjoyed mediocre success with Halifax in the BL in 1967. Greg gave the finest performance of his career when he stormed to an 18-point maximum and led a determined Australian team to a 68-40 win, to level the series.

AUSTRALIA 68: G. Kentwell 18, J. Airey 17, G. Guasco 14, J. White 9, K. Torpie 6, J. Boulger 4, B. Bryden dnr, B. Collins dnr.

ENGLAND 40: K. McKinlay 12, E. Boocock 11, N. Boocock 9, T. Betts 4, R. Wilson 3, B. Landels 1, R. Trigg 0, C. Pratt 0.

There was a three-week break before the final Test at Adelaide, and with everything riding on it the Lions drafted in an ex-Halifax rider – thirty-seven-year-old Bryan Elliott. However, Australia seemed to have saved their trump card until last when they introduced twenty-seven-year-old Charlie Monk into the side. The enigmatic Monk was by far the most successful of all the ex-Provincial League riders in the British League. He caused a sensation by winning the prestigious 'Internationale' at Wimbledon in the new league's inaugural year, and, in 1967, only Briggs stood between him and the top spot in the BL riders' averages.

England got off to a super start when McKinlay and Wilson scored a 5-1 over Airey, and Eric Boocock and Terry Betts looked set to do the same in heat 2 before Kentwell split them. The Monk-Guasco pairing looked formidable on paper, but, although Monk led for most of heat 3, Nigel Boocock wore him down, and won the race for England to lead by 6 points. The Aussies were desperately trying to re-establish them-selves as a top speedway nation, and needed to win this one to prove it. A concerted effort saw them draw back level by the end of heat 8, but the Lions immediately struck back with maximum heat wins from Trigg and Nigel Boocock, and Wilson and Elliot who was riding in place of McKinlay.

From that point on, England never let go. Eric Boocock romped to another 18-point maximum, and skipper Nigel Boocock had another exceptional match. By the end of heat 15 England had won the match, and the Ashes, in a highly successful reopening of the cross-hemisphere contest.

Before returning home, England embarked on a five-match Test Series in New Zealand, which they won 4-1.

AUSTRALIA 46: C. Monk 12, G. Kentwell 11, G. Guasco 8, J. Airey 6, J. Boulger 6, D. Pettijohn 3, T. Harding 0.

ENGLAND 62: E. Boocock 18, N. Boocock 15, R. Wilson 11, R. Trigg 6, T. Betts 5, B. Elliott 4, K. McKinlay 3.

Australia hibernated through the British speedway season as England took on, and beat, Poland and the Soviet Union. As Great Britain they failed to match the might of the Swedes, but, come the winter, they were off down under again to do battle with the Kangaroos.

AUSTRALIA v ENGLAND TEST SERIES 1968/69

1st Test	Melbourne	Nov 23rd	'68	Aust 43	Eng 65	W
2nd Test	Adelaide	Dec 6th	'68	Aust 61	Eng 47	L
3rd Test	Sydney	Dec 14th	'68	Aust 68	Eng 40	L
4th Test	Brisbane	Jan 11th	'69	Aust 51	Eng 57	W
5th Test	Sydney	Jan 18th	'69	Aust 60	Eng 48	L

Australia win series 3-2

The Lions touring team of 1968/69 retained their top three as the Boocock brother and Ken McKinlay all returned. This time, Ken had a fellow Scot on board in twenty-two-year-old Jim McMillan, who was one of the rising stars of the British League. Mike Broadbanks was of course an experienced England international, who had toured with the Lions eight years earlier, and Mike bought along his Swindon teammate, twenty-four-year-old Bob Kilby, another rider who was heading towards a 9-point average in the BL. The seventh man was Eric Boocock's partner in crime at Halifax, thirty-year-old Dave Younghusband, who had been kept off the top of the Dukes averages for the last two years only by Boocock himself.

The Australian team was again led by Jim Airey, who had enjoyed his most successful season ever with Wolverhampton in 1968, and for the first Test, at **Melbourne**, Gordon Guasco, Charlie Monk and the Poole Pirates' skipper, thirty-three-year-old Geoff Mudge, joined him. Twenty-eight-year-old John Langfield had never ridden in Britain, but after only one season at Sydney, he was the most talked-about rider in Australia. One of his teammates was a familiar face – thirty-nine-year-old Peter Moore, who had quit racing in Britain in 1967. John Dewhurst completed the Aussie line-up.

Australia were dealt a blow when, prior to the match, Gordon Guasco was injured in a car accident. Although afternoon rain soaked the track, it didn't prevent the track record from being broken three times, twice by Airey, and finally by Eric Boocock. Jim Airey defeated Nigel Boocock twice, but they were the only points that the gritty Yorkshireman dropped all night as he led England to a convincing 22-point win.

AUSTRALIA 43: J. Airey 13, G. Mudge 12, C. Monk 8, J. Langfield 8, J. Dewhurst 2, P. Moore 0.

ENGLAND 65: N. Boocock 16, E. Boocock 14, K. McKinlay 13, J. McMillan 8, D. Younghusband 7, B. Kilby 7.

Guasco returned for the second Test, at Rowley Park **Adelaide**, and with Boulger and Kentwell also in the squad, the Aussies looked a much tougher proposition. Although Monk was outstanding for the home team, the Lions suffered some bad luck on the night. It began as early as heat 1 when Kilby crashed into the fence and wrote his bike off, bringing reserve Mike Broadbanks into play for the remainder of the match. Nigel Boocock was also unlucky, falling while in an unbeatable position and in a later race his bike seized up. It said much for the good spirit of the competition that Monk loaned Nigel his bike for the final race, in which Booey and Jim McMillan scored a maximum heat win, but by then it was too late.

With Guasco looking far from fit, England held their own until heat 8, when a 4-2 to Australia put them 2 points ahead. The turning point was heat 9, when Boocock fell and the Roos went a further 2 points in front. From that point on they never looked back.

AUSTRALIA 61: C. Monk 18, J. Airey 16, J. Langfield 8, J. Boulger 7, G. Mudge 6, G. Kentwell 4, G. Guasco 2.

ENGLAND 47: K. McKinlay 13, E. Boocock 11, N. Boocock 9, J. McMillan 8, D. Younghusband 3, M. Broadbanks 3, B. Kilby 0.

Australia turned up the heat in **Sydney**, with four riders scoring double figures. Ken McKinlay gave his usual superb performance but, apart from McMillan and Eric Boocock, Mac received little support. The other four England riders scored only 6 points between them, as the Aussies took the lead in the series with a 28-point win.

AUSTRALIA 68: J. Airey 16, J. Langfield 15, C. Monk 12, J. White 12, G. Kentwell 8, J. Boulger 5, G. Mudge dnr.

ENGLAND 40: K. McKinlay 17, J. McMillan 9, E. Boocock 8, N. Boocock 4, M. Broadbanks 1, B. Kilby 1, D. Younghusband 0.

The home side got off to a bad start in the fourth Test, at **Brisbane**, and that was even before the match had begun. While Greg Kentwell was on a practice lap, his chain snapped and he was tossed into the fence and broke his arm. They were already without Guasco, who had withdrawn from the series, and Langfield and Boulger were also absentees. With the introduction of Les Bentzen, Bert Kingston and Kevin Torpie, to join Monk, Airey and White, the Australians looked weak, and it seemed a great opportunity for England to level the series.

Nigel Boocock and McMillan opened proceedings with a 4-2 over Airey, but in the following heat, further disaster struck the Roos when

Bentzen clashed with Eric Boocock on the first bend. The resulting crash saw the Aussie taken to hospital with head injuries. Eric Boocock was badly shaken and, after two more rides, he withdrew from the meeting, to be replaced by Dave Younghusband.

Local rider Brian Loakes was hastily recruited by the home team and, under the circumstances, he rode with great credit to score 6 points on his international debut. However, the Lions were not about to waste the golden opportunity that had been given to them. Led by skipper Nigel Boocock, they took the lead in heat 13 and hung on until the end.

AUSTRALIA 51: J. White 12, J. Airey 11, C. Monk 10, B. Kingston 8, B. Loakes 6, K. Torpie 4, L. Bentzen 0.

ENGLAND 57: N. Boocock 16, K. McKinlay 12, M. Broadbanks 10, B. Kilby 8, J. McMillan 6, D. Younghusband 3, E. Boocock 2.

Langfield and Boulger were back in the Aussie ranks for the Fifth and deciding Test, back at **Sydney**, and twenty-five-year-old local rider Geoff Curtis was brought in at reserve. Thunderstorms were forecast for the day of the match and, although they never materialised, the lightning that lit the skies was a dramatic backdrop for the finale.

The nerves showed in the opening heats, which were littered with false starts, but Australia had opened up a 4-point lead by heat 7. Curtis received a big cheer when he made his debut in heat 7, in place of Kingston, and the Sydney rider won his first race for his country with partner Monk crossing the line behind him for a maximum heat win. In heat 9, Langfield and White recorded their second 5-1 to take the home side into the interval 10 points ahead.

Curtis was again called upon for the first race after the break, but his luck had already run out as he was struck by an object thrown up by another rider's back wheel, leaving him with a bad cut near to his eye. England staged a comeback and, in heat 11, the impressive Lions pairing of Nigel Boocock and Jim McMillan took maximum points from the equally impressive White-Langfield pairing, to put England back in the match.

The tension mounted, as the races became more thrilling and McMillan had the stadium on its feet with a death-or-glory last bend overtaking manoeuvre of Charlie Monk in heat 11. But the Aussies refused to be denied. Over the next few races, they rebuilt their lead, and when Geoff Curtis defied the doctor's advice, and returned to beat Broadbanks for third place in heat 16, the Aussies were clear and had regained the Ashes.

AUSTRALIA 60: J. Airey 17, J. White 14, C. Monk 12, J. Langfield 7, G. Curtis 4, J. Boulger 3, B. Kingston 3.

ENGLAND 48: N. Boocock 13, K. McKinlay 12, E. Boocock 11, J. McMillan 11, M. Broadbanks 1, B. Kilby 0, D. Younghusband 0.

The Aussies had wanted it and now they had achieved it. They reckoned that the victory had once again established them as one of the top speedway nations. A three-match Test Series would await them in England, to be staged in the forthcoming 1969 British speedway season.

England not only faced Australia that year, but also their antipodean cousins, New Zealand. Ivan Mauger had won the 1968 World Championship and Ronnie Moore had returned to Britain. Along with Barry Briggs, the Kiwis had the best heat leader trio ever seen in world speedway. However, apart from Bob Andrews, who had emigrated to New Zealand, but was riding for Cradley, the Kiwis were suspect in the lower order. But such was the power of their top three, that they won the three-match Test Series in England in 1969.

ENGLAND v AUSTRALIA TEST SERIES 1969

1st Test	Poole	May 28th	'69	Eng 66	Aust 42	W
2nd Test	Sheffield	June 5th	'69	Eng 69	Aust 39	W
3rd Test	Wolverhampton	July 4th	'69	Eng 73	Aust 35	L

England win series 3-0

The 1969 Test Series against Australia was an ill-conceived idea. If the motive was revenge, then fair enough, but the fact was Australia were just not strong enough. In the late sixties, England had a stable packed with very good riders, and, although the winter touring team was a fairly good line-up, the Boococks and McKinlay apart, England could have sent out over a dozen riders who were equally as good as the other four.

Gordon Guasco had returned to Britain, and in the first Test he was riding on his home track at Poole, alongside his club skipper, Geoff Mudge. Airey and Monk were, of course, the Australian spearhead, and Johnny Boulger was there too, but at that stage, they began to run out of ideas. Twenty-one-year-old Garry Middleton was one of the most unforgettable riders of his era. He was rude, arrogant, obnoxious and dangerous and even today he remains the rider in speedway history with the largest collection of black eyes. He arrived in Britain in 1967 and rode for no fewer than three clubs in his debut year. He had now settled at Hackney (where George Hunter thumped him on his home debut) but, as of that moment, his talent had not yet caught up with his mouth. Dennis Gavros had been with Halifax since their return to speedway in 1965 and had improved his average every year; currently he was boasting 6 points plus. Finally there was Peter Vandenberg, who was the thirty-three-year-old skipper of Wolverhampton and who had a decade of British speedway under his belt.

Confident England decided to pick thoroughbreds and therefore did not call upon the services of Scottish riders McKinlay and McMillan. The Boocock brothers, Terry Betts, Ray Wilson and Roy Trigg had all served an apprenticeship down under, and they were joined by twenty-five-year-old Martin Ashby, who was doing great things at Exeter. A local rider, twenty-seven-year-old Pete Smith, was making his debut against the Aussies, as was Wolves number one rider, twenty-nine-year-old Norman Hunter.

Hunter sustained a groin injury in his opening ride and withdrew from the meeting, leaving England looking strangely disoriented. By the halfway stage they led by only 4 points. However, after the break, they quickly scored two maximum heat wins to put themselves firmly in the driving seat, as the profitable pairing of Ashby and Nigel Boocock led the Lions to victory. The Poole fans had plenty to cheer about as Pete Smith was brought in to replace Hunter successfully, and club captain Geoff Mudge top-scored for the Roos.

ENGLAND 66: M. Ashby 15, N. Boocock 12, E. Boocock 12, T. Betts 9, P. Smith 9, R. Wilson 6, R. Trigg 3, N. Hunter 1.

AUSTRALIA 42: G. Mudge 13, J. Airey 11, C. Monk 10, G. Guasco 4, G. Middleton 3, J. Boulger 1, P. Vandenberg 0, D. Gavros 0.

The second Test was to be staged at Wolverhampton two nights later, but after two heats, with England leading 8-4, the heavens opened and the match was abandoned. Therefore the match at **Sheffield** on 5 June became the second Test, and England replaced Trigg, Betts and Smith with local rider Arnold Haley, Belle Vue's Tommy Roper and Dave Younghusband. Australia dropped Middleton and Vandenberg, and brought in Greg Kentwell and Cradley's Chris Bass.

Australia were saved from total humiliation by Eric Boocock's bike, which played up all night and kept his score down to 5 points. England were always in front and were never troubled by the Aussies, who had the last man home in all but 2 heats. The Lions kept the crowd interested, by battling from the back when they had to, but apart from the magnificent Airey, Monk and Mudge, the visitors had nothing to offer.

ENGLAND 69: N. Boocock 17, N. Hunter 14, A. Hayley 12, M. Ashby 9, R. Wilson 8, E. Boocock 5, T. Roper 4, D. Younghusband dnr.

AUSTRALIA 39: J. Airey 16, C. Monk 12, G. Mudge 9, D. Gavros 1, G. Kentwell 1, G. Guasco 0, J. Boulger 0.

It was almost a month later that the **Wolverhampton** Test match was rerun, and England decided to give some of the more inexperienced internationals a chance: Roy Trigg and Pete Smith were recalled, Arnold Hayley was given another chance and young Tony Clarke, who was having a great season at West Ham, was given a trial. Australia were in trouble, as they were without Monk and, unfortunately, they did not have the extensive choice of riders enjoyed by their hosts. The best that they could come up with was to enlist the services of twenty-two-year-old Peter Bradshaw from King's Lynn.

The Roos began well when Airey beat Nigel Boocock, and Chris Bass beat Martin Ashby, to score a 4-2 to Australia, but it was the only

ENGLAND

VERSUS

AUSTRALIA

MONMORE GREEN
WOLVERHAMPTON
FRIDAY
JULY, 4, 1969
OFFICIAL
PROGRAMME 1/6
bspa

heat that they won in the entire match, as England ran riot. By heat 4, the Lions had cleared the deficit and led by 10 points. Betts and Wilson led the charge, both scoring 18-point maximums, as Australia were crushed and England whitewashed them to take the 1969 Ashes.

ENGLAND 73: T. Betts 18, R. Wilson 18, N. Boocock 14½, M. Ashby 9½, P. Smith 7, R. Trigg 3, A. Hayley 2, T. Clarke 1.

AUSTRALIA 35: G. Mudge 11, J. Airey 10, G. Kentwell 7, C. Bass 4, G. Guasco 3, P. Bradshaw 0, J. Boulger 0, D. Gavros 0.

The season ended in disaster for England's skipper Nigel Boocock, as he lay in a hospital bed with a hairline fracture of the skull. But he still vowed to lead the Lions on the winter tour of Australia. In the event he didn't make it and Arnold Hayley took his place but, even so, England still maintained a good line-up with Eric Boocock, Ken McKinlay, Ray Wilson, Martin Ashby, Jim McMillan, Hayley and Tony Clarke.

AUSTRALIA v ENGLAND TEST SERIES 1969/70

1st Test	Perth	Nov 21st	'69	Aust 61	Eng 47	L
2nd Test	Adelaide	Dec 5th	'69	Aust 45	Eng 63	W
3rd Test	Sydney	Dec 13th	'69	Aust 50	Eng 58	W
4th Test	Brisbane	Dec 26th	'69	Aust 56	Eng 52	L
5th Test	Sydney	Jan 3rd	'70	Aust 49	Eng 58	W

England win series 3-2

There were a couple of new Aussie faces to the England boys in the first Test, at **Perth**, as Terry O'Leary and Abe Schneider took their places alongside Airey, Monk, Boulger, Kentwell and Western Australia Champion Chum Taylor.

It was not an impressive side on paper, but the Roos got off to a superb start, when Airey and local lad O'Leary, kept Eric Boocock and Arnold Hayley behind them for a maximum opening heat win. However, it was that same England pairing that struck back to score their own 5-1 against Monk and Boulger in heat 7 to level the scores at 21-21. The Aussies were settling down to be more consistent than the Lions and, by the interval, they led by 6 points. In the second half, the England riders began to fade, being consistently out-gated by the opposition and the Roos began to pull away, eventually winning the match by 14 points. Charlie Monk was disappointing, but only Arnold Hayley beat Airey, and Chum Taylor, after finishing third in his opening ride, won the rest of his races.

AUSTRALIA 61: J. Airey 17, C. Taylor 16, J. Boulger 10, G. Kentwell 8, T. O'Leary 7, C. Monk 3.

ENGLAND 47: E. Boocock 10, J. McMillan 10, A. Hayley 9, K. McKinlay 6, R. Wilson 6, T. Clarke 3, M. Ashby 3.

At **Adelaide**, O'Leary and Schneider were replaced by Jack White and Chris Bass, and Australia looked stronger for the inclusion of White. The match at Rowley Park was described as one of the best Test matches ever seen, as it embraced thrilling racing, needle, tension and tragedy. Following three drawn opening heats, England made a breakthrough in heat 4 when Boulger's bike cut out when he was ahead of the field. Ashby immediately took charge, and his partner Tony Clarke passed White to put the Lions in a 4-point lead. The following heat saw Monk as the recipient of another 5-1 courtesy of McMillan and Eric Boocock, and Wilson and McKinlay completed a hat trick in heat 6, as Airey was held in third place. By the interval, England's brilliant team riding had earned them a 35-19 lead.

In heat 12, With Chum Taylor out in front, Wilson and Monk were engaged in a torrid battle, in which Charlie showed the Englishman the fence on a number of occasions during the three laps. However, Wilson was a firebrand – he always had been. In the mid-sixties he had been a nightmare, as his enthusiasm far exceeded his talent, and he was involved in a catalogue of crashes and clashes. He was far more accomplished as a rider by the end of the decade – world class in fact. But he had lost none of his daring, and refused to budge, relegating Monk to third place, and giving Charlie a warning gesture at the end of it, to the delight of the crowd.

England had the match tied up at the end of heat 15, but the following race cost them dearly. Once again Monk was cast in the role of villain as he flicked his wheel out at Martin Ashby, resulting in both riders crashing and Ashby sustaining a broken ankle. When Monk was excluded, the atmosphere got nasty for a while as beer cans were hurled over the fence (they must have banned the bottles after Terry Betts had stopped one with his head). But when Taylor won the rerun, calm was restored.

AUSTRALIA 45: J. Airey 15, J. Boulger 9, C. Taylor 8, C. Monk 7, J. White 3, C. Bass 3, G. Kentwell 0.

ENGLAND 63: R. Wilson 16, E. Boocock 13, J. McMillan 11, T. Clarke 10, M. Ashby 8, K. McKinlay 5, A. Hayley 0.

It had been a superb win for the Lions; but now, of course, they were down to the minimum six riders. Howard Cole, the twenty-six-year-old King's Lynn rider was also wintering in Australia and he answered an appeal to join them for the third Test, at **Sydney**. Australia did not have the services of Chum Taylor and Greg Kentwell, but welcomed back John Langfield and Bert Kingston. Trevor Harding replaced Chris Bass.

Ray Wilson had been the forerunner of a new breed of young English riders. They were more Polish in their style than the traditional English riders; that style was to open the throttle wide and hang on for dear life. It was all a bit hairy in the learning stages, but highly effective when brought under control. Hayley and Clarke were riders from the 'Polish school'. The huge Sydney Showground track had been the graveyard of many accomplished English riders but these two English lads loved it and proved it to great effect in the third Test.

Airey and Kingston were a constant thorn in England's side. In fact Jim was unbeaten throughout the match, but the Lions were the better team and were always in control, taking the match by 8 points, and leading the series 2-1.

AUSTRALIA 50: J. Airey 18, B. Kingston 9, J. White 9, C. Monk 7, J. Boulger 4, J. Langfield 3, T. Harding 0.

ENGLAND 58: J. McMillan 13, T. Clarke 11, A. Hayley 11, R. Wilson 9, E. Boocock 9, K. McKinlay 3, H. Cole 2.

For the fourth Test, at **Brisbane**, Australia built the team around Airey, Monk, Bert Kingston and Jack White. Garry Middleton was recalled and Doug White and Steve Reinke made their debuts as the Aussie reserves. The Lions retained Howard Cole.

An intense battle began from the minute the tapes went up. Airey and Kingston's opening 5-1 was followed by a McKinlay-Clarke maximum heat win in heat 2. The Aussies, in heat 4, answered a 4-2 to England in the next heat with a 4-2, and so it went on. As the match progressed, McKinley's bike began to give out and Boocock was also struggling with his. But at the end of 16 heats, the scores were tied. The pairing of Airey and Kingston had been a feature of the match, and, in heat 17, they dealt England a killer blow with a maximum heat win over Cole and Clarke. It left Haley and Wilson with a mountain to climb in the last race. Jack White made sure that they didn't climb it as he headed them both home to win the match for Australia, who levelled the series. Man of the match was undoubtedly the Roos reserve, Doug White, who subsequently turned out to be the match-winner.

AUSTRALIA 56: J. Airey 14, J. White 13, D. White 11, B. Kingston 10, G. Middleton 6, C. Monk 2, S. Reinke 0.

ENGLAND 52: T. Clarke 13, R. Wilson 11, A. Hayley 10, J. McMillan 8, E. Boocock 5, K. McKinlay 3, H. Cole 2.

Meanwhile, back in Blighty, Nigel Boocock had made a remarkable recovery and the Speedway Board of Control, in recognition for all the years that Nigel had successfully ridden for his country, agreed to pay his fare to Australia in time for him to ride in the Fifth and final Test, at **Sydney**. Boocock would have walked over, if he had had to. Booey was one of speedway's hardest nuts and, after all, he had only had a fractured skull.

After a trial ride the day before the match, Boocock senior was declared fit and took his place as the England reserve. Australia hung on to Airey, Kingston, Jack White and Doug White and recalled Chum Taylor and

Greg Kentwell, with Bill Landels being named as reserve (which meant that he had now represented both England and Australia).

England skipper Eric Boocock lodged a complaint before the match, about the starting tapes being too loose, as they were being moved considerably by the wind. Although nothing was done about this, his complaint was proven justified, as broken tapes and false starts marred the meeting. In heat 4, with the Lions 11-7 ahead, Eric launched a protest, laying his bike across the track and, as a result, he was excluded from the race. Ken McKinlay had suffered an engine failure in his first outing and was replaced in his second by Nigel Boocock, who made a stunning comeback by winning his first race. In the interval Eric Boocock again complained, this time about his opposing captain, Jim Airey's, starting techniques, but even so, apart from his exclusion, Eric was so far unbeaten, and England were 9 points in front.

Eric went on to be unbeaten throughout the second half and young Lions Clarke and Hayley were superb: the result was a 58-49 win for England. They all rode like heroes, none more so than Nigel Boocock. There had been disappointments on the Australian side during the series, especially with the performance of Charlie Monk. But England had had their traumas too, with the mechanical gremlins that plagued McKinlay and, to a lesser extent, Eric Boocock, and the loss of Ashby. In reality, they were worthy winners of the Ashes.

AUSTRALIA 49: J. Airey 15, C. Taylor 9, B. Kingston 7, J. White 7, G. Kentwell 7, D. White 3, B. Landels 1.

ENGLAND: 58: E. Boocock 15, A. Hayley 14, T. Clarke 13, N. Boocock 6, J. McMillan 4, R. Wilson 4, K. McKinlay 2.

England again returned via New Zealand and took on the Kiwis (who included Ronnie Moore and World Champion Ivan Mauger), and won all three Test matches. The incredible Nigel Boocock top-scored for the Lions in the last two matches.

CHAPTER 5

THE SEVENTIES

ENGLAND v AUSTRALIA TEST SERIES 1970

1st Test	Hackney	April 17th	'70	Eng 30	Aust 24	Abandoned
2nd Test	Newcastle	April 20th	'70	Eng 29	Aust 31	Abandoned
3rd Test	Cradley Heath	May 11th	'70	Eng 70	Aust 38	W

England win series 1-0

There was a lack of credence given to the England/Australia Test matches in this new era, as was shown by the fact that the first two matches, which were rained off, were never restaged. With speedway booming again, the Swedes were the new enemy, and still too strong to be taken on by England. However, the Scandinavians still faced a Great Britain team. Because Mauger, Briggs, and Moore were more or less guaranteed a place in the British team, it made the competition for the remaining places fierce, and consequently the English riders, and therefore England, were riding most competitively.

For the first Test, at **Hackney**, the Aussies named Airey, Monk, and Mudge as their heat leaders, to be paired with Gordon Guasco, Peter Bradshaw and Gary Middleton. Neil Street was named as reserve. England went with Nigel Boocock, Terry Betts and Trevor Hedge, and their respective partners were Colin Pratt, Martin Ashby and Tony Clarke. A couple of youngsters were chosen as reserves, the first one being former Division Two Riders' Champion, twenty-year-old Grahame Plant of

Leicester. His fellow reserve was another former Division Two star, Martyn Piddock.

Australia, who were without John Boulger, put up a great fight. In fact during the first half Airey was unbeaten and Monk dropped only 1 point, to Colin Pratt. Even so, England were strong throughout and, at the interval, they led by 6 points but, unfortunately, weather conditions were so bad by then that the meeting was abandoned.

ENGLAND 30: C. Pratt 7, T. Clarke 6, N. Boocock 5, T. Hedge 5, T. Betts 4, M. Ashby 3. G. Plant dnr, M. Piddock dnr.

AUSTRALIA 24: J. Airey 9, C. Monk 8, G. Middleton 3, G. Mudge 3, P. Bradshaw 1, G. Guasco 0, N. Street 0.

Three nights later, they tried again, at **Newcastle**, with much the same outcome. The Boocock brothers, Betts, Wilson, Hayley and Reg Luckhurst, who had first ridden for Great Britain five years earlier against the Soviet Union, represented the Lions. Tommy Roper and local rider Russ Dent were the reserves.

Boulger returned for Australia, and they also featured Halifax's Les Sharpe, who had got off to a flying start that season. Mudge was dropped to reserve with Peter Vandenberg and Pete Bradshaw was rested.

Once again the Aussies looked determined, led by the impressive Jim Airey. But, come heat 10, by which time the visitors held a 2-point lead, the weather again intervened, and proceedings were bought to a halt.

ENGLAND 29: N. Boocock 9, R. Wilson 7, T. Betts 7, E. Boocock 6, A. Hayley 0, R. Luckhurst 0, T. Roper dnr, R. Dent dnr.

AUSTRALIA 31: J. Airey 10, G. Guasco 6, L. Sharpe 4, G. Middleton 4, J. Boulger 4, C. Monk 3, G. Mudge dnr, P. Vandenberg dnr.

A couple of weeks later, Britain's monsoon had ended, and the third Test match, at **Cradley Heath**, could be completed. Australia kept the same squad that had been leading by 2 points at Newcastle when the heavens had opened, but England, sensing that this may be the deciding match, beefed up their team. The Boococks and Betts were retained.

Wilson, Trevor Hedge, and home rider Roy Trigg were drafted in and Hayley was dropped to reserve.

Australia made a shock start with a 5-1 in the opening heat, when Airey and Sharpe led Nigel Boocock and Hedge home, and they continued their form in heat 2 when Gary Middleton led Eric Boocock home, followed by Boulger. However, that was to be the extent of the Roos success and indeed the only heats that they won. The Aussies crumbled under the determined Lions onslaught, and their early advantage was lost as early as heat 5. The visitors were good opposition, but they had caught England when they were totally on song. The Lions fought tenaciously for every point and won most.

As the match was won fairly early on, the main point of interest was to see if Betts could score a maximum. The impressive Les Sharpe denied him this, in his last race. At twenty-four years old, Sharp was looking like a future World Champion. He had already spent two mediocre years in the BL, but, in 1970, he got it right, and, at the time of the third Test, he had over a 10½-point average. Incredibly, well before the end of the season, he retired from British speedway, as the climate did not suit his health, and Australia and Halifax were robbed of one of their finest riders.

ENGLAND 70: T. Betts 17, E. Boocock 13, N. Boocock 13, R. Wilson 10, T. Hedge 9, R. Trigg 8, A. Hayley dnr.

AUSTRALIA 38: L. Sharpe 14, G. Middleton 9, J. Boulger 5, J. Airey 4, C. Monk 4, G. Guasco 2, P. Vandenberg 0, G. Mudge 0.

Two months later, both teams were in mourning, as indeed was the whole of speedway, due to an infamous accident known as the Lokeren Tragedy. A minibus carrying riders who had competed on the continent crashed in Belgium with tragic results. Aussie international Peter Bradshaw and fellow countryman and rider Malcolm Carmichael were killed in the crash. England too suffered, as international Martin Piddock lost his life, along with Gary Everett and the legendary speedway veteran Phil Bishop. England and Great Britain international Colin Pratt sustained such serious injuries that he never rode again.

AUSTRALIA v ENGLAND TEST SERIES 1970/71

1st Test	Perth	Nov 20th	'70	Aust 58	Eng 50	L
2nd Test	Perth	Nov 27th	'70	Aust 61	Eng 46	L
3rd Test	Adelaide	Dec 4th	'70	Aust 55	Eng 53	L
4th Test	Sydney	Dec 26th	'70	Aust 52	Eng 56	W
5th Test	Brisbane	Jan 2nd	'71	Aust 54	Eng 54	D
6th Test	Brisbane	Jan 9th	'71	Aust 54	Eng 54	D
7th Test	Sydney	Jan 30th	'71	Aust 56	Eng 52	L

Australia win series 4-1 with 2 Tests drawn

Such was the success of the 1969/70 Australian Test matches, that the '70/71 series was increased to seven matches in total. Once again, England put together a competitive team to do battle, and again it included two Scots. Inevitably, rider/manager Ken McKinlay signed on, and so did Jimmy McMillan

Skipper Nigel Boocock made the trip without brother Eric, but he had some familiar faces with him in Roy Trigg, Bob Kilby and Arnold Hayley. Finally, the Lions bought a new face to Australia – Chris Pusey. The twenty-year-old Belle Vue rider was one of the most spectacular riders in British speedway and one of its hottest prospects. The beginning of the seventies bought a great infusion of colour onto speedway tracks. Gone were most of the traditional black leathers, as, seemingly, the entire colour spectrum lent itself to speedway leathers. There were red ones, blue ones, red and blue ones, white ones, yellow ones – you name it and you saw it in the seventies. Every rider was so different, that it became difficult to stand out from the crowd. Pusey, who was one of the most flamboyant characters in the sport, found a way, when he got himself a set of polka-dot leathers that certainly set him apart.

England arrived in Western Australia to find the Aussies in crisis. Eight days after being involved in a track accident at New South Wales' Liverpool Raceway, Gordon Guasco had lost his life. His great friend, soul mate and Australian captain, Jim Airey, was also in a financial wrangle with the Sydney Showground promoters. The Showground was the venue for two of the Test matches, and he withdrew his services, leaving Australia without two of it's mainstays.

England were not without their own problems. Jim McMillan had broken his leg riding for Great Britain in Sweden in October, but even so, he was given the nod over Tony Clarke to make the Australian trip. He brought with him a doctor's certificate that pronounced him fit to ride in December, and he was therefore ruled out of only the first Test. With only six riders available for the first match, in **Perth**, the Lions approached Australian-based Scot Bill Landels. But Bill was expecting to ride for Australia in the match and was therefore not available. In the event, the night before the match, Landels was informed that he couldn't ride for the Roos because he was Scottish, and although he was again offered the England reserve jacket, he ducked out of the meeting all together in disgruntlement. He had of course represented both countries in Australia in the past. Local rider, Peter Boston, was in fact placed at number seven for the Lions, but he was not used.

The Aussies still had Chum Taylor, John Boulger and John Langfield, and prodigal Les Sharpe, who had presumably reacclimatised, came into the team. The other two riders were unknown to the Brits – twenty-four-year-old government electrician Laurie Hodgson and Brian O'Leary.

In the first part of the Australian season, Chum Taylor had been virtually unbeatable around Claremont, but Booey saw him off in the first heat and Roy Trigg followed suit in heat 6. However, with Kilby and McKinlay struggling, the hosts took a 6-point lead into the interval. England flourished briefly in the second half with a maximum heat win from Haley and Kilby over Les Sharpe in heat 11, but a 5-1, from Taylor and Hodgson in a later heat, sealed the Lions fate. Laurie Hodgson in fact proved to be the match winner for the Aussies with 12 points on his debut, but equally impressive for England was Chris Pusey, who had three race wins and also scored 12 points.

AUSTRALIA 58: J. Langfield 13, L. Hodgson 12, C. Taylor 11, B. O'Leary 9, L. Sharpe 8, J. Boulger 5.

ENGLAND 50: N. Boocock 15, C. Pusey 12, A. Hayley 12, R. Trigg 5, B. Kilby 4, K. McKinlay 2. P. Boston dnr.

At **Perth**, Garry Middleton replaced John Boulger in the Australian team, and Les Leisk was named as reserve. England were strengthened by the return of Jim McMillan. Laurie Hodgson looked set to do some further damage to the Lions when he won his opening race, but, in his next, Kilby and Hayley pegged him back to third place. However, he soon put that setback behind him and was unbeaten for the rest of the meeting. Kilby and Hayley took another maximum heat win in heat 8, but England were still not able to break away, and the scores were tied at 27-27 going into the interval.

Australia came back strongly from the break, but heat 11 brought controversy to the match. Les Sharpe was excluded after he fell on the Fowlhouse Corner. The first attempt at a rerun saw Hayley break the tapes, which bought about a fine rather than exclusion. After conferring, both Hayley and Kilby returned to the pits to refuel. The remaining Aussie, John Langfield realised that they had both exceeded the two minutes' time allowance, and circled the track, claiming the race by default. Kilby was actually away from the line for approximately six minutes, but eventually took his place at the gate ready to ride. The clerk of the course was having none of it and straddled Kilby's bike, insisting that he leave the track. As tempers frayed, and the Swindon rider got close to losing his temper, disaster was averted when skipper Boocock took matters into his own hands and pulled Kilby from his bike and escorted him back to the pits. From that point on, England lost their edge, and the Roos romped home.

AUSTRALIA 61: L. Hodgson 16, J. Langfield 14, C. Taylor 13, L. Sharpe 6, B. O'Leary 6, G. Middleton 5, L. Leisk 1.

ENGLAND 46: A. Hayley 14, C. Pusey 10, N. Boocock 8, B. Kilby 5, K. McKinlay 3, R. Trigg 3, J. McMillan 3.

In the third Test, at **Adelaide**, England began to run out of luck. McMillan cried off, after injuring his leg in the previous Test, and George Hunter, who was himself based in Adelaide that winter, was brought in. Hunter was one of the top performers at Newcastle and was an ex-Provincial League rider, who was one of the sensations of the British League in its inaugural year, but it could be argued that he was now past his peak. So was McKinlay for that matter, but both riders were still capable of beating the best on their day.

Australia, with the inclusion of Charlie Monk and John Boulger, who joined Hodgson, Langfield, and Taylor, looked stronger than in the previous two matches. Chris Bass and Jack White were also given a run.

In heat 2, disaster struck the Lions when Arnold Hayley fell awkwardly and broke his collarbone, thereby booking an early passage back to England. After losing their top scorer to that point, England could have collapsed. In fact they put on their best performance since their arrival. They lost the match by 2 points, but after the loss of Hayley, the Lions had encountered even more bad luck.

Roy Trigg was sensational. He had dropped only 1 point, to John Boulger, in his first five rides, but in his last, he was comfortably in front of partner Pusey with half a lap remaining, and set for a 5-1, when his carburettor came adrift, costing Triggy 3 points and England the match. Nigel Boocock was involved in an alarming spill in heat 10 when he was rounding Jack White and the Aussie completely rode across him, sending both the men and their machines into the fence. The trailing Charlie Monk negotiated his way through the melée to take the 3 points as the Lions were robbed of yet another opportunity.

Wee Georgie Hunter proved to be a superb reserve for England, and rode like a demon. But if the visitors were waiting for the Hodgson bubble to burst, it showed no signs of doing so, as Laurie clocked up another 14 points.

AUSTRALIA 55: L. Hodgson 14, C. Monk 14, J. Langfield 12, J. Boulger 9, C. Bass 4, C. Taylor 2, J. White 0.

ENGLAND 53: R. Trigg 14, N. Boocock 12, G. Hunter 12, K. McKinlay 7, C. Pusey 5, B. Kilby 3, A. Hayley 0.

England kept the series alive with a 4-point win over Australia at the **Sydney** Showground. McKinlay and Boocock paved the way with a 5-1 in the opening heat, but the Aussies hit back with a maximum heat win in heat 4, against the previously successful England pairing. The 5-1's continued as Hodgson and Boulger kept Hunter and Kilby behind them in the next race, only for Trigg and Pusey to repeat the feat for the Lions in the following heat, in which Gary Middleton sustained a shoulder injury that subsequently caused him to withdraw from the meeting. Another 5-1 from Booey and Mac ensured that England carried a 2-point lead into the break.

By heat 15, the Lions led by 4 points, and, at last, Lady Luck smiled upon them. Chum Taylor and the Roos' reserve Bob Valentine were leading Pusey and Trigg when Pusey fell on the last lap, and Triggy was forced onto the infield to miss his partner. The race was stopped, and a rerun was ordered, but Taylor protested that the race couldn't be stopped on the last lap, and Australia were awarded the 5-1. England protested that Trigg had been forced off the track to avoid an accident and their protest was upheld. In the subsequent rerun, the Aussies were again well away, when Valentine fell in the same place that Pusey had done, and, on the last corner, Taylor suffered an engine failure, leaving Trigg to blast through for the win. The Lions did not look a gift horse in the mouth, and Pusey saved the day by shooting past Langfield and Bert Kingston to win the final race and secure the win.

AUSTRALIA 52: J. Langfield 13, J. Boulger 8, L. Hodgson 8, B. Kingston 8, C. Taylor 7, B. Valentine 5, G. Middleton 3.

ENGLAND 56: N. Boocock 14, C. Pusey 13, B. Kilby 10, R. Trigg 8, K. McKinlay 6, G. Hunter 5.

Australia were at a disadvantage for the fifth Test, at **Brisbane**. Laurie Hodgson had been injured at Rowley Park and therefore Steve Reinke was called in to replace him with Doug White taking the reserve spot. Although far from fit, Jim McMillan was named as the Lions reserve.

Again McKinlay and Boocock opened with a 5-1, but the Roos immediately struck back with two maximum heat wins in the next three races to forge ahead. Even though Mac and Booey headed home Boulger and Reinke in heat 7, Georgie Hunter and Bob Kilby were proving to be a suspect pairing for England, and the Aussies began to pull away.

A disgraceful refereeing decision in heat 13 cost England the match. Bert Kingston was left at the gate, and stayed there. With the other three riders in full flight, he refused to move and the race was stopped. Upon his exclusion, Kingston leaped from his machine and climbed the steward's rostrum to lodge a protest. As he did so, a dozen or so spectators staged a sit-in on the track. The referee reversed his decision and Kingston went out and won the rerun, to put the Aussies 12 points in front.

England were down, but not out. By that time, McMillan had been called in to replace Hunter, and the courageous Scot, along with a rejuvenated Bob Kilby, took maximum points in the following heat. Trigg and Pusey followed suit in the next race, and, when Boocock and McKinlay completed England's third consecutive 5-1, the scores stood level. The final two heats were drawn, making the final score 54-54.

AUSTRALIA 54: J. Langfield 12, B. Kingston 11, J. Boulger 10, J. White 9, D. White 7, S. Reinke 5, C. Taylor 0.

ENGLAND 54: R. Trigg 14, N. Boocock 13, B. Kilby 9, K. McKinlay 8, C. Pusey 6, J. McMillan 4, G. Hunter 0.

Hodgson returned to the home team for the sixth Test, at **Brisbane**, but he seemed far from fit. With everything to ride for the tension was high, and the tapes were broken nine times throughout the match, regardless of the $5 fines imposed. Every point was fought for, but, come the final race, England had to have the first two men home to win the match and stay in the series. Roy Trigg led the field but Chris Pusey, despite a valiant effort, was unable to pass Jack White, and the Aussies regained the Ashes, by virtue of another drawn match.

Boocock, surely the greatest Lion's skipper ever, had played the true captain's role and led by example, scoring 16 points. Superb support from Hunter and Trigg almost pulled it off for England, but a mere 2 points from McKinlay sealed their fate.

AUSTRALIA 54: B. Kingston 14, J. Boulger 11, J. Langfield 9, J. White 9, D. White 7, L. Hodgson 2, S. Reinke 2.

ENGLAND 54: N. Boocock 16, R. Trigg 12, G. Hunter 10, C. Pusey 7, B. Kilby 5, K. McKinlay 2, J. McMillan 2.

For the final Test, at **Sydney**, Australia were without Boulger and Langfield. Bob Valentine, Kevin Torpie and Bob Humphries joined

Kingston, Hodgson and the Whites. Ken McKinlay had been involved in a car accident prior to the match and did not appear for England. It was another close-run affair, but Bert Kingston put on the best performance of his entire career to lead the Aussies to a 4-point win. Even so he was overshadowed by Chris Pusey, the 'Polka Dot Kid', who dropped his only points of the night to the Roos' top scorer. Chris' spectacular style had made him the Australian's favourite English rider on the tour.

AUSTRALIA 56: B. Kingston 18, L. Hodgson 12, J. White 10, B. Valentine 5, K. Torpie 4, B. Humphreys 4, D. White 3.

ENGLAND 52: C. Pusey 16, N. Boocock 10, R. Trigg 8, B. Kilby 7, J. McMillan 7, G. Hunter 4, K. McKinlay dnr.

The Lions had done well under adverse conditions. The loss of Hayley was obviously significant, and the inclusion of McMillan, at the expense of Tony Clarke, in retrospect was probably unwise, but that is by no means meant to criticise Jim's efforts. Unfortunately, the tour had a tragic postscript. Laurie Hodgson had begun it as an unknown and ended it as a star. British promoters lined up to sign him for the 1971 season with Exeter winning the race. However, a few weeks before he was due to commence his British career, Laurie was involved in a track accident that left him paralysed.

AUSTRALIA v ENGLAND TEST SERIES 1971/72

1st Test	Sydney	Nov 13th	'71	Aust 60	Eng 48	L
2nd Test	Brisbane	Nov 20th	'71	Aust 61	Eng 47	L
3rd Test	Brisbane	Nov 27th	'71	Aust 46	Eng 61	W
4th Test	Adelaide	Jan 7th	'72	Aust 57	Eng 51	L
5th Test	Melbourne	Jan 22nd	'72	Aust 44	Eng 64	W
6th Test	Perth	Jan 28th	'72	Aust 49	Eng 59	W
7th Test	Perth	Feb 4th	'72	Aust 31	Eng 77	W

England win series 4–3

Ken McKinlay was conspicuous by his absence from the Lions touring team of 1971/72, but England were still captained by Nigel Boocock, with George Hunter, Jim McMillan and Chris Pusey all returning to Australia. Thirty-year-old Wembley rider Bert Harkins completed a trio of Scots, and all three arrived in Australia via the USA where they had ridden alongside Jim Airey, Barry Briggs and Ivan Mauger, in a United Kingdom side that lost a 3-match Test Series to the United States. Besides Harkins there were another couple of new faces in Coventry rider Tony Lomas and Malcolm Simmons of King's Lynn. If anything, England looked slightly stronger than the year before.

The Kangaroos were led once again by Jim Airey, who seemed to have patched up his difference with the **Sydney** promotion, and, for the first Test at the Showground, he was joined by John Langfield, John Boulger, Jack White, Kevin Torpie, Bill Landels and John Bowerman.

A slow start by Boocock took its toll on England, and, with McMillan being the only English rider to win a race in the first half, the Aussies led by 14 points at the interval stage. Nigel sorted himself out in the break and dropped only 1 point in the second half of the match, but with both Airey and Langfield being on top form, England were only able to reduce the deficit by 2 points over the remaining 9 heats. Airey was robbed of a maximum by an engine failure in his last race, but Langfield's 16 points were the subject of some controversy.

The orange-leathered Australian had been riding on an illegal 22in rear wheel, which had been banned by the FIM (the world governing body). When Nigel Boocock, acting in his capacity as England manager, protested, it was pointed out that the wheel had never officially been banned down under – the world maybe, but not Australia. Following some heated discussions, it was agreed that the Langfield would not use the wheel in the remainder of the series.

AUSTRALIA 60: J. Langfield 16, J. Airey 15, J. White 12, K. Torpie 7, J. Boulger 6, B. Landels 3, J. Bowerman 1.

ENGLAND 48: J. McMillan 14, N. Boocock 11, M. Simmons 8, G. Hunter 6, C. Pusey 5, B. Harkins 3, T. Lomas 1.

Great Britain were now established as the greatest speedway nation, but the Swedes were still a mighty force in world speedway, and the Aussies booked them in for a Test Series that ran concurrent to the England Test Series. Before the second England Test, the Swedes made their debut, and got hammered by the Roos, as most of the visitors chose the wrong gearing. It was proof that racing in Australia was different. Some of us had sat at home, eating our Christmas dinners, reading the *Speedway Star*, wondering why a 10-point average British rider had only scored only a few points in a Test match: this was an indication as to the reason why. The tracks were much bigger, therefore a different set-up was required, and also a different technique. Maybe the Swedes had won some sympathy for the English riders who had failed to make an impact in Australia in the past.

The action moved to **Brisbane** for the second Test, and the match was dominated by the Boulger-White pairing which had an incredible five consecutive maximum heat wins to their credit, before their eventful last outing. With Boulger out in front, White tried an outside move on Chris Pusey, but ended up on his backside. The Australian managed to convince the referee that he was blameless, and was allowed back into the rerun. Once again White found himself behind Pusey, and, when he clipped the English rider's back wheel, the Aussie tumbled heavily into the safety fence. Upon his return to the pits, the other Australian riders jostled Pusey, but, by that time, Australia were easy winners.

AUSTRALIA 61: J. Boulger 15, J. White 13, J. Langfield 8, K. Torpie 8, J. Airey 6, T. Hart 6, S. Reinke 5.

ENGLAND 47: N. Boocock 13, T. Lomas 10, J. McMillan 9, C. Pusey 8, B. Harkins 4, M. Simmons 3, G. Hunter 0.

The following week was a bad one for the Aussies, and it was their own fault. The second match against the Swedes took place on 26 November at Perth, with the third match against England taking place the following night, again at **Brisbane**. Logistically, it meant that the home side had to field two different teams. Boulger and Chum Taylor at Perth, and Airey and Langfield at Brisbane headed them, and, in the event, they lost both matches.

Greg Kentwell replaced Boulger, but he was pointless, however Tony Hart, who replaced him three times, proved to be a lively reserve. Heavy track conditions favoured the Lions, and, on the night, they were superior in all departments. England lost Jim McMillan after two rides when a stone pierced his goggles and injured his eye, but he returned from the ambulance room to help out in the pits for the remainder of the match. Chris Pusey was the star of the night, blasting to a superb 18-point maximum, and leading the Lions to a 15-point victory.

AUSTRALIA 46: J. Airey 10, T. Hart 10, J. White 7, J. Langfield 7, S. Reinke 6, K. Torpie 6, G. Kentwell 0.

ENGLAND 61: C. Pusey 18, N. Boocock 13, T. Lomas 9, B. Harkins 7, M. Simmons 7, G. Hunter 5, J. McMillan 2.

It was over a month before the series was resumed at **Adelaide**, but after that time, the England squad, whose riders had been engaged in various open meetings, were back to full strength, with McMillan having recovered. Even though they were at full strength, they were not back to full fitness. A few days before the fourth Test, Boocock was involved in an accident at the Sydney Showground that saw him lose a considerable amount of skin from one side of his body. Even so, he and partner Pusey still won the New South Wales Pairs Championship, but Nigel turned up at Rowley Park in some pain. Not only that, but all his gear had gone astray too.

The Aussies put out a fine line-up with Boulger returning to the team, and Charlie Monk making his debut in the series. Chris Bass replaced Kevin Torpie, and nineteen-year-old Phil Crump made his debut at reserve.

On a hot sticky night, a near capacity crowd watched one of the closest and toughest Test matches ever fought, as Australia crept a couple of points ahead, only for England to draw back level on numerous occasions. Boocock's misery continued as he suffered bike problems, and he eventually replaced himself with reserve George Hunter. The Lions all fought like tomcats, Jim McMillan leading with an impressive display of riding, but, despite that, the Australian big guns had too much firepower for the Pommies, and a 6-point win for the Roos took them to within one match of winning the series.

AUSTRALIA 57: J. Airey 18, J. Boulger 16, C. Monk 14, J. White 6, J. Langfield 2, P. Crump 1, C. Bass 0.

ENGLAND 51: J. McMillan 12, B. Harkins 9, C. Pusey 9, T. Lomas 6, M. Simmons 6, N. Boocock 5, G. Hunter 4.

The all-important fifth Test, at **Melbourne**, was the subject of more lunacy, with Australia splitting the team once again to take on Sweden the same night at Brisbane. Langfield and Monk were retained, Greg Kentwell and Neil Street were recalled, and Jack Biggs returned to the team, twenty-five years after making his debut for the Roos. John Dewhurst and Phil Crump completed the side.

Australia had been known to bend the rules on the odd occasion, such as Langfield's illegal wheel, and in fact an earlier match in the series had seen Jim Airey stop a race with the black flag. But in heat 12 at Melbourne, Langfield committed a professional foul. With Lomas and Pusey heading for a comfortable 5-1, Langfield slid to earth and lay on the track until the race was stopped. Not only was he allowed in the rerun, but he and partner Kentwell won it, serving a great injustice on England.

Young Phil Crump, with only one British season under his belt, at Second Division Crewe, was the star on the Australian side, but the young Lions were roaring, as Lomas, Pusey, Simmons and McMillan all scored double figures, and George Hunter stormed back to top form. It all proved too much for the Roos, who lost by 20 points, which kept the English hopes alive.

AUSTRALIA 44: P. Crump 12, J. Langfield 10, J. Dewhurst 9, G. Kentwell 5, J. Biggs 3, N. Street 3, C. Monk 2.

ENGLAND 64: G. Hunter 15, C. Pusey 13, J. McMillan 11, T. Lomas 10, M. Simmons 10, B. Harkins 4, N. Boocock 1.

Airey and Boulger returned for the sixth Test, at **Perth**, and Chum Taylor and Les Sharpe gave Australia a strong top four, but they opted for local riders to fill the other three places, and Les Leisk, Brian O'Leary and Doug Underwood left them with a weak tail end.

By now, the Lions had bit between their teeth, and Hunter began proceedings with a win in the opening race. Although they provided the following six race winners, the Aussies showed no interest in team riding. In fact, in heat 2, Taylor and Leisk were so intent on racing one another, when in a 5-1 position, that they forgot all about Chris Pusey, who split them on the last lap. England, by contrast, were team-riding very well, and when Boocock won a titanic four-lap battle with Taylor in heat 8, and Hunter took third place, it proved to be the turning point of the match.

Reserve Bert Harkins was bought into the fray in heat 11, and he led Pusey home for maximum points over Taylor. Two races later, Boulger received the same treatment from them, and, when Simmons and McMillan took maximum points in heat 14, England were well on their way. The Lions stormed to a 20-point victory to come back from the dead, and level the series, to set up a last match decider.

AUSTRALIA 49: J. Airey 16, C. Taylor 10, L. Sharpe 10, J. Boulger 8, L. Leisk 4, B. O'Leary 1, D. Underwood 0.

ENGLAND 59: C. Pusey 13, N. Boocock 12, M. Simmons 11, B. Harkins 9, J. McMillan 8, G. Hunter 5, T. Lomas 1.

The final Test was also ridden at **Perth**, and Australia were found to be in disarray. The selectors were trying frantically to put together a team, as few of the Australian riders wanted to be in it. Airey cried off with illness, and Boulger was riding in the South Australian Championship, leaving Langfield and Taylor as the Aussie spearhead. Les Sharpe, Jack White and Les Leisk were recalled and Jim Ryman was named as their number six.

England had saved their best performance until last. Despite some shenanigans, usually involving John Langfield, that caused the match to run for 2½ hours, the Lions remained unfazed, and completely destroyed the Aussies. The home team were given another lesson in team riding, and, after 6 heats, they trailed by 21-8. At this point they were hit by another blow as Chum Taylor withdrew from the meeting and Brian O'Leary was brought in to replace him.

None of the politics, however, should detract from England's performance, which was stunning on the night. Harkins, who had steadily improved throughout the series, dropped his only point to Langfield, and such was the might of the England riders that poor old Tony Lomas, at reserve, never got an outing.

AUSTRALIA 31: J. Langfield 14, J. White 6, L. Leisk 4, J. Ryman 3, C. Taylor 2, L. Sharpe 1, B. O'Leary 1.

ENGLAND 77: B. Harkins 17, N. Boocock 16, M. Simmons 16, C. Pusey 10, G. Hunter 9, J. McMillan 9.

After a poor start, England, against all odds, had regained the Ashes, in what was one of the Lions' finest performances overseas. Nigel Boocock had to take a lot of the credit. He had left a few layers of skin behind in Sydney, and, although he must have been in great pain initially, he still made his services available, and just shrugged off the injury, as he always did. Over the years, Nigel had become a great leader of men, and it was he who forged together the tremendous team spirit of the 1971/72 England touring team. By contrast, the Australians were sadly lacking in that department that same year. It almost led to the team falling apart, and it certainly lost them the Ashes, but at least they had the consolation of beating the Swedes in the other Test Series.

All three teams had met in mid-December at the Sydney Showground in a triangular tournament, and England (who were billed as Britain), won that event too. They finished just one point ahead of Australia with Sweden trailing in third place.

England and Australia clashed briefly in the 1972 British speedway season, in an Inter Nations Championship contested between themselves and Sweden, New Zealand and Norway-Denmark. They met at Halifax where the Roos were beaten 48-30 in the final match of the tournament, which left England as the winners and Australia in fourth place.

AUSTRALIA v ENGLAND TEST SERIES 1972/73

| 1st Test | Perth | Nov 17th | '72 | Aust 60 | Eng 48 | L |
| 2nd Test | Adelaide | Nov 24th | '72 | Aust 50 | Eng 58 | W |

3rd Test	Sydney	Dec 23rd	'72	Aust 63	Eng 45	L
4th Test	Sydney	Dec 30th	'72	Aust 58	Eng 50	L
5th Test	Brisbane	Jan 6th	'73	Aust 71	Eng 36	L
6th Test	Brisbane	Jan 13th	'73	Aust 58	Eng 50	L
7th Test	Sydney	Jan 22nd	'73	Aust 62	Eng 46	L

Australia win series 6-1

Of the victorious 1971/72 England side, only Nigel Boocock and Chris Pusey returned. Pusey bought with him two of his Belle Vue teammates – Eric Broadbelt and Peter Collins. Collins was the latest sensation in British speedway, who, in his first full season at Belle Vue that same year, had averaged over 8 points a match, and looked well set for stardom. Arnold Hayley and Bob Kilby were old hands down under, but another new face completed the squad – twenty-one-year-old Barry Thomas from Hackney made his antipodean debut. Thomas had been the 1970 British Junior Champion, and, like Collins, he was one of England's precocious young talents. This was certainly the youngest England side to have toured Australia, but certainly not the strongest; but at least, consisting of exclusively English riders, they could call themselves England with some conviction.

The tour began at **Perth**, and Australia fielded a strong side in Jim Airey, Chum Taylor, John Boulger and John Langfield, with Les Sharpe, Les Leisk and Bob O'Leary filling in the gaps.

The English riders, especially Kilby and young Collins had done well in the pre-series open meetings, but in the first Test they were disappointing. The early heats were close-run affairs, and it looked as though the meeting would be close, but two maximum heat wins in heats 6 and 7 gave the Aussies an advantage that they subsequently built upon.

John Langfield was getting a reputation as the Australian villain, and, in a first half race, he took his bike out onto the track to coast around for a lap while a race was in progress. When he got around to the start line again, the starter pulled his bike to the infield and a confrontation took place. In the first race of the second half, Langfield was left at the tapes and left his bike on the track when he walked to the infield, to have further words with the starter. The race was consequently stopped, but he was allowed in the rerun (only in Australia), solely to do a lap beforehand, waving to the crowd, for which he was soundly booed. He finished in third place when the race was finally completed.

Jim Airey was never a lover of the Claremont track, but he got it right in the first Test and scored a blistering 18-point maximum. But he was made to sweat when a burst water main flooded the track at the pits gate in heat 14. Jim had a plane to catch for his next meeting in less than an hour, and, after maintenance had solved the problem, and the match was completed, he shot from the stadium still in his leathers.

England were still in the match with three heats left, but a grandstand finish by the Roos saw them win the match by 12 points.

AUSTRALIA 60: J. Airey 18, J. Boulger 14, L. Sharpe 8, C. Taylor 8, L. Leisk 6, J. Langfield 4, B. O'Leary 2.

ENGLAND 48: B. Kilby 13, N. Boocock 11, C. Pusey 8, A. Hayley 7, P. Collins 7, B. Thomas 2, E. Broadbelt 0.

In the South Australian Championship, Johnny Boulger retained his title, but he was hard pushed by Pusey and Boocock. Pusey was involved in a remarkable incident in the second Test, at **Adelaide**. Australia had only retained the services of Boulger and Langfield, having received the crippling news that captain Jim Airey had broken a bone in his his arm, teaching youngsters how to ride mini-bikes. The rest of the team was made up of Bob Valentine, Phil Crump, Steve Reinke, Chris Bass and Kym Amundson.

There was some tremendous riding in the first half and, at the end of it, England led by 6 points, before the match turned into a Wild West Show. In the interval the water truck began watering the track, and, although the English riders complained, they were ignored. Chris Pusey, he of the short fuse, attempted to flag the truck down, but was almost run over when the driver did not change course, and the Polka Dot Kid was left hopping around the track, clutching his right leg. When the truck eventually stopped, on the other side of the track, Pusey crossed the infield to make his way towards it.

A fight broke out between the irate Englishman, the truck driver, the tractor driver, several corner stewards and ambulancemen, and only ended when Chris, who was being held by several men, was knocked to the ground.

30. *Above:* Australians Jack Young and Bob Duckworth, 1955.

31. *Right:* Dick Bradley, Split Waterman and Alan Hunt 'Singing in the Rain' in the mid-1950s.

32. The Legendary Ronnie Moore, 1956.

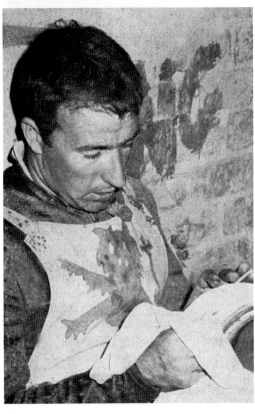

33. Roy Trigg successfully toured Australia with the Lions in the late 1960s.

34. Howard Cole leads Jim Airey and Tony Clarke in the fourth Test at Brisbane, 1969/70.

35. Jim Airey and Gordon Guasco with Australian team manager the legendary Johnnie Hoskins in 1970.

36. *Right:* Chris Bass, Australian star of the late 1960s.

37. *Below:* Barry Thomas in action in 1972/73.

38. *Left:* Eric Broadbelt.

39. *Below:* Jim McMillan, Doug Wyer, Kevin Holden and Chris Morton.

40. Phil Crump and Billy Sanders in 1978.

41. *Above:* Australasia 1978. From left to right: Mitch Shirra, Billy Sanders, Bruce Cribb, Ivan Mauger, John Titman, Larry Ross, John Bouleer, Phil Crump.

42. *Below:* England 1978. From left to right: Alan Grahame, Les Collins, Peter Collins, Malcolm Simmonds, Michael Lee, John Berry (manager), Steve Bastable, Chris Morton, Tony Davey.

43. Kenny Carter.

44. Larry Ross.

45-7. *This page and opposite:* Action from the 1986 Test match at Birmingham.

48. *Above:* Ryan Sullivan and Paul Thorpe in the 1995 Test series.

49. *Opposite:* Jason Crump (with flag) and Leigh Adams celebrate.

50. Action from the 1996 series, which England won 2-0.

51. Kelvin Tatum and Steve Schofield (inside) hold out Jason Crump (left) and Shane Bowes at Poole in 1996.

52. Lion Killers at Eastbourne, 1997. From left to right, back row: Leigh Adams, Shane Parker, Neil Street (manager), Jason Lyons, Steve Johnson. Front row: Mark Lemon, Craig Boyce, Jason Crump.

53. Mark Loram on the outside of Jason Crump at Eastbourne, 1998.

A public announcement was made that Pusey was excluded from the remainder of the match. Nigel Boocock then stated that England would not continue without their fiery teammate. Negotiations took place at the starting line before the announcement was made that 'Australia had won the match by default, and the rest of the programme would consist of stock-car races plus solo scratch and handicap races'. Two stock-car races were run before a further announcement was made, that Pusey had requested that his team continue without him, which they did with a vengeance, and won by 8 points.

AUSTRALIA 50: J. Boulger 16, B. Valentine 14, J. Langfield 9, P. Crump 8, C. Bass 1, K. Amundson 1, S. Reinke 1.

ENGLAND 58: A. Hayley 14, P. Collins 14, N. Boocock 10, B. Thomas 9, E. Broadbelt 5, C. Pusey 4, B. Kilby 2.

Australia's bad luck continued, as they were shaken to hear that fifty-year-old Jack Biggs had been killed in a track crash at Bendigo near Melbourne. Jack had been one of the Aussies' finest servants, having ridden for his country as recently as the previous year.

The third Test, at **Sydney**, was staged in a heat wave, which meant awkward track conditions for both sides. Jim Airey stepped in as the home team manager, and the riders at his disposal were Boulger, Langfield, Valentine, Torpie, Jack White, Bill Landels and reserve, the ill-fated Barry Van Praag. Barry never enjoyed the good fortune of his father, Lionel. Later on that season, a bad crash saw him confined to a wheelchair, until he died from a heart attack in 1990.

The Aussies opened with two maximum heat wins, and never looked back, as Pusey and Broadbelt struggled on sick motors. Hayley never got going, and Kilby was an unimpressive reserve. Young Peter Collins was the man of the match and was only robbed of a maximum by a flat tyre in heat 14.

AUSTRALIA 63: J. Boulger 15, J. White 15, B. Valentine 13, J. Langfield 7, B. Landels 6, K. Torpie 6, B. Van Praag 1.

ENGLAND 45: P. Collins 15, N. Boocock 12, E. Broadbelt 8, A. Hayley 5, B. Thomas 2, C. Pusey 2, B. Kilby 1.

England were unfortunate to lose the fourth Test, at the **Sydney** Showground, when they were the victims of a couple of questionable decisions, and they also lost their best rider Peter Collins in a last heat crash. With Jack White being unavailable, Australia brought in Bob Humphreys who rode for King's Lynn in the British League, but it was Kevin Torpie who proved to be the match winner for the Roos.

Australia were ahead by 32-22 at the interval stage, but England skipper Boocock led a revival, with three incredible last-to-first races in the second half which had the spectators on their feet. At the end of heat 13, the Lions had pulled back to within 6 points, but a photo finish in heat 15 saw Langfield get the decision over Pusey even though the English rider appeared to have got the drop on him, which even Aussie team manager Airey admitted. The Lions were left needing a 5-1 in the final heat to force a draw, and Collins and Pusey faced the highly successful pairing of Boulger and Torpie.

English hopes rose when Boulger missed the gate but, on the apex of the first corner, Pusey collided with Collins, and a horrendous crash was the result with sparks flying from the Showground's concrete fence, as both Lions cartwheeled around it. Fortunately, both riders walked away, but for Collins, it was the end of his highly successful tour, as he was unable to continue riding. Bob Kilby stepped in as a replacement in the rerun, but finished in third place.

AUSTRALIA 58: J. Boulger 15, K. Torpie 11, B. Valentine 11, J. Langfield 11, B. Landels 8, B. Van Praag 2, B. Humphreys 0.

ENGLAND 50: N. Boocock 12, P. Collins 11, A. Hayley 9, B. Kilby 6, C. Pusey 5, B. Thomas 5, E. Broadbelt 2.

Australia crushed England to win the series at **Brisbane**. Their most successful pairing was split to place Valentine with Boulger, and Jack White with Torpie, and Steve Reinke was paired with Doug White, with John Titman at reserve. There were other English riders wintering in Australia, and the Lions distress call was answered by Collins' Belle Vue team mate Alan Wilkinson for the fifth Test.

A heat 4 crash saw Jack White taken to hospital, and Barry Thomas' bike taken to the scrap heap for the night, but, with Boocock sporting a foot injury from the previous Test, England were never in the match, despite a dazzling display from Pusey, who ruined Johnny Boulger's maximum. The Australian victory saw them regain the Ashes.

The sixth Test was also staged in Brisbane, and the Roos replaced Landels with Bob Gourlay, and England retained Wilkinson. Despite having lost the series, the Lions put on a determined display, and, at last, reserve Bob Kilby rode like he did week after week in the British League. He stepped in for Wilkinson on four occasions, and, after collecting three easy heat wins; he seemed set for a fourth when he suffered an engine failure. The scores were level after 15 heats, but in the next race, Thomas fell and injured his knee. Kilby's bike failed in the penultimate heat, and the Aussies took full advantage to record an 8-point win.

AUSTRALIA 58: J. Boulger 15, S. Reinke 11, J. White 9, D. White 8, J. Titman 8, K. Torpie 6, B. Gourlay 1.

ENGLAND 50: N. Boocock 10, A. Hayley 10, C. Pusey 10, B. Kilby 9, B. Thomas 7, E. Broadbelt 4, A. Wilkinson 0.

Airey and Langfield both returned for the final Test match, at **Sydney**, and were joined by Boulger, Valentine, Landels, Van Praag and Geoff Curtis. England recruited their old pal Georgie Hunter to replace Wilkinson, and in fact the Scot topped the Lions' scorechart. Boocock was still suffering with a foot injury, and Barry Thomas at reserve was a virtual passenger, with stitches in an infected knee.

Langfield stormed back to top form with an 18-point maximum, but although Boocock complained that the perpetual villain was riding an oversize motor, the result of the match stood. Boulger was again superb, and dropped his only point of the night to Hunter. Although the Aussies were an out-of-balance side, their top three were good enough to win the match for them.

AUSTRALIA 62: J. Langfield 18, J. Boulger 17, J. Airey 14, B. Van Praag 7, B. Valentine 5, B. Landels 1, G. Curtis 0.

ENGLAND 46: G. Hunter 11, C. Pusey 9, N. Boocock 9, A. Hayley 9, E. Broadbelt 5, B. Kilby 3, B. Thomas 0.

Although England had surrendered the Ashes, they had handled themselves with pride, and had ridden much better than their single match victory suggested. Had Peter Collins not been injured, they may well have added to that, for rarely had an English rider made such an impact on his debut in Australia as PC. Boocock, of course, never gave in, and Pusey was always good value for money, but Kilby rarely showed the form that had made him one of the top Brits in England.

The Lions made their way back home, once again via New Zealand, and rode a four-match series against the Kiwis, who were led by Ronnie Moore, who had retired from British speedway at the end of the 1972 season. New Zealand featured Ivan Mauger and Barry Briggs in two of the matches, and won them both. However in the matches in which they were absent, England were the victors, and the series was drawn 2-2.

Mauger had been having pretty much his own way in the World Championship; he completed a hat-trick of victories between 1968 and 1970. But his former pupil, the Great Dane, Ole Olsen, eclipsed him in 1971. Mauger was far from finished however, and was the current World Champion, having regained the title in 1972. Briggo too had announced his retirement from British speedway at the end of 1972 (although he did return in 1974). With him and Moore retiring, it marked the end of an era.

World speedway was changing, as shown by the fact that in the 1972 World Championship, the USSR had no fewer than six finalists. England had a fair contingent with the Boocock boys and John Louis, but Australia had been having a lean time of it in the competition. Their only finalist since 1963 had been Jim Airey in 1971. Jim had his best season ever in British speedway that year, and had scored 8 points in the final. He shocked the world of speedway by announcing his retirement from Britain at the end of that season. He explained that he was desperate to become World Champion, but, after just one World Final appearance, in Gothenburg, he knew he never would be, and Airey never raced in the British League again.

The Lions once again briefly met the Aussies in the 1973 British speedway season, when they clashed in the ambitious Daily Mirror International Tournament, which featured England, Australia, New Zealand, Sweden, Poland, the Soviet Union and Norway-Denmark.

Rarely, if ever, has such a star-studded tournament been staged. Moore and Briggs returned to take part for the Kiwis, and Airey made final appearances in Britain. The old rivals met at King's Lynn in July, and England, who were the eventual winner of the tournament, won the match by 10 points.

AUSTRALIA v GREAT BRITAIN TEST SERIES 1973/74

1st Test	Perth	Nov 23rd	'73	Aust 53	Brit 55	W
2nd Test	Perth	Dec 7th	'73	Aust 33	Brit 75	W
3rd Test	Adelaide	Dec 15th	'73	Aust 44	Brit 64	W
4th Test	Sydney	Jan 5th	'73	Aust 50	Brit 58	W
5th Test	Brisbane	Jan 12th	'74	Aust 46	Brit 62	W
6th Test	Brisbane	Jan 19th	'74	Aust 60	Brit 47	L
7th Test	Sydney	Jan 26th	'74	Aust 53	Brit 55	W

Britain win series 6-1

In the previous year, and at any time previously, the visitors would have been called England. However, maybe due to England's success in the Daily Mirror tournament, elitism had crept into the Lion's camp, and the inclusion of Scots McMillan and Hunter (who had both ridden for England in Australia previously) necessitated the tourists being called Great Britain. Collins Broadbelt and Nigel Boocock all returned, and speedway's inseparable friends, twenty-six-year-old Doug Wyer, and twenty-five-year-old Reg Wilson supplied the new faces. Since Airey's departure from Sheffield, Aussie Bob Valentine had taken over as the number one rider at Owlerton, but Wyer and Wilson were acknowledged as being the backbone of the Northern side. For once the Lions had a non-riding manager, as Reg Fearman returned to Australia twenty-three years after he had made his debut there as an England rider.

For the first Test match, at **Perth**, the Aussies hit a snag when John Boulger declared himself unavailable as he was awaiting surgery for a cartilage injury. John Langfield was also absent. Jim Airey had already declined to ride in the series, which put Australia into trouble. They did, however, feature their latest star – eighteen-year-old Billy Sanders – who had already got two British seasons under his belt with Ipswich. The ever-improving Bob Valentine joined him. Home track rider Bob O'Leary, Les Leisk, Bob Humphries, Peter Thompson and Glyn Taylor completed a modest Australian line-up.

Despite their modesty, the Roos led the match for the first 11 heats, but the Brits began to get used to the sprawling Claremont track, and, when McMillan and Wilson scored a 4-2 in the following heat, it began a revival for the Lions that saw them pip the home team by 2 points by the end of the match. Peter Collins was just as impressive as he had been twelve months earlier, and for Australia, Bob O'Leary made the most of his home track knowledge.

AUSTRALIA 53: B. O'Leary 15, B. Sanders 11, B. Valentine 9, B. Humphreys 6, L. Leisk 6, P. Thompson 5, G. Taylor 1.

BRITAIN 55: P. Collins 15, N. Boocock 10, R. Wilson 10, J. McMillan 6, E. Broadbelt 6, D. Wyer 5, G. Hunter 3.

The action remained in **Perth** for the second Test, but without Valentine. The Aussies looked even more vulnerable than they had in the previous Test. Chum Taylor and Phil Crump were brought in, but Britain gave the Aussies a thorough trouncing, with no fewer than five Lions scoring double figures in this one-sided match.

AUSTRALIA 33: B. Sanders 8, B. O'Leary 7, C. Taylor 6, L. Leisk 4, B. Humphreys 4, P. Crump 3, P. Thomson 1.

BRITAIN 75: J. McMillan 15, G. Hunter 15, R. Wilson 14, N. Boocock 14, P. Collins 12, E. Broadbelt 4, D. Wyer 1.

The third Test, at **Adelaide**, was rained off and restaged on the same night as the New South Wales Championship at Sydney. This featured Bob Valentine, so the home team were robbed of his services once again. Langfield, Crump and Leisk all returned and Lou Sansom, who rode in Britain for Second Division Workington, was given his first full cap. Robin and Kym Amundson completed the Australian team.

As expected, the Aussies proved poor fare against a British team whose confidence was growing by the match. Sansom made an impressive debut, but, apart from him and Steve Reinke, the rest of the Aussies had little to offer as they were once again well beaten. A poor crowd was an indication of the Australian public's disenchantment with the sides that their country was putting out to represent them at an international level. But things got worse. All in one night, they were dealt a triple blow as skipper Langfield announced his retirement from Test racing, and, back in Sydney, after winning the New South Wales title, Jim Airey announced his retirement from speedway. In the same meeting, Geoff Curtis was tragically killed in a heat 11 crash.

AUSTRALIA 44: L. Sansom 13, S. Reinke 12, B. Sanders 7½, J. Langfield 7½, P. Crump 2, R. Amundson 1, K. Amundson 1.

BRITAIN 64: P. Collins 15, J. McMillan 13, G. Hunter 11, N. Boocock 10, E. Broadbelt 6, D. Wyer 5, R. Wilson 4.

At least Boulger was back for the fourth Test, at **Sydney**, for which only Reinke and Sanders were retained. Greg Kentwell and Bill Landels returned to join Ricky Day and nineteen-year-old Second Division rider, Phil Herne, from Birmingham. The Roos looked lively as Boulger won the opening race, and Sanders won heat 2. However the Lions immediately hit back with two maximum heat wins but, by the half way stage, with Britain 6 points ahead, Billy Sanders remained the only unbeaten rider. However, he had an unfortunate second half to the match as he was beaten by Hunter, excluded for breaking the tapes in heat 13 and suffered an engine failure in his final outing. Steve Reinke on the other hand was unbeaten after the interval, but Britain would not be denied, and took the Ashes with an 8-point win.

AUSTRALIA 50: S. Reinke 13, J. Boulger 11, B. Sanders 11, G. Kentwell 5, R. Day 5, P. Herne 4, B. Landels 1.

BRITAIN 58: R. Wilson 14, P. Collins 12, G. Hunter 10, E. Broadbelt 9, J. McMillan 6, N. Boocock 5, D. Wyer 2.

Australia retained Boulger, Sanders and Reinke for the fifth Test, at **Brisbane**, and brought in local riders Jack White, Kevin Torpie, Bryan Loakes and John Titman. By the break, Boulger had dropped his only point to Reg Wilson, but in the interval, he decided that the pain from his recent knee operation was too great, and he withdrew from the meeting to leave the Roos at the mercy of the rampant Lions. With Sanders having an off-night, the Aussies had little to offer, as Britain stormed to their fifth consecutive win in the series. Wilson had hit a purple patch for the visitors, and even improved on his impressive display at Sydney by dropping his only point to Steve Reinke.

AUSTRALIA 46: S. Reinke 11, J. Titman 9, J. Boulger 8, J. White 7, K. Torpie 6, B. Loakes 3, B. Sanders 2.

BRITAIN 62: R. Wilson 17, P. Collins 12, N. Boocock 11, G. Hunter 11, E. Broadbelt 7, D. Wyer 4, J. McMillan 0.

The teams remained in **Brisbane** for what was the Aussies only win of the series. Phil Crump and Lou Sansome replaced Boulger and Sanders, and the home team took full advantage of the Collins-Hunter pairing, who were very subdued on the night. The match was not without incident however. After heat 16, the Aussies had already won the match, but in the penultimate heat, Jack White was the victim of some first-bend bunching and found himself pushed into the fence. When his exclusion was announced, the spectators were in uproar, and 200 of them stormed onto the track and refused to move until White had been reinstated. The match was held up until the police arrived and broke up the protest.

With the remaining riders preparing for the rerun, Eric Broadbelt was riding around to the starting tapes when a spectator crossed the track and collided with him. Eric fell from his bike, which toppled onto the spectator breaking his leg.

AUSTRALIA 60: S. Reinke 15, J. Titman 13, J. White 10, P. Crump 9, K. Torpie 8, L. Sansome 3, B. Loakes 2.

BRITAIN 47: R. Wilson 14, N. Boocock 9, E. Broadbelt 9, J. McMillan 6, P. Collins 4, G. Hunter 4, D. Wyer 1.

The Roos appeared to be doomed before the start of the final Test, at **Sydney**, when the news arrived that both Steve Reinke and John Titman were flood-bound in Brisbane. Already without Boulger, Australia struggled to get a side together at such short notice, but John Langfield ended his retirement and came to the rescue. In desperation, the Aussies drafted in veteran Bob Sharp and Paul Johnson.

The Aussie camp had a problem with Johnson however. English born, Paul was now regarded as a Kiwi, and the home team did not want to run the risk of protest from the opposition. But with the Ashes in the bag, Johnson programmed only as reserve, and with a total of 2 points from him in the match, no such British protest was forthcoming.

Britain led by 8 points at the interval, but Ricky Day had an exceptional match for the Aussies, and they staged a comeback, entering the final heat needing a 5-1 to draw the match. Langfield and Kentwell faced George Hunter and Peter Collins, but Hunter burst through the tapes and was excluded. Doug Wyer was brought in to replace him and, on the second attempt, Collins was controversially excluded for balking Langfield. On the third attempt to start the final heat, all three riders appeared to go through the tapes, but both Aussies led the race. Langfield struggled to protect the slower Kentwell, and took Wyer's front wheel at one stage of the race, but this only inspired Doug to overtake him on the last lap to secure victory for the Lions.

After the race, Langfield publicly apologised for riding dangerously around the British rider, but even so Australia deserved full credit for the fight they showed with the limited resources that they had available.

AUSTRALIA 53: J. Langfield 16, B. Sanders 14, R. Day 11, P. Herne 8, G. Kentwell 2, P. Johnstone 2, R. Blackadder 0.

BRITAIN 55: P. Collins 14, R. Wilson 13, E. Broadbelt 10, D. Wyer 6, G. Hunter 5, J. McMillan 4, N. Boocock 3.

It had been a hugely successful tour for the Lions. Apart from the Test matches, they had beaten South Australia at Whyalla, Ole Olsen's Seven at Liverpool, an Australian Select at Newcastle and a Jerilderie Park Select, also at Newcastle. The British riders, especially Peter Collins, were successful in the open meetings also, and the reason for the success of the tour was credited to Reg Fearman, Britain's (or England's) first manager down under. He had earned his corn and had taken as much pressure as possible off the riders, making their arrangements, and allowing them to concentrate on their racing. It was a luxury that had been missed by Jack Parker and Ken McKinlay, and was now enjoyed by Nigel Boocock.

AUSTRALIA v GREAT BRITAIN TEST SERIES 1974/75

1st Test	Brisbane	Nov 30th	'74	Aust 62	Brit 45	L
2nd Test	Brisbane	Dec 7th	'74	Aust 50	Brit 58	W
3rd Test	Newcastle	Dec 20th	'74	Aust 63	Brit 45	L
4th Test	Sydney	Dec 21st	'74	Aust 55	Brit 53	L
5th Test	Liverpool	Dec 26th	'74	Aust 57	Brit 51	L
6th Test	Adelaide	Jan 3rd	'75	Aust 59	Brit 49	L
7th Test	Perth	Jan 17th	'75	Aust 46	Brit 61	W

Australia win series 5-2

The 1974/75 touring team had a familiar look about it. In fact no fewer than five of the previous year's team returned; only Collins and Hunter did not make the trip. Once again the Lions had a team manager, as this time Exeter promoter Wally Mawdsley stepped into the breach. He brought with him, one of his Championship-winning Falcons, Kevin Holden, who was averaging around 7 points a match at the County Ground. Chris Morten was named as the British reserve. Eighteen-year-old Mort had also averaged around 7 points at Belle Vue in the 1974 season and was one of the hottest prospects in British speedway, but he had sustained a shoulder injury towards the end of the season, and the tour marked his return to riding.

As a team, they weren't too bad, but they were certainly not the best touring team of recent years. Peter Collins, John Louis, Terry Betts, Eric Boocock, Martin Ashby, Dave Jessup and Malcolm Simmons were now the top English riders, and they were all conspicuous by their absence. Such was the magnitude of world-class English riders, that they now stood alone as a nation, as the Great Britain team had been disbanded.

In 1974, England rode Test Series against Sweden, Poland, and the Soviet Union, and never lost a match, and they ended the British season by winning the World Team Cup in Poland. It was the first time that an English team had won the Word Championship since the competition had begun in 1960.

Phil Crump had by now established himself as the top Australian in British speedway, riding for Newport, and Billy Sanders was now the number one rider at Ipswich. These two riders, along with John Titman, formed the nucleus of the 1974/75 Australian team. John Boulger was not competing in the series, but Langfield had returned and Bryan Loakes, Steve Reinke, and Steve Koppe joined him for the opening Test at **Brisbane**.

John Titman had not returned to England for the 1974 season, but he showed no signs of rustiness, as he blasted his way to 16 points, and led Australia to a 17-point win. The Brits were consistently out-gated by the determined Aussies, but they did have the man of the match in Doug Wyer who dropped only 1 point – to Titman. At the end of the meeting Mawdsley asked for a meeting with the Australian Speedway Control Council to establish some ground rules for the remainder of the series. Britain were unhappy with the starting procedures, and the way that the referee had allowed bunching on the first turns, but the fact remained that Australia were the better team on the night: 3 points from McMillan and 2 from Broadbelt had spelled disaster for the visitors.

AUSTRALIA 62: J. Titman 16, P. Crump 12, B. Sanders 11, B. Loakes 10, S. Reinke 8, J. Langfield 5, S. Koppe 0.

BRITAIN 45: D. Wyer 17, R. Wilson 11, N. Boocock 9, J. McMillan 3, C. Morton 3, E. Broadbelt 2, K. Holden 0.

The following week, **Brisbane** was again the host, for the second Test, and the Aussies kept the same team. On an ill-prepared track, gating was at a premium, and Britain got it right. Boocock and Broadbelt opened proceedings with a 5-1 over Loakes and Reinke, and Titman and Langfield suffered the same fate against Wilson and Holden in heat 2. Australia rallied in the second half, but Wyer and Wilson held the Lions together. Wilson was unlucky in heat 13, when he was well in front on the last lap when his magneto came adrift, but an improved performance by Eric Broadbelt saw the Brits home to level the series.

AUSTRALIA 50: J. Titman 11, P. Crump 11, J. Langfield 8, B. Sanders 8, B. Loakes 6, S. Koppe 4, S. Reinke 2.

BRITAIN 58: D. Wyer 14, R. Wilson 13, E. Broadbelt 12, N. Boocock 6, J. McMillan 5, K. Holden 4, C. Morton 4.

Following a two-week layoff, the Lions faced two Test matches in as many days: the first being held at **Newcastle**. The inclusion of Bob Valentine and Phil Herne made Australia formidable opponents, and Robbie Blackadder was making his debut at reserve. Crumpie hit top form, and none of the Brits could live with him, as he scorched around Jerilderie Park, to record an 18-point maximum. Sanders was almost as good, and the Lions didn't have an answer to it. Boocock had a poor match, and Kevin Holden failed to score, as the Brits were beaten 63-45.

AUSTRALIA 63: P. Crump 18, B. Sanders 15, P. Herne 10, B. Valentine 9, J. Langfield 7, J. Titman 2, R. Blackadder 2.

BRITAIN 45: D. Wyer 10, R. Wilson 9, J. McMillan 8, E. Broadbelt 8, N. Boocock 5, C. Morton 5, K. Holden 0.

A day later, and Crumpie was at it again, in **Sydney**, with another 18-pointer in the fourth Test. Billy Sanders also repeated his previous performance, as Australia moved into a 3-1 lead. Blackadder and Valentine were replaced by Ricky Day and Paul Johnson, and the loss of Valentine almost cost the Roos the match, as, after 16 heats, the tourists led by 2 points. But Crump and Titman turned the tables in the penultimate heat when they scored a 5-1 over Boocock and Broadbelt.

AUSTRALIA 55: P. Crump 18, B. Sanders 15, J. Langfield 9, P. Herne 6, J. Titman 4, R. Day 2, P. Johnson 1.

BRITAIN 53: D. Wyer 12, E. Broadbelt 11, R. Wilson 9, J. McMillan 9, N. Boocock 8, C. Morton 4, K. Holden 0.

Australia won the Ashes on Boxing Day, at **Liverpool**, in the first official Test match ever staged there. The 310m circuit was the smallest in the country, and therefore suited the Lions, but they were beaten by an uncommon amount of bad luck. There was no fence between the track and the tarmacadamed car circuit, and both Crump and Titman on occasions rode outside the speedway perimeter, without recourse from the referee – not that he would have seen them, as he was situated in the centre of the arena. Even so, the Brits were determined to put on a good show, and, after a poor start, they pulled back to within 4 points after heat 11. Chris Morton had wrecked his bike in an earlier crash with Billy Sanders, but, sat astride Broadbelt's machine, he partnered Kevin Holden to an unlikely maximum heat win over the previously unbeaten Valentine-Herne pairing to level the scores in heat 12. However, Crump, Sanders and Valentine sealed the Lions' fate in the later heats.

AUSTRALIA 57: P. Crump 14, B. Sanders 14, B. Valentine 13, J. Titman 8, P. Herne 5, J. Langfield 2, B. Humphreys 1.

BRITAIN 51: J. McMillan 11, E. Broadbelt 8, R. Wilson 8, D. Wyer 8, N. Boocock 7, K. Holden 7, C. Morton 2.

The sixth Test, at **Adelaide**, was run more on the lines of a rodeo than a speedway match. All of the races were started with an elastic band, and after every three races, there were two other events of motorised racing. Proceedings were reduced to the farcical between heats 12 and 13 when, not only was there an interval, but a 4-lap sidecar handicap championship was run, followed by the 4-lap Topline Paint Solo Handicap event. Even though Australia did not have Valentine and Herne, they still were too much for the Brits to handle, as Crump roared to a paid maximum and Sanders dropped his only point to McMillan.

AUSTRALIA 59: P. Crump 17, B. Sanders 16, J. Titman 9, J. Langfield 8, K. Amundson 4, L. Sansome 4, P. Thompson 1.

BRITAIN 49: J. McMillan 10, R. Wilson 9, D. Wyer 9, E. Broadbelt 7, C. Morton 6, N. Boocock 6, K. Holden 2.

Britain received some consolation in the final Test, at **Perth**, when Chris Morton cut loose, and top scored for the tourists with 14 points. With the series already won, the Aussies didn't field their strongest side and paid the price for it as they lost the match by 16 points.

AUSTRALIA 46: J. Titman 15, P. Crump 12, J. Langfield 11, B. Sanders 6, P. Thompson 2, D. Underwood 0.

BRITAIN 61: C. Morton 14, D. Wyer 12, R. Wilson 10, E. Broadbelt 10, J. McMillan 8, N. Boocock 6, K. Holden 1.

Britain rode two further matches on their tour, beating both North Queensland and Rockhampton. The Lions had had their share of mechanical problems (as usual), but the team lacked the balance of the touring teams of the previous few years. Wilson and Wyer were the backbone of the side, but the old hands had not done so well. Nigel Boocock had struggled mechanically, but the reality of it was that, at thirty-seven years of age, his career was in decline. He had certainly been one of England's greatest-ever riders, but, although he led the British Lions in Australia, he was no longer being selected to represent England back in Britain. There had been Parker, there had been McKinlay, and there had been Boocock. Jack and Ken had been the English kings of Australia, and had been forced to abdicate. Now it was Nigel's turn.

Much the same could be said about Jim McMillan. The rider who turned England into Britain flourished briefly – but he was not the Mac of old. And Kevin Holden, on his first visit down under, never got to grips with the situation. Chris Morton of course realised his potential at the end, but he was typical of a veritable stable of stars that England had at that time. If the Ashes were to be won the following winter, then more of them would have to make the trip.

Australia seemed to have a future World Champion in Phil Crump, with Billy Sanders not far behind him. Valentine and Boulger were also world-class riders, but in the winter of 1974/75, England could have sent out two or three teams that would have won the Test Series – but they failed to do so. It was an indication as to how the Ashes were becoming devalued.

AUSTRALIA v ENGLAND TEST SERIES 1975/76

1st Test	Perth	Nov 14th	'75	Aust 41	Eng 67	W
2nd Test	Perth	Nov 28th	'75	Aust 34	Eng 74	W
3rd Test	Newcastle	Dec 5th	'75	Aust 32	Eng 76	W
4th Test	Sydney	Dec 6th	'75	Aust 38	Eng 70	W
5th Test	Liverpool	Dec 26th	'75	Aust 47	Eng 61	W
6th Test	Sydney	Dec 27th	'75	Aust 62	Eng 45	L
7th Test	Brisbane	Jan 10th	'76	Aust 50	Eng 57	W

England win series 6-1

With the absence of Jim McMillan for the 1975/76 visit to Australia, the tourists once again became England, but only Chris Morton and Doug Wyer were retained from the previous year. The team did however contain another old hand, as Chris Pusey returned. But the Lions boasted an even bigger gun in Peter Collins. In the two years since his previous visit, Collins had developed into a world-class rider of the highest calibre. He had finished fifth in the 1975 World Final, and, although Mauger and Ole Olsen were regarded as the best two riders in speedway, Peter looked set to topple both. Chris Morton's elder brother Dave was making his debut for the Lions down under but it was not his first visit as he had won the 1975 New Zealand Championship. Two young 'virgins' completed the team; although the term had probably never been used before when describing Reading's twenty-two-year-old glamour boy John Davis. Oxford's Gordon Kennett was also making his first visit to Australia. Both were part of the crop of up-and-coming English riders who promised success for the mother country for years to come. Reg Fearman, once again, took over as the England team manager.

Australia had, however, not had the same success rate in finding new talent. Crump had progressed, and had finished on the same points tally as Collins in the World Championship, and Sanders had become one of the top riders in the British League. Phil Herne was also beginning to make a name for himself in Britain, but with Johnny Boulger again opting not to ride in the Test Series, Australia's chances looked slim, and indeed a rout took place.

For the opener, at **Perth**, the Aussies fielded Crump, Peter Thompson, Glyn Taylor, Les Leisk, Bryan O'Leary, Mick McKeon and Rod Chessell. Crumpie was superb, dropping his only point of the match to Doug Wyer, but the rest of the Roos were completely outclassed. John Davis made a superb debut, becoming the Claremont track record holder in heat 4, but, by the end of the match, the record belonged to Wyer, who became the new holder in heat 17. A 5-1 by Chris Morton and Wyer in heat 2 put the Lions on track for a win, and they never looked back.

AUSTRALIA 41: P. Crump 17, G. Taylor 9, M. McKeon 5, P. Thompson 4, L. Leisk 4, R. Chessell 2, B. O'Leary 0.

ENGLAND 67: P. Collins 14, J. Davis 12, C. Morton 12, C. Pusey 9, D. Wyer 9, D. Morton 9, G. Kennett 2.

The action stayed in **Perth** for the second Test on the following Friday, and the Aussies called up reinforcements Billy Sanders, John Langfield and Phil Herne to join Crump, Taylor, Thompson and Leisk. But, as a team, they failed to match even the poor performance of the week before. Crumpie was again superb, this time dropping his only point to Collins, who, in turn, dropped his only point to Phil. Davis and skipper Pusey were a sensational pairing for England, and were beaten only by Crump throughout the entire match. It was usually the tourists who suffered mechanically in Australia, but on this occasion, the home team were the recipients of mechanical gremlins as Sanders, Langfield and Herne all ground to a halt at one time or another.

AUSTRALIA 34: P. Crump 17, J. Langfield 5, P. Herne 5, B. Sanders 2, P. Thompson 2, G. Taylor 2, L. Leisk 1.

ENGLAND 74: P. Collins 17, C. Pusey 15, D. Wyer 13, J. Davis 12, C. Morton 9, D. Morton 7, G. Kennett 1.

At **Newcastle**, Australia put out their best team, with only Boulger missing. Bob Valentine, Gary Middleton and John Titman were recruited to join Crump, Sanders, Langfield and Herne, as the Roos desperately tried to stem the tide, but, inexplicably, their downward spiral continued. Even Crumpie was brought to heel as the Lions ran amok, led by a Collins maximum. The England reserve Kennett also got into the act by scoring 9 points from five rides. With the fourth Test only twenty-four hours away, the Aussies only chance of retaining the Ashes was to naturalise Ivan Mauger and Ole Olsen in double quick time. At the end of the match, Reg Fearman was forced to leave the tour to attend to personal business.

AUSTRALIA 32: P. Crump 7, J. Titman 7, B. Sanders 6, P. Herne 4, B.Valentine 3, J. Langfield 3, G. Middleton 2.

ENGLAND 76: P. Collins 18, J. Davis 15, C. Morton 13, D. Wyer 12, D. Kennett 9, C. Pusey 6, D. Morton 3.

England regained the Ashes, at **Sydney**, on 6 December. With Valentine and Middleton being unavailable, Ricky Day was brought in, and Mitch Shirra, who was a Kiwi, made his debut. Crump was back on form for Australia, but he couldn't save them. Only an engine failure prevented Collins from scoring a maximum, but no such misfortune dogged Wyer, as he scooped the pool.

AUSTRALIA 38: P. Crump 15, P. Herne 9, J. Langfield 8, R. Day 3, J. Titman 2, B. Sanders 1, M. Shirra 0.

ENGLAND 70: D. Wyer 18, P. Collins 14, J. Davis 11, D. Morton 8, C. Morton 8, C. Pusey 7, G. Kennett 4.

Billy Sanders at last came good in the Fifth test, at **Liverpool**, to score 11 points. Terry Sutherland made his debut for the Roos, but, despite another fine showing from Crump, the England steamrollering continued, and the Aussies were once again crushed, in what was their most humiliating series ever.

AUSTRALIA 47: P. Crump 17, B. Sanders 11, P. Herne 7, T. Sutherland 4, G. Middleton 3, M. Shirra 3, J. Langfield 2.

ENGLAND 61: P. Collins 17, D. Wyer 13, C. Morton 9, J. Davis 7, G. Kennett 7, C. Pusey 5, D. Morton 3.

The England team arrived at **Sydney** to find the Showground track four inches thick with new dirt in some places. It hadn't been watered or bedded down, and rain and watering just before the start of the match made the track treacherous. There was drama in heat 3 when Peter Collins hit an inconsistent patch and lost control, jarring his arm in the process. The Sydney promotion was requested by England's new manager John Berry to take some dirt off the track, but suspecting that they had found the Lion's achilles heel, they refused. The referee was then called in to inspect the track, but once he had established that it was of an oval shape, devoid of any dead animals, and that there was some dirt on it, he declared it fit for racing.

The Lions skipper Chris Pusey was fatalistically heard to suggest 'someone's going to get hurt out there', and it was him, in the very next race. He hit a deep patch when chasing John Langfield, and when the Aussie locked up, Chris hit his back wheel, crashed into the fence, and was hit by third-placed Billy Sanders. The England skipper was taken to hospital with a suspected broken leg, which fortunately proved to be a chipped bone in his right knee, along with various cuts and bruises.

Berry had had enough and withdrew his troops saying that he did not wish to have a death on his conscience. After a considerable delay, and the England camp had calmed down and taken into considera-tion the Australian spectators, the Lions unloaded their equipment and agreed to continue. However, they did so under Berry's instructions that they must not take any risks, and must not try to overtake on the impossible surface.

Collins completed only three rides before he withdrew from the match, and with Davis being the only English rider to make the gate, the Aussies finally won a match.

AUSTRALIA 62: P. Herne 16, P. Crump 15, B. Sanders 11, R. Day 7, J. Langfield 6, T. Sutherland 4, S. Mountford 3.

ENGLAND 45: J. Davis 15, D. Wyer 10, D. Morton 9, C. Morton 5, G. Kennett 3, P. Collins 2, C. Pusey 1.

For the final Test, at **Brisbane**, England called upon Malcolm Simmons, who was spending the winter riding at Perth. Malcolm was down on power in his first two rides, and packed up in his last outing before the interval. Rain had left the track wet and greasy, and the Australians' superior gating gave them an advantage in the opening heats, resulting in a 6-point lead by heat 11. However, as the track began to dry out, the Lions began to claw their way back into the meeting, and when stand-in skipper Doug Wyer beat Crump in heat 13, it proved to be the turning point of the match. Simmons bounced back with two heat wins, as England took the initiative, and stretched for home, to win the series 6-1.

AUSTRALIA 50: P. Crump 17, B. Sanders 8, J. Titman 7, P. Herne 7, R. Henderson 6, M. Farrel 4, N. Coddington 1.

ENGLAND 57: P. Collins 15, D. Wyer 13, J. Davis 10, M. Simmons 7, D. Morton 7, C. Morton 5, G. Kennett 0.

Once again the Lions returned to England via New Zealand, where they scored over 80 points in each of the three Test matches against the Kiwis who were poor fare without Ivan Mauger.

At that time, England were the greatest speedway nation on earth. In the 1975 season they had retained the World Team Cup, won the Daily Mirror International Tournament, beaten the Poles 3-1 in Poland, beaten the Swedes 5-0 in Sweden and beaten the Rest of the World in England.

The 1976 British season bought its share of success for both teams. England's John Louis and Malcolm Simmons won the World Pairs Championship in Sweden, and Peter Collins fulfilled his promise and became World Champion in Poland, with Simmons taking silver and Phil Crump bronze. Australia took their revenge on England for the humiliating winter tour, by sensationally knocking the Lions out of the World Team Cup competition in a qualifier at Ipswich, and even went on to win the event, in their finest hour. However the traditional Lions winter tour of Australia was put on ice as the Australian promoters balked at the escalating costs.

AUSTRALIA v ENGLAND TEST SERIES 1978

1st Test	Newcastle	Jan 2nd	'78	Aust 38	Eng 70	W
2nd Test	Brisbane	Jan 7th	'78	Aust 51	Eng 57	W
3rd Test	Brisbane	Jan 14th	'78	Aust 61	Eng 47	L
4th Test	Sydney	Jan 20th	'78	Aust 53	Eng 55	W
5th Test	Adelaide	Feb 3rd	'78	Aust 56	Eng 52	L
6th Test	Sydney	Feb 11th	'78	Aust 47	Eng 61	W
7th Test	Perth	Feb 24th	'78	Aust 38	Eng 70	W

England win series 5-2

It was not until the winter of 1977/78 that the hostilities recommenced. When they did the Aussies were immediately up against it. Phil Crump had broken his leg in the 1977 season and was therefore not available, and the promoters had failed to agree financial terms with Billy Sanders. They had also placed a six-week ban on John Boulger, which meant that he would miss the first Test match, and their plans to include Mitch Shirra were scuppered when he pledged his allegiance to New Zealand.

With the matches not commencing until the beginning of January, the Lions did not fly out until Boxing Day, and they were a mixture of experience and youth. They were certainly way short of England's best team, but considering the last tour, and the bill of fare that the Aussie promoters seemed to have waiting for them, it seemed only appropriate to dilute the team a little.

Peter Collins, Doug Wyer, John Davis, Gordon Kennett and Alan Wilkinson provided the Lions experience, while twenty-one-year-olds Keith White and Neil Middleditch (son of Ken) made their Aussie debuts. Reg Fearman returned as team manager.

For the first Test, at **Newcastle**, Australia built their team around Titman, Herne and John Langfield. Ricky Day, Terry Sutherland, Robbie Blackadder and Wayne Forrest filled in the gaps, but there was only one way that this match was going to go – and it did. Collins cruised to an untroubled maximum and Davis was beaten only by Titman, as England thundered to a 32-point victory. It was difficult to criticise the Lions' performance, but in reality, the Australian team would have been hard pressed to beat any club side in the British League.

AUSTRALIA 38: J. Titman 12, P. Herne 11, R. Day 7, T. Sutherland 3, J. Langfield 3, R. Blackadder 2, W. Forrest 0.

ENGLAND 70: P. Collins 18, J. Davis 17, D. Wyer 11, G. Kennett 10, A. Wilkinson 6, K. White 5, N. Middleditch 3.

England also won the second Test, at **Brisbane**, but it was against another sub-standard team. Boulger returned, but Herne was absent, so Steve Koppe, Mick McKeon, Mike Farrell, Neil Coddington and Ken Murray made up the remainder of the home team. Boulger split the Belle Vue pairing of Wilkinson and Collins twice, but he was the only rider to do so, as they roared to four maximum heat wins. But Wyer had a subdued night, and the Aussies managed to make a match of it. England failed to wrap up the match until heat 17, but they never looked seriously challenged.

AUSTRALIA 51: J. Titman 14, J. Boulger 13, S. Koppe 9, M. McKeon 9, M. Farrell 5, N. Coddington 1, K. Murray 0.

ENGLAND 57: P. Collins 14, A. Wilkinson 12, J. Davis 12, G. Kennett 7, D. Wyer 6, K. White 5, N. Middleditch 1.

The third Test was originally scheduled for Liverpool, but a rain-off meant that it was staged at **Brisbane** the following Saturday. With his pay dispute settled, Billy Sanders returned to an Australian team that retained Boulger, Titman, Koppe McKeon and Farrell. With Herne also returning, the Aussies began to gain some semblance of a national team. Sanders was the star of the match, being beaten only by Collins, and establishing a new track record. He was well supported by the Titman-Boulger pairing that scored 14 out of a possible 15 points in their last three outings. England led by 2 points at the interval stage, but the superior gating of the Aussies saw them stage a comeback, to overtake the Lions, and comfortably win the match.

AUSTRALIA 61: B. Sanders 17, J. Titman 15, J. Boulger 10, M. McKeon 10, S. Koppe 5, M. Farrell 2, P. Herne 2.

ENGLAND 47: P. Collins 16, J. Davis 11, G. Kennett 10, A. Wilkinson 4, K. White 4, D. Wyer 2, N. Middleditch 0.

Australia were without Boulger for the fourth Test. at **Sydney**, but, following their victory at Brisbane, the Roos' desire had been reawoken, and they put up a strong fight. The scores were level at the interval stage, with Sanders unbeaten, but the Collins-Wilkinson pairing scored vital 5-1s in heats 13 and 16 to propel England 8 points ahead. Australia hit back with a 5-1 in the penultimate race, and, when Wyer fell and dislocated his shoulder in the final race, a draw looked to be on the cards; but Gordon Kennett split Herne and Titman to give England a 2-point win in the best match of the series so far.

AUSTRALIA 53: B. Sanders 15, J. Titman 11, P. Herne 7, M. McKeon 7, M. Farrell 7, R. Day 5, W. Forrest 1.

ENGLAND 55: P. Collins 14, J. Davis 10, A. Wilkinson 9, D. Wyer 8, K. White 7, G. Kennett 7, N. Middleditch 0.

Boulger returned for the fifth Test, at **Adelaide**, and Tony Boyle was also given a run in the Australian team. Disaster hit England as early as heat 2, when John Davis crashed and needed thirty-six stitches in his left leg and ten stitches in his right heel. Despite that, and an exclusion of Kennett for exceeding the time limit, the Lions still led by 4 points after heat 10. Titman and Herne scored a maximum heat win over Middleditch and White in the next race to level the scores, and a further 5-1 in heat 14 put the Aussies ahead. Australia won the match in heat 17 when Boulger and the impressive Boyle held back White and Middleditch, although Wyer and Kennett's 5-1 in the final heat closed the deficit to only 4 points. The series now stood at 3-2 to England.

AUSTRALIA 56: J. Boulger 14, B. Sanders 14, J. Titman 13, M. McKeon 6, T. Boyle 5, P. Herne 4, M. Farrell 0.

ENGLAND 52: D. Wyer 11, P. Collins 11, A. Wilkinson 10, G. Kennett 9, N. Middleditch 6, K. White 5, J. Davis 0.

Lloyd Cross replaced Boyle for the sixth Test, at **Sydney**, and Davis also returned to the England fold. Both teams had to battle against a mischievous starting gate, and the first three heats were started off the flag, causing the usual controversies. Collins led the England charge, dropping his only point to Mick McKeon, and John Davis, sporting more stitches than a patchwork quilt, rode like a hero. A telling factor was the performance of Gordon Kennett who had his finest match so far in the land down under. After taking an early lead, the Lions were always in command, and a mere 5-point return from Johnny Boulger sealed Australia's fate, as England retained the Ashes with a 14-point win.

AUSTRALIA 47: B. Sanders 13, J. Titman 13, M. McKeon 6, J. Boulger 5, L. Cross 5, M. Farrell 4, P. Herne 1.

ENGLAND 61: P. Collins 17, G. Kennett 15, J. Davis 11, D. Wyer 9, A. Wilkinson 7, K. White 2, N. Middleditch 0.

Boulger was again absent for the final Test, at **Perth**. But Sanders, Titman, McKeon and Herne formed the nucleus of the Australian side. Lloyd Cross was recalled and Glyn Taylor and Mick Moores completed the side. It was far from being the strongest team that had faced England in the series, and the Lions thrashed them unmercifully. The first three heats yielded 15 points to the Lions, as they scored three successive maximum heat wins, and it was not until heat 8, that an Australian crossed the finishing line in first place (Billy Sanders). The Aussies provided only a further three race winners in the entire match, as they were savaged by the hungry Lions.

AUSTRALIA 38: M. McKeon 12, B. Sanders 10, J. Titman 6, P. Herne 5, G. Taylor 3, M. Moores 1, L. Cross 1.

ENGLAND 70: P. Collins 18, G. Kennett 14, J. Davis 14, D. Wyer 12, K. White 8, A. Wilkinson 4, N. Middleditch dnr.

ENGLAND v AUSTRALASIA TEST SERIES 1978

1st Test	Bristol	July 21st	'78	Eng 52	Aust 56	L
2nd Test	Birmingham	July 24th	'78	Eng 59	Aust 49	W
3rd Test	Ipswich	Aug 10th	'78	Eng 51	Aust 57	L
4th Test	Hull	Aug 16th	'78	Eng 36	Aust 70	L
5th Test	Hackney	Aug 18th	'78	Eng 56	Aust 52	W

Australasia win series 3-2

The situation remained that Australia were not strong enough to take on England in Britain. As a matter of fact, at the end of the seventies, no speedway nation was. It was therefore decided to resurrect Australasia, to keep the Ashes alive in Great Britain. And so a five-match series was staged in 1978.

Just before the first Test, at **Bristol**, Gordon Kennett went down with a dose of the flu, but England still looked rock-solid. Simmons, Collins and Chris Morton headed the team that was littered with young talent. Michael Lee of King's Lynn was the current young sensation of world speedway, and was on a meteoric rise to fame. Steve Bastable, the twenty-two-year-old from Cradley Heath was also one of England's precocious talents. Steve's Cradley teammate, twenty-four-year-old Alan Grahame, twenty-six-year-old Tony Davey from Ipswich, and Peter's twenty-year-old younger brother, Les Collins, completed the England squad.

The Australasian squad comprised four Aussies – Crump, Sanders, Titman, and Boulger – and they were joined by four Kiwis. Larry Ross, the twenty-four-year-old Wimbledon rider, twenty-year-old Coventry sensation Mitch Shirra, skipper Ivan Mauger, and Bristol's own Bruce Cribb. Mauger, although undoubtedly still world class, was not the perpetual scoring machine that he had been in the early part of the decade, His place as one of speedway's all-time greats was already assured when he equalled Ove Fundin's five World Championship victories in 1977. Thus, he entered the series as World Champion.

Mauger in fact had a stinker of a night as he experimented with his carburettor and chose to miss a couple of rides. However, his inspiration and motivation as captain was a key factor in the result of the match. England's number one Peter Collins scored only 4 points, and was dropped from two races, as the Australasians took an unexpected victory by 4 points. England team manager John Berry was critical of a number of his riders, but the Lions, and the British public had taken the colonials too lightly – the series was clearly not going to be a walk in the park.

ENGLAND 52: M. Simmons 15, T. Davey 10, C. Morton 10, A. Grahame 7, P. Collins 4, M. Lee 3, S. Bastable 3, L. Collins 0.

AUSTRALASIA 56: P. Crump 17, J. Titman 13, L. Ross 12, B. Sanders 10, J. Boulger 2, I. Mauger 1, M. Shirra 1, B. Cribb 0.

The victors replaced Mitch Shirra with Phil Herne for the second Test, at **Birmingham**, and the Lions bought in Gordon Kennett and Dave Morton for Les Collins and Alan Grahame. Again Mauger failed to get his usual haul of points as he was excluded for breaking the tape in one race, and fell in another, injuring his knee. With Boulger failing once more, England took advantage of the situation and Mike Lee at last showed why he had finished fourth in the 1977 World Final. The Anzacs began the match with a 5-1, but this was quickly neutralised, and England led by 8 points after 6 heats, never looking likely to lose from that point on.

ENGLAND 59: M. Lee 15, M. Simmons 12, G. Kennett 9, D. Morton 8, P. Collins 7, T. Davey 5, C. Morton 2, S. Bastable 1.

AUSTRALASIA 49: B. Sanders 11, P. Crump 11, L. Ross 11, J. Titman 9, I. Mauger 3, B. Cribb 3, P. Herne 1, J. Boulger 0.

John Berry called up John Louis to ride on his home track at **Ipswich**. Thirty-seven-year-old Louis had not begun his speedway career until 1970, but he was an immediate sensation, and finished third in the 1975 World Championship. Twenty-five-year-old Dave Jessup made his return to the England side after injury, and Terry Betts was named as reserve, as the Morton brothers and Steve Bastable were rested. Shirra replaced Cribb for Australasia. It looked as though Berry had got it right when England stormed into a 10-point lead, but the visitors changed their tyres in the interval and it was a different team that contested the second half of the match. Mauger, who had netted only 2 points in the first half, shot to a win in heat 10, and Crump headed the pack in the following race. In heat 13, Ross and Mauger scored a maximum heat win, and, when they repeated the feat in heat 16, it paved the way for a win for the Commonwealth riders.

ENGLAND 51: T. Davey 14, M. Lee 11, J. Louis 10, M. Simmons 7, P. Collins 5, G. Kennett 4, D. Jessup 0, T. Betts dnr.

AUSTRALASIA 57: B. Sanders 14, J. Titman 14, I. Mauger 10, L. Ross 10, P. Crump 6, M. Shirra 2, P. Herne 1, J. Boulger 0.

The fourth Test, at **Hull**, was a travesty. After two rained off attempts to run the 1978 British Final, the only date that seemed to be left was 16 August, the same night as the fourth Test. With all of England's top riders contesting the British Final, the series was lost at the Boulevard. The Lions took on a strange look, as Ian Cartwright and Kevin Jolly were called up. Chris Pusey, Neil Middleditch and Terry Betts were recalled, and Hull's Graham Drury and Frank Auffret were conscripted. Second Division rider Tom Owen completed the squad. The Australasians were exempt from the British Final, and were therefore at full strength, the result being that they destroyed England and won the Ashes.

ENGLAND 36: T. Owen 10, I. Cartwright 7, F. Auffret 7, K. Jolly 6, N. Middleditch 3, C. Pusey 2, T. Betts 1, G. Drury 0.

AUSTRALASIA 70: P. Crump 16, B. Sanders 15, L. Ross 13, J. Titman 9, M. Shirra 7, I. Mauger 7, J. Boulger 3, B. Cribb dnr.

The top names returned for the final Test at **Hackney**, determined to show that they would have won the series but for a quirk of fate. But, by the same token, the Anzacs were just as determined, and the match was not a walkover for the Lions. By heat 10, the home side were 10 points in front, but Australasia staged a comeback, and drew level with two heats remaining. A maximum heat win from Jessup and Simmons in the penultimate heat swung the match in favour of the Lions, and a heat win in the final heat by Tony Davey settled the match in England's favour.

ENGLAND 56: M. Lee 12, M. Simmons 10, D. Jessup 10, P. Collins 9, J. Louis 9, T. Davey 3, G. Kennett 3, B. Thomas dnr.

AUSTRALASIA 52: B. Sanders 12, I. Mauger 12, M. Shirra 11, J. Titman 7, P. Crump 5, L. Ross 5, J. Boulger dnr, B. Cribb dnr.

England were left shell-shocked. They may have lost the series on a technicality, but even so, they were not expecting to be seriously challenged by the colonials. As soon as the domestic season was over, the Lions flew to Australia, hell bent on revenge.

AUSTRALIA v ENGLAND TEST SERIES 1978/79

1st Test	Perth	Nov 17th	'78	Aust 39	Eng 69	W
2nd Test	Adelaide	Nov 24th	'78	Aust 45	Eng 63	W
3rd Test	Liverpool	Nov 25th	'78	Aust 47	Eng 60	W
4th Test	Newcastle	Dec 1st	'78	Aust 50	Eng 58	W
5th Test	Sydney	Dec 2nd	'78	Aust 51½	Eng 56½	W
6th Test	Brisbane	Jan 1st	'79	Aust 50	Eng 58	W
7th Test	Brisbane	Jan 6th	'79	Aust 43	Eng 65	W

England win series 7-0

England took a strong, if young, side to Australia for the winter of 1978/79. They were hand picked by Nigel Boocock who appointed himself team mentor/reserve. Nigel had in fact retired from British League racing at the end of the 1975 season, and emigrated to Australia, but the lure had been too great and he had returned to ride for his current team Bristol. Although in the twilight of his career, he remained immensely popular with the Australian spectators and was now a resident of Queensland. Along with Boocock, Doug Wyer and Gordon Kennett provided the experience necessary to guide the youngsters though the tour. Cradley Heath provided three of the team members in Steve

Bastable, Alan Grahame and Phil Collins. Eighteen-year-old Phil was the younger brother of Peter and Les Collins and, after beginning his career at Ellesmere Port, he had been signed by Cradley for an unheard of transfer fee of £15,000. Collins was the current British Junior Champion, and was one of the most exciting riders in speedway. Current British Champion Michael Lee was making his Australian debut.

The Aussies were without Mick McKeon who was recovering from a broken wrist, and Phil Crump was not returning from England until mid-December. Although Sanders and Titman were in the team, the supporting cast of Danny Kennedy, Steve Koppe, Mike Farrell, Dave Shields and Mick Moores did not look strong enough to cope with the Lions in the first Test, at **Perth**, and indeed they were not.

One week prior to the match, Lee sounded off a warning when he won the King of Claremont title on the same track, and, in the series opener, he again showed his liking for the track by storming to an 18-point maximum. His partner Bastable finished behind him on four occasions in a celebration of young English speedway talent. Collins and Grahame were also impressive visitors, as England never displayed a weak link, and Boocock gave himself only one outing. Old hands Titman and Sanders tried in vain to stem the tide, but the tide steadily developed into a tidal wave that washed the Aussies away. The 18,000 crowd were of the opinion that they had just seen one of the best England sides ever to appear in Australia.

AUSTRALIA 39: J. Titman 14, B. Sanders 9, S. Koppe 5, D. Kennedy 4, M. Moores 4, M. Farrell 3, D. Shields 0.

ENGLAND 69: M. Lee 18, D. Wyer 11, S. Bastable 10, A. Grahame 10, P. Collins 10, G. Kennett 9, N. Boocock 1.

Australia were desperately in need of a transfusion of new blood, and for the second Test, at **Adelaide**, Rowley Park specialist John Boulger was brought into the side, along with Phil Herne. Sanders, Titman and Koppe were retained and Kym Amundson and Robert Maxfield completed the squad.

Once again the Lions heat leaders were superb, and Kennett equalled the four-year-old track record on his way to 16 points. Lee continued to enthral the Aussie spectators with another display of riding that belied his young years, as the Roos once again had no answer to the Lions' supremacy.

AUSTRALIA 45: B. Sanders 13, P. Herne 8, J. Boulger 8, J. Titman 7, S. Koppe 5, R. Maxfield 4, K. Amundson 0.

ENGLAND 63: M. Lee 17, G. Kennett 16, D. Wyer 13, A. Grahame 7, S. Bastable 6, P. Collins 4, N. Boocock dnr.

Immediately the match was over the bikes were hosed down, and a frantic scurry began to get to **Liverpool** for the third Test, which was on the very next day. Ricky Day, Glen McDonald and Phil Cain joined Sanders, Titman and Herne, and Gary Guglielmi, the controversial twenty-year-old Coventry rider, made his debut against the Lions.

The match proved to be England's toughest so far. There was no time for any practice on the Liverpool circuit, and trouble hit the Lions' camp as early as heat 2 when a snapped con-rod left Lee with a wrecked motor. Gordon Kennett was controversially excluded in heat 9, when he was adjudged to have brought down Glenn McDonald, but a television rerun proved that this was not the case. Phil Collins was also excluded in the first half when both of his wheels crossed the white line, and Australia went into the interval 1 point in front. However, led by the brilliant Kennett-Grahame pairing, and Mike Lee on borrowed equipment, England got their heads down, to cruise to another impressive win.

AUSTRALIA 47: B. Sanders 16, J. Titman 10, G. Guglielmi 7, R. Day 7, P. Herne 6, G. McDonald 1, P. Cain 0.

ENGLAND 60: G. Kennett 14, M. Lee 12, D. Wyer 12, A. Grahame 9, S. Bastable 9, P. Collins 3, N. Boocock 1.

On the 1 December, Australia attempted to stay in the competition at **Newcastle**. Mick Moores replaced Phil Cain, but he, of course, was not the answer. Although Sanders and Titman were the best riders on view, the Roos were once again trampled. The scores were the closest so far, but the Lions total was affected by a couple of engine failures and three exclusions. Even so, another rock solid performance saw them retain the Ashes with some style.

AUSTRALIA 50: B. Sanders 15, J. Titman 14, P. Herne 9, R. Day 6, G. McDonald 3, G. Guglielmi 2, M. Moores 1.

ENGLAND 58: D. Wyer 11, G. Kennett 11, S. Bastable 9, M. Lee 8, P. Collins 8, A. Grahame 7, N. Boocock 4.

By now, Nigel Boocock was playing host to the England team, as the entire squad moved into his house for the next few weeks. They had only twenty-four hours to prepare for the fifth Test, at **Sydney**, and experienced mechanical problems throughout the match; Bastable rode all night with the wrong timing and Kennett experienced float level problems that kept him down on power. Australia, who kept the same team, took full advantage of the situation. The match was close up until the final stages, when England's superb second strings came through to win the match for the Lions.

AUSTRALIA 51½: B. Sanders 16, J. Titman 15, P. Herne 8½, R. Day 7, G. McDonald 5, G. Guglielmi 0, M. Moores 0.

ENGLAND 56½: D. Wyer 16, M. Lee 15, G. Kennett 11, A. Grahame 8, S. Collins 4½, S. Bastable 2, N. Boocock dnr.

A month elapsed before the sixth Test, at **Brisbane**, was ridden, and by that time Mick McKeon had recovered and joined the Australian team, as did Farrell and Koppe. Neil Coddington and Neil Murray also joined Titman and Sanders. However, by this time, England were unstoppable. Doug Wyer scored his first full maximum for the Lions as they powered to another win and threatened a complete whitewash of the Aussies.

AUSTRALIA 50: B. Sanders 13, M. Farrell 13, M. McKeon 10, J. Titman 7, S. Koppe 6, N. Coddington 1, K. Murray 0.

ENGLAND 58: D. Wyer 18, G. Kennett 14, M. Lee 14, S. Bastable 5, P. Collins 4, A. Grahame 3, N. Boocock dnr.

Phil Crump finally joined the Australian team five nights later, again at **Brisbane**, and Billy Sanders dropped down to reserve. England were completely unfazed by such tactics and completed the expected whitewash with a workmanlike demolition of their hosts. Alan Grahame had an unfortunate end to the tour when he crashed and sustained a broken collarbone and dislocated shoulder, but by that time the business had been done. There was a nice touch at the end of the match, when Boocock came out to replace Grahame in heat 18 and won his last ever race for England.

AUSTRALIA 43: J. Titman 14, P. Crump 11, S. Koppe 7, M. Farrell 6, B. Sanders 4, D. Kennedy 1, R. Blackadder 0.

ENGLAND 65: D. Wyer 14, M. Lee 14, G. Kennett 13, P. Collins 9, S. Bastable 7, A. Grahame 5, N. Boocock 3.

For only the second time in forty years, England had not lost a Test match in Australia. Not only that, but they won another four matches against club sides as well. Every single rider had been superb, and the youngsters had exceeded all expectations. The tourists even went back to England and beat the English World Team Cup team.

Australia were a team in turmoil. All too often, their top stars had shown a reluctance to ride for their country, and now Australia was being looked upon as a training ground for the young England internationals. The Aussies in fact were running out of top riders. Boulger's career was in decline, and Crump and Sanders were their only two true world-class riders. Titman was always a good rider at club level and had his best season ever in Britain, and had also reached the World Final that year. He deserved a medal for his efforts, but, at almost thirty years of age, he was unlikely to improve. Australia needed time to regroup. England gave them three years in fact, as they did not tour again until the winter of 1981.

ENGLAND v AUSTRALASIA TEST SERIES 1979

1st Test	Wimbledon	July 12th	'79	Eng 61	Aust 47	W
2nd Test	Swindon	July 27th	'79	Eng 67	Aust 41	W
3rd Test	Ipswich	Aug 2nd	'79	Eng 60	Aust 48	W
4th Test	Cradley Heath	Aug 22nd	'79	Eng 72	Aust 36	W
5th Test	Halifax	Oct 14th	'79	Eng 68	Aust 40	W

England win series 5-0

Ivan Mauger, at almost forty years of age, was enjoying a renaissance in his career, and was riding almost as well as he ever had. But a heavy schedule and a niggling back injury prompted him to ask to be omitted from any of the Australasian Test matches, and this put the Anzacs at a distinct disadvantage. For the first Test, at **Wimbledon**, they built their team around Crump, Sanders and Larry Ross, with Titman, Shirra and Cribb as second strings. Gary Guglielmi and Steve Koppe, who was now linked with Exeter, were the reserves.

England had a strong opening pairing in Simmons and Jessup, and their second pairing of Lee and Kennett also looked good. With John Davis and Peter Collins forming the third pairing, things looked grim for the visitors. Chris Morton and home rider Roger Johns were the Lions reserves. However, no one had told the Australasians that things looked grim for them, and a 5-1 from Crump and Titman in heat 7, and some furious riding from the rest of the team in the first half, saw the Australasians take a 2-point lead into the interval. Two maximum heat wins in the second half put England on the road to victory. But it wasn't easy in this cracker of a match.

ENGLAND 61: J. Davis 13, D. Jessup 12, M. Lee 11, P. Collins 9, M. Simmons 9, G. Kennett 7, R. Johns 0, C. Morton dnr.

AUSTRALASIA 47: P. Crump 13, L. Ross 12, B. Sanders 11, B. Cribb 5, J. Titman 4, M. Shirra 2, G. Guglielmi 0, S. Koppe 0.

With Mitch Shirra reportedly injured, Ivan Mauger was persuaded to step in for the Anzacs at **Swindon**, and Phil Herne and John Boulger, who was having a thin time of it at Leicester, replaced Guglielmi and Koppe. England brought Morton into the main body of the team, and eighteen-year-old whizz-kid Kenny Carter made his debut at reserve.

When Crumpie broke the Blunsdon track record in heat 2, and Sanders won the following race, it seemed that England had another tough match on their hands, but, led by Jessup and Lee, the Lions began to forge ahead. With the match under control, England team manager John Berry gave Carter an outing in heat 12, and he responded by winning the race ahead of partner Peter Collins. In the last few heats, Australasia staged a minor comeback, but Lee and Morton closed proceedings with a 5-1 for the home side.

ENGLAND 67: M. Lee 16, D. Jessup 15, C. Morton 11, P. Collins 9, M. Simmons 8, J. Davis 4, K. Carter 4.

AUSTRALASIA 41: I. Mauger 12, P. Crump 10, B. Sanders 10, L. Ross 8, J. Titman 1, P. Herne 0, B. Cribb 0, J. Boulger 0.

Gary Guglielmi was given another chance at **Ipswich**, but when Titman and Herne failed to turn up, Poole's Danny Kennedy and Steve Koppe were hastily drafted into the side, making the Aussies looked decidedly weak. England brought in home riders John Louis and Kevin Jolly, and twenty-two-year-old Joe Owen from Hull made his debut against the colonials.

Crump and Sanders made a fight of it, and the match never lacked interest; but the absentees were missed too much. Guglielmi was a lively reserve and his efforts were worth far more than his pointless return. Only 4 points separated the teams at the halfway stage, but, once again, England increased the pressure in the second half to cruise home. Mike Lee robbed Phil Crump of a maximum in the final heat as England won the Ashes.

ENGLAND 60: M. Lee 16, D. Jessup 11, P. Collins 9, J. Louis 7, K. Jolly 7, J. Owen 7, G. Kennett 2, M. Simmons 1.

AUSTRALASIA 48: P. Crump 17, B. Sanders 15, L. Ross 9, D. Kennedy 6, S. Koppe 1, B. Cribb 0, G. Guglielmi 0.

With the fourth Test, at **Halifax**, postponed, the next meeting took place at **Cradley Heath**. Herne and Titman both turned up, but the visitors were without injured Billy Sanders. Shirra and Boulger returned and twenty-four-year-old Aussie John McNeill from Leicester made his debut. For England, Heathens Phil Collins and Alan Grahame joined Jessup, Davis, Lee, Morton and Peter Collins.

The two Cradley riders plugged any gaps that may have existed in the England team, as they stormed to their biggest win of the series. Only ex-Heathen Bruce Cribb beat 'Big PC', and 'Little PC' scored paid 14 points for England.

ENGLAND 72: Peter Collins 17, D. Jessup 16, Phil Collins 11, J. Davis 10, A. Grahame 8, M. Lee 8, C. Morton 2.

AUSTRALASIA 36: P. Crump 12, L. Ross 6, J. Boulger 6, J. Titman 6, B. Cribb 5, J. McNeill 1, M. Shirra 0, P. Herne 0.

The rearranged match, at **Halifax**, was not ridden until almost two months later. When it was, Sanders and Phil Herne had both been struck down by flu and Phil Crump was a non-starter. Halifax's own Mick McKeon made his debut in the series with Leicester's Mike Farrell. Shirra, Boulger, Guglielmi and Ross joined them. England paraded a watered-down northern-flavoured side. Phil Collins, Ian Cartwright and Steve Bastable, with Joe Owen being named as reserve, partnered John Davis, Reg Wilson and Kenny Carter. Even so, the Lions were too strong for the depleted Australasians, and, but for an impressive display from Shirra, the result may have been embarrassing for the visitors,

ENGLAND 68: J. Davis 15, R. Wilson 14, K. Carter 14, I. Cartwright 10, S. Bastable 9, P. Collins 6, J. Owen dnr.

AUSTRALASIA 40: M. Shirra 15, L. Ross 8, M. Farrell 8, M. McKeon 7, J. Boulger 1, G. Guglielmi 1.

CHAPTER 6

THE EIGHTIES

AUSTRALIA v YOUNG ENGLAND TEST SERIES 1981/82

1ˢᵗ Test	Perth	Nov 27ᵗʰ	'81	Aust 54	Eng 54	D
2ⁿᵈ Test	Mildura	Dec 13ᵗʰ	'81	Aust 54	Eng 54	D
3ʳᵈ Test	Liverpool	Dec 19ᵗʰ	'81	Aust 41	Eng 66	W
4ᵗʰ Test	Newcastle	Dec 20ᵗʰ	'81	Aust 59	Eng 49	L
5ᵗʰ Test	Brisbane	Jan 9ᵗʰ	'82	Aust 46	Eng 62	W

England win series 2-1 with two Tests drawn

By the time touring recommenced in the winter of 1981, there had been changes in world speedway. Ivan Mauger had officially become the greatest speedway rider ever, by winning the World Championship for a record breaking sixth time in 1979. Michael Lee had ended Ivan's reign the following year (when Billy Sanders finished in third place), and American Bruce Penhall was the current World Champion. Penhall was one of the many flamboyant Yanks who had invaded the British League over the previous few years, and the USA were now a major power in World Speedway. Ole Olsen had also bred a fine crop of young Danish riders, and Denmark too had emerged as major players in world speedway. The USA and the Danes were now England's biggest rivals, and both were worthy of annual Test Series in Britain. England had peaked in 1980, winning the World Pairs Championship, the World Team Cup Championship and the Individual

World Championship, but, sadly, Australia had slipped from world prominence.

England therefore assembled a team of youngsters to tour Australia in the winter of 1981/82 for a five-match Test Series. They were to tour under the name of Young England, and this was given full approval by the British Control Board. John Davis and Alan Grahame, at twenty-seven were the oldest members in the England camp, and also returning to Australia was Phil Collins. Phil brought with him the youngest brother of the Collins' dynasty, twenty-year-old Neil from Edinburgh. Phil's Cradley teammate, Alan Grahame, also took a younger brother with him, as twenty-four-year-old Birmingham rider Andy Grahame joined the party. Twenty-year-old Kevin Smith from Poole Pirates was taking his first look at Australia, and twenty-year-old Kenny Carter completed the side.

Carter, in no time flat, had established himself as England's new number one rider, finishing fourth in the 1981 classic World Final at Wembley, and winning the British League Riders Championship at Belle Vue. At the end of the British season, only World Champion Penhall headed Kenny in the BL riders' averages. Carter had quickly developed into an immensely talented rider, with a heart as big as a bucket, but, unfortunately, he had the mouth to match it. Pint-sized Kenny was a blunt Yorkshireman who was just as aggressive off-track as he was on it. His caustic comments had upset many during his short time in the sport, and a personal feud was developing between him and Bruce Penhall.

Kenny hated the Americans, and he hated the Danes and the Swedes. He even hated the French – and they didn't even ride speedway. He was brash, he was arrogant, he was obnoxious – he was Kenny Carter – he was great. A week before the opening Test, Carter won the 'King of Claremont' at Perth with a stunning 24-point maximum.

The Aussies had little new to offer. Crump and Sanders were still two of the world's finest, but Titman had not been so impressive in Britain, and Leicester had transfer-listed him at the end of the 1981 season.

For the first Test, at **Perth**, Glyn Taylor, Les Sawyer, Gary Guglielmi and Clayton Isbel joined the three aforementioned riders. The Australians had more experience, but the young Lions made up for that with sheer determination, and the blend made for a sensational match. The Lions, once again managed by Nigel Boocock, took an early advantage with two maximum heat wins in the second and third races, but Sanders and Sawyer headed Andy Grahame home in heat 6, and the Aussies began to claw their way back into the match. Another 5-1 in heat 12 saw the Roos take the lead for the first time, but Alan Grahame and John Davis put the Lions back ahead in heat 14. A nail-biting finish saw Australia needing a 5-1 in the final heat to win the match, but some last lap heroics by Andy Grahame saw him split race-winner Guglielmi and Phil Crump, to force a draw for England. Amid all of the action, Kenny Carter again showed his liking for the Claremont circuit by coasting to a majestic 18-point maximum.

AUSTRALIA 54: B. Sanders 14, G. Taylor 12, P. Crump 9, G. Guglielmi 9, L. Sawyer 8, J. Titman 2, C. Isbel 0.

ENGLAND 54: K. Carter 18, J. Davis 12, Andy Grahame 10, Alan Grahame 9, P. Collins 3, K. Smith 1, N. Collins 1.

The second Test took place in **Mildura** and the Aussies retained only Crump, Sanders and Titman, and recalled John Boulger, Danny Kennedy and brought in Rod North and Terry Tulloch. After 18 heats, the teams were again deadlocked. Crump hit top form, and this time it was he who was unbeaten. Kennedy and Sanders were also superb. But apart from these three, Australia lacked the steam. England, on the other hand had more strength in depth, but without the big scorers, it served only to even things out.

AUSTRALIA 54: P. Crump 18, D. Kennedy 16, B. Sanders 11, J. Titman 5, R. North 3, T. Tulloch 1, J. Boulger 0.

ENGLAND 54: P. Collins 13, K. Carter 11, Alan Grahame 11, Andy Grahame 6, N. Collins 6, J. Davis 4, K. Smith 3.

At **Liverpool**, England at last made a breakthrough. Ironically Australia put out their best team so far, but Crump had one of his worst internationals ever, and Danny Kennedy failed to score. For England, Carter was back to his magnificent best, and skipper John Davis had his best match to date. The result was a comfortable win for Young England, who broke the stalemate and took the lead in the series.

AUSTRALIA 41: B. Sanders 10, G. Guglielmi 10, P. Herne 7, J. Titman 7, P. Crump 6, D. Mills 1, D. Kennedy 0.

ENGLAND 66: K. Carter 18, J. Davis 15, Andy Grahame 11, Alan Grahame 9, P. Collins 8, N. Collins 4, K. Smith 1.

The Aussies hit back immediately at **Newcastle** the following night. With John Davis and Alan Grahame being plagued with problems, Australia took full advantage.

AUSTRALIA 59: P. Crump 13, B. Sanders 11, J. Titman 11, G. Guglielmi 11, P. Herne 7, D. Kennedy 5, R. Blackadder 1.

ENGLAND 49: K. Carter 12, Andy Grahame 12, Alan Grahame 8, P. Collins 8, J. Davis 6, N. Collins 2, K. Smith 1.

What followed was the usual crop of problems that had threatened to ruin tours many times in the past. The fifth match, scheduled for Boxing Day in Canberra was hit by rain, and the local promotor promptly rearranged the match for the following day. However, Crump and Kennedy were appearing in a World Championship qualifying round, and the Australian Control Board refused to recognise the meeting, which England won 59–49. The Fifth and final Test was therefore ridden at **Brisbane** on 9 January, but matters had put further tours in jeopardy.

Gary Guglielmi was an unlikely hero, top scoring for the Aussies in his finest international performance. But England were not about to be denied twice, and put on a superb team performance. As Crump again failed to make an impression, this time it was the Lions' turn to take advantage, no one more so than Carter who roared to his third maximum of the series to collect the Ashes for Young England. Unbeknown to anyone at the time, the tour was the last official England tour of Australia to date.

AUSTRALIA 46: G. Guglielmi 15, B. Sanders 11, P. Crump 7, D. Kennedy 5, N. Coddington 5, J. Titman 3, S. Koppe 0.

ENGLAND 62: K. Carter 18, Alan Grahame 15, Andy Grahame 11, J. Davis 9, P. Collins 6, K. Smith 2, N. Collins 1.

So, the training had been completed successfully, and the young Lions had been triumphant, but, in reality, the mighty England had had their day. They still had a crop of veritable world-class riders, but the charismatic Americans had captured the British public's imagination, and were beginning to match England in Britain. The Danes continued to progress, and would soon have a monopoly on world speedway that had previously not been seen, as Erik Gundersen, Hans Nielsen and Jan Pedersen would rule world speedway with an iron fist.

England suffered a huge blow when Mike Lee went errant. In the early part of the eighties, when he still had so much more to give, young Lee went off the rails and got into all sorts of trouble, and for some time, he was even banned from the sport. Missed meetings, motoring offences and drug offences saw the flawed genius eventually retire from speedway, and thus was lost one of the greatest-ever English riders. If Michael Lee had stayed on the straight and narrow, he would have been remembered as the greatest English rider of all time.

Australia suffered too, even more tragically. In 1985, Australian Champion Billy Sanders, who was at that time back at Ipswich, took his own life. The thirty-year-old was found in woodlands, close to Foxhall Heath, in a friend's car with a length of tubing running from the exhaust to the inside of the vehicle.

ENGLAND v AUSTRALASIA TEST SERIES 1985

1st Test	King's Lynn	July 23rd	'85	Eng 71	Aust 37	W
2nd Test	Oxford	July 26th	'85	Eng 69	Aust 38	W
3rd Test	Halifax	Sept 15th	'85	Eng 53	Aust 55	L

England win series 2-1

In 1985, after suffering defeats at the hands of the USA and Denmark, England needed a confidence boosting Test Series, and, once again, Australasia was reborn, for a three-match series in Britain. Time had moved on, and only Crump, Ross and Shirra remained of the previous Australasian team. Australia supplied twenty-nine-year-old Rod Hunter from Halifax, twenty-six-year-old Steve Regeling from King's Lynn, twenty-two-year-old Steve Baker, also from Lynn and twenty-year-old Dave Cheshire from Wolverhampton. Twenty-three-year-old 'Coventry Kiwi' Dave Bargh completed the side.

England didn't put out their strongest side. The old guard of Carter, Morton, Simmons, Davis and the Collins brothers were all left out in order to give the youngsters a chance to shine. In fact, only Dave Jessup was left in the squad, the reason being that the first Test was being held on his home track at **King's Lynn**. Neil Collins was Dave's partner and England's latest protégé, Coventry rider Kelvin Tatum was the Lions' second heat leader, being partnered by King's Lynn's twenty-six-year-old Richard Knight. Ipswich rider, Jeremy Doncaster and Belle Vue's nineteen-year-old firebrand, Andy Smith, completed the main body of the team. Cradley's twenty-year-old Simon Cross and Oxford's twenty-one-year-old Marvyn Cox were England's two reserves.

Richard Knight was an early casualty, when Lynn teammate Steve Regeling sent him crashing in heat 11, and Richard was forced to withdraw from the meeting with double vision and a severe headache. Even so, the Anzacs were disappointing opposition for the Lions. The rapidly improving Tatum scored his first (paid) maximum for England and Doncaster dropped his only point to Australasian skipper Regeling. With Simon Cross proving to be a splendid reserve for the home side, the visitors were never in it. Dave Jessup put on a superb display in his 106th (and last) match for England.

ENGLAND 71: K. Tatum 17, J. Doncaster 17, D. Jessup 15, S. Cross 9, A. Smith 7, R. Knight 5, N. Collins 1.

AUSTRALASIA 37: P. Crump 9, S. Regeling 8, L. Ross 6, R. Hunter 6, M. Shirra 5, D. Bargh 2, D. Cheshire 1, S. Baker 0.

The Australasians changed their reserves for the second Test, at **Oxford**, as the twenty-seven-year-old Aussie from National League Poole, Stan Bear, was brought into the team along with teammate Ray Dole. England made two changes as Jessup and Neil Collins were dropped in favour of home rider, Simon Wigg and John Davis. As a spectacle, the match was a non-event caused by the Anzacs reluctance to race. Crump again failed to get going, and their other big gun, Larry Ross, failed to score a point. Once again Tatum made great strides in his international career, dropping his only point to Mitch Shirra, and his partnership with young Smithy dropped only 3 points to the opposition in six outings. The home rider, Simon Wigg, was robbed of a maximum only by an engine failure in heat 17.

ENGLAND 69: K. Tatum 17, S. Wigg 15, A. Smith 10, R. Knight 10, N. Collins 9, J. Davis 5, S. Cross 2, M. Cox 1.

AUSTRALASIA 38: P. Crump 9, M. Shirra 9, R. Hunter 9, D. Bargh 7, S. Regeling 3, R. Dole 1, L. Ross 0, S. Bear 0.

The third Test, at **Halifax,** was not staged until 15 September, and by that time, England had failed miserably in the World Team Cup Final in Long Beach USA. The meeting had been an intriguing clash of the home side and Denmark, which the Danes won, but third placed England had scored only 13 points.

The Lions tracked Tatum, Smith, Knight, Neil Collins and John Davis, and, with the series already won, they bought in new blood, in the form of twenty-year-old Carl Blackbird, twenty-four-year-old Peter Carr and twenty-one-year-old Neil Evitts. Despite losing Crump with an ankle injury after three rides, the Australasians fought for every point. England lost Evitts with a foot injury in heat 8, and despite a brilliant maximum from Tatum, the Lions never led throughout the match. They looked set to, when Davis was winning heat 16, but an engine failure put paid to that. However, they had still drawn level by the last heat. But Shirra denied Steve Collins, and Baker, surprisingly, held Knight at the back for the Aussies to score a match-winning 4-2.

ENGLAND 53: K. Tatum 17, A. Smith 12, J. Davis 8, N. Collins 7, P. Carr 4, R. Knight 3, N. Evitts 2, C. Blackbird 0.

AUSTRALASIA 55: L. Ross 13, D. Bargh 13, R. Hunter 10, M. Shirra 10, S. Regeling 4, S. Baker 3, P. Crump 2.

As Denmark continued to rule world speedway, they became the focus of England's attention for the next few years, along with America, as the British public lost interest in Australia. Phil Crump retired from British racing at the end of the 1986 season, as the last truly great Australian rider at that time. However, all was not lost for the Aussies. Although they were not enjoying a high profile in the British League, the National League held the key to the Aussies' future, as riders such as Troy Butler, Craig Boyce, Leigh Adams and Todd Wiltshire all began to make a name for themselves.

Australia had suffered an awful blow with the death of Billy Sanders in 1985, but the following year, it was England's turn. On 21 May 1986, Kenny Carter murdered his wife with a shotgun and then turned the weapon on himself, taking his own life. Not only had England lost their number one rider, but also world speedway had lost one of its most charismatic characters.

1987 saw the Aussies say goodbye to some of their legends as Dickie Case, Arthur Payne, Lionel Van Praag and the great Jack Young all passed away.

A loose connection remained between England and Australia, as English riders continued to tour Australia in the winter. The 1987/88 tourists called themselves the Young Lions, and were led by Gary Havelock and Paul Thorpe. They won a seven-match Test Series against Australia by 5-2, but Crumpie was the top scorer in the series.

The following year, there was a marathon nine-match Test Series between an Australia Select side and an England Select side. The English team featured Kelvin Tatum and Jeremy Doncaster, but although Crump only made one appearance in the series, the visitors did not have things all their own way and won the series by only one match.

In the winter of 1989/90, the tourists took out one of their best unofficial squads – featuring Tatum, Doncaster, Havelock, Paul Thorp and Steve Schofield – and the Aussies hammered them 5-1, with one match drawn. Crump rode in every match and showed that he was still a match for anyone in his own country, but the Aussies success was not just down to him. There was an 18-point maximum from eighteen-year-old Leigh Adams at Adelaide, there was an 18-point maximum from twenty-year-old Todd Wiltshire at Newcastle and young Mick Poole scored 16 points at Paramatta – the Aussies were evolving again.

CHAPTER 7

THE NINETIES

There were no more matches between the legendary rivals until 1991 when a three-team Test Series in Britain between the rapidly emerging Sweden, Australia and England was staged. The three-match series was won by Sweden from runners-up England. It was still early days for the new Australia, although they did visit Poland and win a three-match series over there.

By the early nineties, the Danish reign of terror was all but over. Erik Gundersen and Jan Pedersen had retired through injury, and Hans Nielsen stood alone as the last Great Dane. Although the Americans were still feisty opponents, a Test Series against the Danes was no longer viable, and England needed new opponents. They challenged Australia in 1992, to a three-match Test Series.

ENGLAND v AUSTRALIA TEST SERIES 1992

1st Test	Oxford	April 10th	'92	Eng 73	Aust 35	W
2nd Test	Reading	June 15th	'92	Eng 55	Aust 53	W
3rd Test	Peterborough	July 5th	'92	Eng 49	Aust 59	L

England win series 2-1

The Aussies got off to a bad start when Troy Butler picked up an injury prior to the series, and Mick Poole and Jason Lyons had club matches on the same night as the first Test, at **Oxford**. They were already without Todd Wiltshire, who had broken his pelvis the previous

269

winter in Australia. However, they still had their best asset in Swindon's Leigh Adams, and, together with the two-time Australian Champion – Eastbourne's Glen Doyle – and the current Australian Champion from Oxford, twenty-four-year-old Craig Boyce, he completed the Australian heat leader trio. They were paired with the experienced Steve Regeling, young Shane Parker and Mark Carlson. Tony Langdon and Tony O'Brien were the reserves.

England managers Eric Boocock and Colin Pratt took the opportunity to try out some of the England youngsters. Dean Barker was brought in to partner his friend and Oxford teammate, Martin Dugard. Twenty-one-year-old Mark Loram was paired with home rider Marvyn Cox, and twenty-two-year-old Chris Louis partnered skipper Gary Havelock. The Lions' reserves were nineteen-year-old Dave Norris and Dean Standing.

England began with a 5-1 and never let up on their depleted opponents. Parker, Adams and Boyce were the only three Aussie riders to compete against the Lions, who were led by Dugard with an 18-point maximum on his home track.

ENGLAND 73: M. Dugard 18, G. Havelock 14, M. Cox 11, D. Barker 10, C. Louis 9, M. Loram 7, D. Standing 3, D. Norris 1.

AUSTRALIA 35: L. Adams 11, S. Parker 10, C. Boyce 9, G. Doyle 2, M. Carlson 2, S. Regeling 1, T. O'Brien 0. T. Langdon 0.

At **Reading**, Boocock and Pratt stayed with their youth policy for the second Test. Havelock was replaced by Jeremy Doncaster, Loram and Louis were retained, and home riders Dave Mullett and Ray Morton joined Andy Smith to make up the Lions' top six. Dean Barker was dropped to reserve with Dean Standing.

The Aussies looked a much fitter outfit with the return of Troy Butler. Boyce Parker and Adams were the visitors' heat leaders, with twenty-two-year-old birthday boy Jason Lyons, and Peterborough's Steven Davies joining Butler as the second strings. Shane Bowes and Dave Cheshire were the reserves. England lost Andy Smith in a heat 4 crash that left him badly shaken with a cut eye. Dean Barker stood in for Smith in heat 11, and he too was a casualty as he was involved in a three-man pile-up that saw him taken to hospital with a suspected broken arm.

By the interval, Leigh Adams was unbeaten, and England had only a 4-point lead. Local hero Dave Mullett got the better of Leigh in heat 10, and was the only rider to do so all night. But the Lions were unable to increase their lead until Mullet and Doncaster scored a maximum heat win in heat 15. When Butler and Parker hit back for the visitors in the penultimate heat, it meant a last heat decider, and Ray Morton got the biggest cheer of the night when he split winner Boyce and Bowes, to give England a 2-point win. Reading riders Mullett and Morton, who were both making their full England debuts, won the match, and the Ashes, for the Lions.

ENGLAND 55: D. Mullett 14, M. Loram 12, R. Morton 11, C. Louis 6, J. Doncaster 6, D. Barker 3, D. Standing 2, A. Smith 1.

AUSTRALIA 53: L. Adams 17, C. Boyce 13, T. Butler 11, S. Parker 7, S. Bowes 4, J. Lyons 1, S. Davies 0, D. Cheshire 0.

The final Test took place at Second Division **Peterborough**, and Australian manager Neil Street made only one change, replacing Shane Bowes with home rider Mick Poole. England retained Loram and Louis, recalled Dugard and Havelock, placed Norris and Barker at reserve and brought in Wolves rider Grahame Jones and Bradford's twenty-two-year-old Sean 'the Prawn' Wilson.

The Aussies, led for the first time by skipper Mick Poole, came to fight. And, even though Martin Dugard broke the Alwalton track record in the opening heat, by heat 4, Australia led by 4 points. The match quickly developed into a no-holds barred contest that saw some torrid first bend action. Heat 8 was typical of this, as both Dugard and Lyons refused to give an inch. The resulting crash saw both teams lose a rider for the rest of the match. With Chris Louis suffering from tonsillitis, it left England virtually as a six-man team, with their reserves unable to fill the gaps. Australia on the other hand had Peterborough's top rider Steven Davies at reserve, and when he stepped in for Lyons, the Aussies pulled away to record a famous win.

ENGLAND 49: S. Wilson 12, G. Havelock 12, M. Loram 10, M. Dugard 5, G. Jones 4, C. Louis 4, D. Norris 2, D. Barker 0.

AUSTRALIA 59: L. Adams 13, C. Boyce 12, S. Parker 11, M. Poole 10, S. Davies 5, T. Butler 5, J. Lyons 3, D. Cheshire 0.

Although the Aussies had lost the series, they had won a match, and won it convincingly and deservedly. England certainly did not field its strongest side in any of the three matches, choosing to give their young-sters a chance. Even so, Australia were the younger side in all three Tests, and they were without one of their top riders, Todd Wiltshire. A specta-tor at the match was the Peterborough reserve, sixteen-year-old Aussie Jason Crump, the son of Phil Crump. What he wouldn't give to ride for Australia.

ENGLAND v AUSTRALIA TEST SERIES 1995

1st Test	Poole	Aug 23rd	'95	Eng 58	Aust 50	W
2nd Test	Sheffield	Aug 24th	'95	Eng 35	Aust 73	L
3rd Test	King's Lynn	Oct 21st	'95	Eng 49	Aust 59	L

Australia win series 2-1

Young Crumpie did get his chance, but not until 1995. By that time, he was a star in the British Premier League with Poole, and was also the current World Under-21 Champion. With Boyce and Adams, both having improved, and twenty-year-old Ryan Sullivan making a name for himself in Britain, Australia were now considered to be of sufficient strength seriously to take on England in Britain. It was a time of change in world speedway, with the introduction of the Grand Prix that same year, and Craig Boyce had been the only Aussie regular in the inaugural series, finishing eleventh overall.

A three-match series was arranged between the two great rivals, and the first match was staged at **Poole** in August. England were at a disad-vantage from the off, being without Mark Loram and Martin Dugard, but they still had skipper John Louis and Gary Havelock. Since the teams last met, twenty-two-year-old Joe Screen had become an England regular and he currently headed the Premier League riders' averages. He took his place alongside Sean Wilson, Paul Thorp and ex-Pirate Steve Schofield. Alun Rossiter and Ben How were the England reserves.

Australia were also understrength, being without the services of Sullivan, but Crump, Boyce and Adams were a powerful spearhead, and Shane Parker, Jason Lyons and Mick Poole were more than useful second-strings. However, England took an early lead when Crump spluttered to a halt in heat 2, and two races later, Boyce took a knock that left him in third place. It gave England an 8-point cushion to take into the interval, but Crump and Boyce fought like tigers to pull the deficit back to 4 points after heat 13. Apart from his engine failure, Crump dropped only 1 point to Joe Screen, and, apart from his third place, Boycie won his other five races. But Adams had an awful night and his two points handed the match to England on a plate.

ENGLAND 58: C. Louis 14, J. Screen 11, S. Schofield 10, G. Havelock 9, P. Thorp 8, S. Wilson 6, A. Rossiter dnr, B. How dnr.

AUSTRALIA 50: C. Boyce, 16, P. Crump 14, S. Parker 8, M. Poole 4, S. Bowes 4, L. Adams 2, J. Lyons 1, G. Bartlett 1.

Twenty-four hours later, Dugard was back in the England team at **Sheffield**, and Schofield dropped down to reserve with twenty-three-year-old Carl Stonehewer. Chris Louis was riding in a league match at Ipswich, and home rider Neil Collins took his place. Australia kept the same team, but they didn't ride like the same team. The Aussies consistently out-gated, out-raced and outclassed the Lions to establish a new record win on British soil. A sadly out of touch Martin Dugard was replaced after only two outings, but reserve Schofield was unable to repeat his impressive Poole performance. Only Thorp beat Boyce, and Crump was beaten only by Havelock, and although England's performance bordered on the pathetic, at least it set the series up for an intriguing last match decider.

ENGLAND 35: P. Thorp 9, J. Screen 9, G. Havelock 9, N. Collins 6, S. Wilson 2, M. Dugard 0, S. Schofield 0, C. Stonehewer 0.

AUSTRALIA 73: C. Boyce 17, J. Crump 16, L. Adams 12, M. Poole 11, J. Lyons 10, S. Parker 7, S. Bowes dnr, G. Bartlett dnr.

The final Test was not staged until the end of October, and, by that time, Hans Nielsen had won the first ever Grand Prix series, to become World Champion for the fourth time. On the eve of the deciding match, the Aussies fired a warning shot in the Premier League Riders Championship at Swindon, when Adams and Crump jointly topped the scorers. With the meeting being decided by a run-off between the top 4 scorers, neither won the title, but both had made an impact.

Australia welcomed Sullivan into the team at **King's Lynn**, but they were dealt a devastating blow when, a few days prior to the meeting, Craig Boyce fell at Exeter and broke his hand, nullifying any advantage that Sullivan may have given them. Shane Bowes was replaced at reserve by twenty-four-year-old Steve Johnson from Long Eaton.

The original date for the match was set for the 22 October, but for one reason or another, it was pulled forward by a day. This played havoc with England team manager John Louis' plans. The rescheduled date meant that Dugard was not available. John already had to juggle riders around with Screen, Dean Barker and David Norris being injured. However, the BSPA did not help matters. Mark Loram had missed the last two matches for his current club Exeter, to ride abroad, and he was therefore not chosen to represent his country. High principles indeed – but this was not the time for high principles. World Longtrack Champion Kelvin Tatum was recalled to the team as the third heat leader alongside Havelock and Chris Louis, and Thorp Schofield and Andy Smith were their partners. Twenty-year-old Paul Hurry of Arena Essex made his debut at reserve, with Sean Wilson.

When Chris Louis beat the Saddlebow Road track record in heat 4, England had a 4-point lead, but Adams and Sullivan hit back with a maximum heat win in heat over Thorp and Havelock. The hapless England pairing were the victims of another 5-1 at the hands of Lyons and Parker two races later, and the Aussies took a 4-point lead. The Lions rallied briefly, but when their top performer Louis suffered an engine failure in heat 11, it left Lyons and Parker to score maximum points again. The only disappointment on the Australian side was skipper Mick Poole, who failed to score on a sick bike in his farewell meeting. The remainder of the team rode as though their very lives depended upon it, and the result was a 10-point win for the Australians, who won the Ashes for the first time in seventeen years.

ENGLAND 49: K. Tatum 15, C. Louis 14, P. Thorp 8, G. Havelock 5, S. Schofield 4, A. Smith 3, P. Hurry 0, S. Wilson dnr.

AUSTRALIA 59: J. Crump 16, J. Lyons 12, L. Adams 12, S. Parker 10, R. Sullivan 8, S. Johnson 1, M. Poole 0, G. Bartlett dnr.

Speedway had become, very much a journeyman's sport. All of the top riders were professional, and had been for many years, and they rode regularly in Poland, Denmark, Sweden and anywhere else they could get a booking during the speedway season. It meant of course that re-scheduled matches were a constant headache, with riders having a diary full of bookings from the very start of the season. The situation was very unpopular with the British promoters, but it was how the riders made their living, and they had only eight months of the year in which to do it.

England had been having a slim time of late. Gary Havelock had won the World Championship in 1992, but since the team's World Team Cup victory in 1989, they had enjoyed limited success, and some of their subsequent performances in the event had been an embarrassment. They were often criticised for lacking commitment, and certainly very few riders seemed to be prepared to drop everything in order to ride for England. England still had world-class riders, but they lacked the fire of Peter Collins, Mike Lee and Kenny Carter. Loram was the closest rider that they had to either, but a slap on the wrist had seen him excluded from the team in 1995, when he may well have reversed the result.

Kelvin Tatum had officially ruled himself out of the 1995 British speedway season, to concentrate on his Longtrack commitments, and in fact had ridden only seven league matches at the time of the final Test, and yet he had been top scorer for the Lions.

All of this only served to highlight the performance of the Australians. A completely new crop of riders had emerged who were young, exciting, determined and totally committed. The parallels were there to compare them to their early predecessors. Adams was the new Vic Huxley. He rode a bike like he was sitting in an armchair, totally at ease, but with a chilling control over his machine. Boyce was the new Lionel Van Praag – class personified. Sullivan was an early day Bluey Wilkinson – the master of the power that could take him around three opponents in one bend. Jason Crump was the new Max Grosskreutz – the warrior. Crumpie had come from good stock. Father Phil had achieved so much in his career, and his grandfather, Neil Street, having also enjoyed an illustrious speedway career, was now his Australian team manager. Jason had come a long way in such a short time. Yes, he was Grosskreutz, but he could also become Huxley, Van Praag and Wilkinson all rolled into one. These were exciting days for Australia. They were back – in a big way.

ENGLAND v AUSTRALIA TEST SERIES 1996

1st Test	Hull	June 12th	'96	Eng 55	Aust 41	W
2nd Test	Poole	July 3rd	'96	Eng 48	Aust 48	D
3rd Test	Wolverhampton	July 15th	'96	Eng 54	Aust 42	W

England win series 2-0 with 1 match drawn

A further three-match Test Series was instigated in the 1996 season, but the first match at Hull proved to be ill-timed for Australia. Leigh Adams was recovering from a broken collarbone, and Ryan Sullivan had been struck down by tonsillitis, leaving the Roos in a state of depletion. For the first time, the matches were being run on the Premier League match formula, which meant that seven man teams contested 16 heats, with the reserves having compulsory rides. Boyce, Parker, Crump, Lyons and Johnson were all fit, and Tony Langdon and Shane Bowes completed the Aussie seven.

England were at full strength, fielding Havelock, Dugard, Louis, Loram, Screen and Tatum, with Paul Thorp at reserve. On paper, it looked one sided, but the Lions were given an early jolt when Boyce and Parker stormed home ahead of Havelock and Dugard in the opening heat. Thorp and Tatum quickly levelled the scores in the following race, but Lyons and Crump hit back with another maximum heat win over Loram and Louis in heat 3. However England battled gamely and, by heat 10, they led by 2 points.

Crump and Lyons had been unbeaten as a pairing up until then but, in that tenth heat, Lyons fell, and it all began to go wrong for the Aussies. Craig Boyce had dropped only 1 point at the halfway stage, but in his remaining three rides he scored only 1 point. This resulted in England increasing their lead to win the match by 14 points, as Crump bowed out with a broken chain in the final heat. Havelock and Dugard were well below par, but the Lions had the match winner in reserve Thorp.

ENGLAND 55: J. Screen 12, P. Thorp 11, C. Louis, 8, M. Loram, 8, K. Tatum 8, G. Havelock 4, M. Dugard 4.

AUSTRALIA 41: J. Lyons 11, J. Crump 10, C. Boyce 6, S. Parker 5, S. Johnson 3, S. Langdon 3, S. Bowes 3.

Adams and Sullivan returned for the second Test, at **Poole**, as Langdon and Johnson made way for them. England made only one change with Wimbourne Road specialist Steve Schofield replacing Thorp at reserve.

In front of Sky Sports television cameras, the two teams put on a display of riveting speedway. As in the first Test, the Aussies opened with a 5-1, only for England to draw back level in the following heat. The Lions were unfortunate to lose Havelock in a heat 6 crash, and the visitors began to establish control of the match, taking a 4-point lead. However, this was television, and a 5-1 by Dugard and Schofield in heat 8, over Parker and Bowes saw the scores level at the halfway stage.

When the match resumed, Australia quickly established a 4-point lead. But again England fought back to level the scores with one race remaining. Louis and Dugard faced a daunting task as they lined up against Adams and the unbeaten Boyce. The Lions' task was made even tougher when Dugard touched the tapes and was excluded, and when his replacement Schofield shot right through them, it left only Chris Louis to face the formidable Aussie pairing. In a grandstand finish, Louis ruined Boyce's maximum, as he heroically led the two Aussies home to rescue England, and draw the match.

There could be no excuses. Australia had the match under control at one stage, and let it go. Crump was still recovering from a wrist injury, and after winning his first three races, he was pointless in his last two, and Jason Lyons struggled with a sick bike all night. But that should not detract from a fine performance by England, who had lost Havelock at a critical time in the match.

ENGLAND 48: J. Screen 12, K. Tatum 9, C. Louis 8, M. Dugard 7, M. Loram 6, S. Schofield 6, G. Havelock 0.

AUSTRALIA 48: C. Boyce 14, L. Adams 11, J. Crump 9, R. Sullivan 8, S. Parker 3, J. Lyons 3, S. Bowes 0.

Once again, in front of the Sky cameras, speedway gave itself a massive shot in the arm, as the two teams served up a veritable feast of overtaking and first rate racing in the final Test match, at **Wolverhampton**. Australia replaced the injured Shane Parker with Steve Johnson, and England recalled Paul Thorp to replace Havelock. With Kelvin Tatum also injured, young Ben Howe was given another chance at reserve.

An engine failure by Thorp allowed the Kangaroos to take an early lead, but sheer determination and skill saw the England riders power their way from behind to take the lead by heat 5. It was a lead that they never relinquished, as time and time again the Lions brought the Monmore crowd to its feet with their overtaking exploits. The Aussies were left needing maximum heat wins in the final two races to draw the match, and they looked set to do it in the penultimate heat when Lyons and Adams shot from the tapes. However Martin Dugard typified England's performance, as he rounded Adams and shot inside Lyons to win the match, and the Ashes, for the home team.

It had been England's finest performance for many a year, silencing their increasing throng of critics. There was no lack of effort, there was no lack of team spirit, and they were the better team on the day. The Aussies too played their part in making the series such a success, as they never stopped fighting, even when victory was beyond their grasp. The spirit, in which the series had been contested, was a throwback to the early days, when they were the two most powerful speedway nations on earth.

As the season closed, American Billy Hamill became the new World Champion. Australia now had three Grand Prix riders in Adams, Boyce and Crump, and Crump became the first Australian rider to win a Grand Prix, when he was victorious at Hackney in the British Grand Prix at the end of August.

ENGLAND v AUSTRALIA TEST SERIES 1997

1st Test	Belle Vue	July 11th	'97	Eng 52	Aust 44	W
2nd Test	Swindon	Sept 14th	'97	Eng 42	Aust 54	L
3rd Test	Eastbourne	Oct 19th	'97	Eng 43	Aust 53	L

Australia win series 2-1

Team manager Neil Street attempted to give Australia a boost by including Todd Wiltshire in the 1997 Test Series. Wiltshire had been one of the top Australian riders in the early part of the decade, finishing third in the 1990 World Final. A bad crash in the 1992 Australian Final left him with back and thigh injuries, and he appeared to be lost to the sport forever. However, Todd began riding again in the winter of 1996, and expressed a wish to resume his career in Britain. Bradford attempted to sign him for the 1997 season, but as he had not competed in the 1997 Australian Championship, he had been refused a work permit. That left Street with only eight first-division riders in Britain, and as Steve Johnson was on World Longtrack duty, the Australian team virtually picked itself for the first Test at **Belle Vue** for forty-five years. The only new face in the Roos' line-up was young Mark Lemon at reserve, who was having an impressive season with Poole.

John Louis, by this time, had a great respect for the Australian team, and exercised caution with his selection of the England team. He went for experience over youth, as British Champion Mark Loram, Overseas Champion Kelvin Tatum, and Grand Prix rider and son Chris Louis, led the Lions. Joe Screen and Martin Dugard made up the top five, as Dean Barker and Gary Havelock took the reserve berths.

The two teams again served up a helping of splendid speedway in a match in which England always had the upper hand. They had greater strength in depth than their opponents as was shown by the fact that Gary Havelock was down at reserve. Gary was still suffering from the back injury that he had collected in the previous year's Test Series, and was far from at his best, but, even so, there was no other speedway nation on earth that could have boasted a rider of his standing at reserve. Joe Screen was resplendent in a set of Union Jack leathers, and only Boyce, in the final heat, robbed him of a paid maximum. Crump had a painful night, taking a couple of nasty tumbles, but a failure by Leigh Adams to get going lost Australia the match.

ENGLAND 52: C. Louis 13, J. Screen 12, M. Loram 8, M. Dugard 7, G. Havelock 5, D. Barker 5, K. Tatum 2.

AUSTRALIA 44: C. Boyce 12, P. Crump 9, J. Lyons 6, R. Sullivan 5, M. Lemon 5, S. Parker 4, L. Adams 3.

Before the second Test, at **Eastbourne**, the Aussies cleaned up in the Intercontinental Final in Sweden with Sullivan, Crump and Boyce taking the first three places. But there was trouble brewing. The match at Eastbourne clashed with Ipswich's league match at Wolverhampton, and England manager John Louis gave son Chris the option of riding in either match. The other England riders were unhappy with this, accusing manager Louis of favouritism toward his son. The BSPA received a letter from Gary Havelock, and his Bradford teammates, Loram and Screen, calling for the resignation of Louis as team manager, and withdrawing their services from the England team unless this was implemented. With only days left before the meeting, the second Test match was cancelled.

It was therefore over two months before the second Test match was ridden, at **Swindon**. By that time, the rebels, after meetings with BSPA, had been brought into line, and John Louis still remained as team manager: for the time being at least. 'The Three' lined up with Chris Louis and Martin Dugard, and Paul Hurry was recalled as number six, with Ipswich's nineteen-year-old sensation Scott Nicholls making his debut at number seven.

The Aussies were without Shane Parker, but Steve Johnson returned to the side, and Neil Street had strategically placed him at reserve, which proved to be a match-winning move. Crump and Boyce were both ex-Swindon number one riders, and Adams was the current top Robin, so Australia were expected to do well at Blunsdon – and they did.

Joe Screen was the only English rider to beat Adams, and Jason Crump also scored double figures for the Roos. Sullivan had a poor night, and, after three outings, Steve Johnson, who was given six outings from which he scored 14 points, replaced him. Australia took an early lead and were 8 points up by the interval, with the match well under control, but England staged a revival in the second half, which saw them close the gap to 2 points with five heats remaining. However, Australia turned up the heat in the later stages to emerge as comfortable winners. One can only speculate as to the atmosphere in the England pits. The rebels had enjoyed mixed fortunes, with Loram staging some breathtaking manoeuvres, and Screen putting in his usual solid performance, but Gary Havelock was pointless.

ENGLAND 42: C. Louis 14, M. Loram 12, J. Screen 9, M. Dugard 4, S. Nicholls 2, P. Hurry 1, G. Havelock 0.

AUSTRALIA 54: S. Johnson 14, L. Adams 13, J. Crump 13, C. Boyce 6, J. Lyons 3, M. Lemon 3, R. Sullivan 2.

The Third, and deciding, Test was finally staged, at **Eastbourne**, in mid-October. The tight Arlington circuit was reckoned to suit the England team, and, as Australia were without Sullivan, an England win did seem to be on the cards. The Lions retained their top five, reinstated Nicholls as reserve, and recalled Davis Norris as their other reserve.

A huge crowd were left shaking their heads in disbelief as Australia roared to an 8-point lead after only 3 heats. Throughout the first half the visitors gave England a lesson in gating, and the Lions' trump card, Martin 'Mr Arlington' Dugard had yet to score a point in front of his home crowd. Martin blew a motor at the gate in his first outing, shed a primary chain on Dave Norris' spare bike in his second, and was left stranded at the gate aboard Mark Loram's steed in his third. With Havelock again struggling with his back injury, Dave Norris was a busy reserve for England. On his home track, Norris was superb, scoring paid 13 points from 6 outings.

By comparison, Australia were trouble-free. With Lemon having his best match so far for the Roos, they coasted to an easy victory and regained the Ashes.

ENGLAND 43: D. Norris 12, J. Screen 9, M. Loram 8, C. Louis 8, S. Nicholls 3, G. Havelock 3, M. Dugard 0.

AUSTRALIA 53: J. Lyons 11, J. Crump 10, L. Adams 10, M. Lemon 9, S. Parker 5, S. Johnson 4, C. Boyce.

ENGLAND v AUSTRALIA TEST SERIES 1998

1st Test	Wolverhampton	July 6th	'98	Eng 55	Aust 41	W
2nd Test	Eastbourne	Aug 1st	'98	Eng 56	Aust 40	W
3rd Test	King's Lynn	Aug 2nd	'98	Eng 37	Aust 59	L

England win series 2-1

Not surprisingly, England had a new team manager in 1998, as another ex-Lion, Dave Jessup, took up the appointment. If that suited Gary Havelock, then he suffered for it, as he was dropped from the team. Louis, Dugard, Loram and Screen were retained, and young Scotty Nicholls, who had shown great improvement during the season, was moved up into the main body of the team. Andy Smith was a somewhat surprise choice as first reserve, and Paul Hurry filled the final place.

Todd Wiltshire had arrived in Britain, one week prior to the first Test, at **Wolverhampton**, to take his place with Oxford for the rest of the season. However, with little time to get organised, he was not called up to ride for his country. The Aussies also received a major blow when Crump injured his ankle at Oxford a few days earlier, and he was a non-starter. Even so, they had a solid look about them with a top five of Lemon, Lyons, Sullivan, Boyce and Adams, and reserves Johnson and Parker.

The Aussies were, however, strangely subdued, with only Lemon and Parker showing any fire. By contrast, England had one of their better nights, with youngsters Nicholls and Hurry being especially impressive. With Lyons, Boyce and Sullivan scoring fewer than 10 points between them, the Roos were dead and buried.

ENGLAND 55: M. Loram 12, P. Hurry 12, C. Louis 11, S. Nicholls 10, J. Screen 5, A. Smith 3, M. Dugard 2.

AUSTRALIA 41: S. Parker 12, M. Lemon 9, L. Adams 8, C. Boyce 5, J. Lyons 3, R. Sullivan 2, S. Johnson 2.

For the second Test, at **Eastbourne**, Crump returned, and Johnson was rested. England, as usual, called up Dave Norris to ride on his home track, and the Second Division Riders Champion, twenty-three-year-old Glen Cunningham, was given an opportunity at reserve.

Australia looked ill at ease on an Arlington track made tricky by a downpour of rain. Mark Lemon fell twice, and Lyons and Parker both took heavy falls, as England capitalised by scoring maximum heat wins in three of the races in which there were fallers. Only Crump and Lemon, before his first fall, performed for the Roos, as the Lions swamped them. The victory meant that the Lions had retained the Ashes. The performances of Boyce and Sullivan prompted the question: 'Had the Aussie bubble burst?'

ENGLAND 56: M. Dugard 13, J. Screen 11, P. Hurry 10, C. Louis 8, D. Norris 8, M. Loram 5, G. Cunninhgham 1.

AUSTRALIA 40: J. Crump 14, J. Lyons 8, L. Adams 7, M. Lemon 5, S. Parker 3, R. Sullivan 2, C. Boyce 1.

What a difference a day makes. Twenty-fours hours later, the two teams met in the final Test, at **King's Lynn**. There were no changes to the Australian team. They only just about had time to refuel, let alone regroup. England replaced Norris with Hurry, and recalled Andy Smith to ride at reserve with Cunningham.

There was no doubt that the Aussies felt more at home on the wide open spaces of Saddlebow Road. Crump and Boyce opened proceedings with a maximum heat win over Louis and Hurry. England hit an early setback when they lost Loram in a heat-3 crash, and it gave Australia the impetus they needed. After nine heats, England had provided only three race winners, and trailed by 10 points. With the series already lost, the Roos were desperate to reestablish their credibility, and did so with chilling determination.

Crump stormed to a paid maximum; he and Boyce were beaten only once in the four races in which they were paired together. It was that race which cost Boyce a paid maximum as he shot back to top form. Sullivan was another Aussie who bore no resemblance to the rider the previous day at Eastbourne, as he, along with Adams, collected paid 11 points. It was all too much for the Lions who provided only a further two race winners in the remainder of the match, as Australia romped to a 22-point win.

ENGLAND 37: C. Louis 13, G. Cunningham 7, M. Dugard 7, J. Screen 5, A. Smith 3, P. Hurry 2, M. Loram 0.

AUSTRALIA 59: J. Crump 14, C. Boyce 11, L. Adams 10, R. Sullivan 10, S. Parker 6, J. Lyons 5, M. Lemon 3.

It was a strange series that had seen the best and the worst of Australia. The following week, Phil Crump visited Britain to see his son Jason ride in the British Grand Prix at Coventry, and was delighted to see his boy lift the British crown for the second year in succession. The year however belonged to Tony Rickardsson, who was the new World Champion. Ryan Sullivan was the highest-placed Australian, finishing in seventh place, one above Crumpie. Chris Louis was the highest placed Brit, finishing fifth.

ENGLAND v AUSTRALIA TEST SERIES 1999

1st Test	Belle Vue	June 11th	'99	Eng 45	Aust 45	D
2nd Test	Hull	June 16th	'99	Eng 56	Aust 40	W
3rd Test	Oxford	June 18th	'99	Eng 60	Aust 30	W

England win series 2-0 with 1 match drawn

With the inclusion of Todd Wiltshire, the Aussies looked stronger than ever in 1999. Todd had lost none of the class that he had possessed some ten years earlier, and he remained one of the fastest trappers in speedway. They had a solid top five in Wiltshire, Crump, Adams, Lyons and Lemon, but the Roos looked especially strong at reserve, tracking Ryan Sullivan and Steve Johnson in the first Test at **Belle Vue**. Dave Jessup took no chances with the England team, calling up Louis, Loram, Dugard, Screen and Nicholls, with Hurry and Norris at reserve.

When Crump and Lyons shot ahead of Louis and Nicholls in the opening heat, it looked as though England were in for a tough night, but Lyons shed a chain and the heat was shared. However, Joe Screen, who was brought up on the Belle Vue track, and England's fastest rising star Scott Nicholls, rode superbly to hold off all Australian efforts to break away. The rest of the Lions gave them good support, and, by heat 9, England led by 9 points, and had the match under control before it all began to go wrong.

The home team had a gremlin in the pits, and it was serving time on Louis and Dugard, as the match turned into a mechanical nightmare for both. After two rides, having been unbeaten by an opponent, Paul Hurry joined them in their misfortunes. The Aussies began to creep back into the match, and, with only two races remaining, they trailed by just 2 points. In the penultimate race, Dugard and Hurry were in a match-winning 4-2 position, when Dugard's bike again spluttered to a halt on the last lap. Sullivan shot through to reverse the heat result and level the scores, setting up a last heat decider. In the final nominated race Scottie Nicholls and the unbeaten Screen faced Crump and Lyons, and Crump flew out of the gate to lead the England riders for six laps, and draw the match.

ENGLAND 45: J. Screen 13, S. Nicholls 11, M. Loram 7, P. Hurry 7, D. Norris 3, M. Dugard 2, C. Louis 2.

AUSTRALIA 45: J. Crump 11, J. Lyons 9, R. Sullivan 9, L. Adams 6, S. Johnson 5, T. Wiltshire 4, M. Lemon 1.

For the second Test, at **Hull,** Street replaced Lemon with Craig Boyce, and Shane Parker moved into the reserve spot in place of the injured Ryan Sullivan. Dave Jessup made only one change, replacing reserve Norris with Second Division rider, twenty-seven-year-old Carl Stonehewer. On the face of it, it seemed a somewhat audacious move, but, subsequently, the selection proved to be inspirational, as Stoney became the match winner for England. On a slightly damp Craven Park track, the Workington star was the only rider who seemed capable of passing. England provided the race winner in the first three heats, and established a 4-point lead. However, a 5-1 by Boyce and Wiltshire in heat 7 got Australia back in the match and, after heat 9, following a fall by Nicholls and an engine failure by Screen, they led by 4 points.

The visitors suffered a blow in heat 13 when an out-of-touch Jason Crump crashed and was taken to hospital with a suspected broken collar-bone. England seized their moment, and Dugard and Stonehewer scored a maximum heat win in the penultimate race to level the scores. Top scorer Chris Louis was an automatic choice for the final heat, but Jessup caused a few raised eyebrows with the nomination of Stonehewer as the other English rider to face Adams and Lyons. Louis led from the gate followed by the two Australians, but Stonehewer would not be denied, and burst past Lyons to take up third place and win the match for England.

ENGLAND 46: C. Louis 12, C. Stonehewer 9, M. Dugard 8, J. Screen 6, M. Loram 5, S. Nicholls 5, P. Hurry 1.

AUSTRALIA 44: L. Adams 12, J. Lyons 10, B. Boyce 8, T. Wiltshire 5, S. Parker 4, S. Johnson 4, J. Crump 1.

Two nights later, at **Oxford**, Sullivan returned for the Aussies, but without Jason Crump they folded. When England skipper Louis and Scott Nicholls scored a maximum heat win in heat 1, it gave the Lions the green light to run rampant against a lacklustre Australian side. The Lions led by 14 points after just seven heats, with Adams and Sullivan failing completely for Australia. Experiencing little sign of resistance, England ran riot, and the points came their way thick and fast for the remainder of the match. They amassed a 30-point win at the end of it.

ENGLAND 60: P. Hurry 12, M. Dugard 10, C. Stonehewer 8, S. Nicholls 8, M. Loram 8, J. Screen 7, C. Louis 7.

AUSTRALIA 30: T. Wiltshire 8, J. Lyons 7, S. Johnson 6, L. Adams 4, C. Boyce 2, R. Sullivan 2, S. Parker 1.

It was a great pity that Australia went out with a whimper, and there was little evidence of the legendary pride and tenacity that the Aussies had become renowned for throughout the world. However, by the end of the 1999 season, they were the new World Champions, having easily won the World Team Cup Final in Czechoslovakia, when England finished in third place.

Although there were no Test matches in the millennium year, England were successful. They were denied the World Team Championship only when Mark Loran fell in a run off for the title with Sweden's Tony

Richardsson. Rather surprisingly, Australia finished in last place in the competition. However the icing on the cake for England came at the end of the 2000 season when Mark Loram became the first Englishman to be crowned World Champion since Gary Havelock back in 1992.

The World Team Cup had been revamped for the year 2001, and was now the World Cup, which was run over a week with two qualifying meetings and a Final at the weekend. England too had a new look. They entered the millennium as Team Great Britain, with Neil Middleditch at the helm as team manager. In a prelude to the World Cup, a Test match was staged between the favourites Australia, and Team GB, at **Ipswich** on 24 May. Long-time Aussie manager Neil Street stayed with his faithful old stagers, but Middleditch was without Screen and Dugard, and built the team around home riders Louis and Nicholls. Hurry was promoted into the top five, along with Loram and Stonehewer, while Gary Havelock was recalled at reserve alongside eighteen-year-old David Howe.

Scott Nicholls was by now pushing Loram for the England number one slot, and at Ipswich, in six outings, he dropped only 3 points; all to Jason Crump, who was unbeaten by an opponent throughout the match. Crump was by now arguably the finest rider in the world. He already had three Grand Prix victories to his credit, and was riding better than ever in 2001. In a hard fought battle, Team GB never gave an inch, but with two races remaining, they were 6 points adrift. However, in the penultimate heat, the Ipswich pairing of Louis and Nicholls struck gold, and scored a maximum heat win over Johnson and Wiltshire to pull back within 2 points of Australia.

Middleditch had no hesitation in sending the home pair straight out again in the nominated final heat, against Crump and Adams. Crumpie, mainly due to his success in the Grand Prix, had developed nerves of steel, and the final race proved a formality for him. Athough Nicholls chased him home, Louis failed to get the better of Leigh Adams, and the Aussies snatched the win.

TEAM GB 43: S. Nicholls 14, M. Loram 11, C. Louis 9, P. Hurry 3, C. Stonehewer 3, G. Havelock 2, D. Howe 1.

AUSTRALIA 47: J. Crump 14, C. Boyce 8, L. Adams 7, R. Sullivan 5, S. Parker 5, S. Johnson 5, T. Wiltshire 3.

In the World Cup at Wroclaw, Poland, Team GB failed to reach the Final, but Australia went all the way and regained the World Championship. The Ipswich Test match was the last one ridden to date between the two old enemies. The following year, in another marathon World Cup at Peterborough, the Aussies retained their World Championship and even staged their own round of the Grand Prix series. With the Grand Prix rounds being increased to ten in total for 2002, it left little room for the likes of Test matches in the British domestic calendar – and there lay a problem.

The reinvention of World Championship speedway had left the British speedway promoters with perpetual headaches. Not only did they have to work their fixtures around the seemingly ever-increasing number of Grand Prix rounds, but also they now had to scratch out a week for the World Cup.

As a spectacle, the speedway Grand Prix is compulsive and utterly absorbing, brilliantly covered by television. But has it turned into a monster, devouring all in its path? Will it be speedway's saviour, or its destroyer? Certainly top-flight speedway in Britain has suffered, and seems likely to continue to do so. Since the birth of speedway, Britain has always had the strongest league racing in the world, hence the adoption of countless foreign riders over the years. Apart from the Eastern Bloc riders in the sixties, if you wanted to make it in speedway, then you had to ride in Britain. Whether or not the Grand Prix will put an end to top-flight league racing in Britain remains to be seen. Maybe it will also put an end to those wonderful England-Australia Test matches.

Those Test matches have attracted thousands upon thousands of spectators through the turnstiles over the years, especially in the thirties and forties. In fact, no other two teams have been watched by so many people over the years. As the Swedes, the Danes, the USA and other speedway nations developed, the rivalry became less intense, but those early days will never be matched or seen again. Tell any speedway promoter today, that, if he staged a match between the best two teams in the world, he could expect a crowd of 50,000 and he would probably ask you what part of the solar system you belonged to, or at least he would question your mentality and parentage.

Those were the days.